ISBN: 9781314558708

Published by:
HardPress Publishing
8345 NW 66TH ST #2561
MIAMI FL 33166-2626

Email: info@hardpress.net
Web: http://www.hardpress.net

# A VILLAGE COMMUNE

LONDON : PRINTED BY
SPOTTISWOODE AND CO., NEW-STREET SQUARE
AND PARLIAMENT STREET

# A VILLAGE COMMUNE

BY

## OUIDA

"L'ÉTAT C'EST MOI"

*A NEW EDITION*

London
CHATTO & WINDUS, PICCADILLY
1882

AL POPOLO ITALIANO
CHE
MOLTO MERITA
E
POCO RICEVE

# A VILLAGE COMMUNE

## CHAPTER I.

Santa Rosalia in Selva is a village anywhere you will betwixt the Adrian and the Tyrrhene seas, betwixt the Dolomites and the Abruzzi. It is not necessary to indicate its geographical position more clearly; it is sufficient to say that it is a little Italian borgo, like many another, lying under the sweet blue skies of this beloved and lovely land that has been mother to Theocritus and Tasso. A village white as a seashore stone: lying along a river green as the Adige; with low mountains in sight across a green table-land of vine and chestnut, olive and corn; with some tall poplars by the water, and a church with a red brick bell-tower, and the bell swinging behind its wooden cage. Across the fields and along the side of the hills are scores of other villages; narrow roads run between them all in a network hidden under vine leaves; and some hundreds of house-roofs make up together what is called the Commune of Vezzaja and Ghiralda. Of this commune the chief place, because the largest village, is Santa Rosalia. Santa Rosalia in Selva; so called because thus named in days when the woods had covered it up as closely as a blackbird's nest is covered with the long leaves that it builds in; Santa Rosalia in Selva, a simple, honest, fresh, and most rural place, with sunburnt women plaiting straw upon its doorsteps, and little naked children tumbling about like Loves escaped from the panels of Correggio; with the daffodils and the odorous narcissus growing in spring-time everywhere among the grass and corn, and in the autumn the ox-carts going with the tubs of gathered grapes slowly down its single street: a street without a paving-stone, and without a shop except the butcher's stall and the grocer's, and one little old dim penthouse-like place where in the gloom an old woman sells cakes and toys and rosaries.

The bright green country lies close about Santa Rosalia, and indeed is one with it, and in summer so overlaps it, and roofs it in, with vine-foliage and clouds of silvery olive leaf that nothing is to be seen of it except the bell-tower of its chief church, San Giuseppe, with a statue of the saint upon its roof pointing heavenward.

Things had always come and gone easily in Santa Rosalia in the old days, and even in the new. With revolutions and the like it had had nothing to do. It never talked politics. When men who had remembered wine ten centimes a flask found it rise to a hundred they scratched their heads and were puzzled; being told it was the cost of liberty, they took the explanation simply as a matter of fact, and thought liberty was a name for the vine disease.

When the church was whitewashed, and the trattoria was turned into the Caffè Vittorio Emanuele, and the conscription placards were pasted on the bridge, and the Imperial taxes established themselves in a brand-new stucco-plastered public office next the butcher's, with a shield upon it, bearing a white cross on a red ground, Santa Rosalia did not take much notice: everything grew dear indeed, but some said it was the gas away in the city did it, and some said it was the railway, and some said it was the king, and some said it was all the fault of liquid manure; but still nobody troubled much about anything, and everybody continued to go to mass, and do his best to be happy, until—the events took place that I propose to record.

The Commune of Vezzaja and Ghiralda, whose centre is the village of Santa Rosalia, is, like all Italian communes, supposed to enjoy an independence that is practically a legislative autonomy. So long as it contributes its quota to the Imperial taxes, the Imperial Government is supposed to have nothing to do with it, and it is considered to be as free as air to govern itself; so everybody will tell you; and so inviolate is its freedom that even the Prefect of its province dare not infringe upon it—or says so when he wants to get out of any trouble.

Anybody who pays five francs' worth of taxes has a communal vote in this free government, and helps to elect a body of thirty persons, who in turn elect a council of seven persons, who in turn elect a single person called a syndic, or, as you would call him in English, a mayor. This distilling and condensing process sounds quite admirable in theory. Whoever has the patience to read the pages of this book will see how this system works in practice.

Now in Vezzaja and Ghiralda the thirty persons do nothing but elect the seven persons, the seven do nothing but elect the one person, and the one person does nothing but elect his secretary; and the secretary, with two assistants dignified respectively by the titles of Chancellor and Conciliator, does everything in the way of worry to the public that the ingenuity of the official mind can conceive. The secretary's duties ought to be simply those of a secretary anywhere, but by a clever individual can be brought to mean almost anything you please in the shape of local tyranny and extortion; the chancellor (*cancelliere*) has the task of executing every sort of unpleasantness against the public in general, and sends out by his fidus Achates, the Usher, all kinds of summons and warrants at his will and discretion; as for the conciliator (*giudice conciliatore*), his office, as his name indicates, is supposed to consist in conciliation of all local feuds, disputes, and debts, but as he is generally chiefly remarkable for an absolute ignorance of law and human nature, and a general tendency to accumulate fees anywhere and anyhow, he is not usually of the use intended, and rather is famous for doing what a homely phrase calls setting everybody together by the ears. It being understood that all these gentry are men who in any other country would be butchers, or bakers, or candlestick makers, it is readily to be understood likewise that they are not an absolutely unmixed boon to the community over which they reign; at their very best they have been book-keepers or scriveners, or bankrupt petty tradesmen who have some interest with the prefect of the province or the syndic of the commune, and as they usually are, all three alike, little Gesslers in temperament and almost uncontrolled in power, it is easy to imagine that their yoke is by no means light upon the necks of their neighbours and subjects, and that they dance the devil's dance, humorously, over its finances and its fortunes. Power is sweet, and when you are a little clerk you love its sweetness quite as much as if you were an emperor, and maybe you love it a good deal more.

Tyranny is a very safe amusement in this liberated country. Italian law is based on that blessing to mankind, the Code Napoléon, and the Code Napoléon is perhaps the most ingenious mechanism for human torture that the human mind has ever constructed. In the cities its use for torment is not quite so easy, because where there are crowds there is always the fear of a riot, and besides there are horrid things called newspapers, and citizens wicked and daring enough to write in them. But away in the country, the embellished and filtered Code Napoléon can work like a steam plough; there is nobody to appeal, and nobody to appeal to; the people are timid and perplexed; they are as defenceless as the sheep in the hand of the shearer; they are frightened at the sight of the printed papers, and the carabinier's sword; there is nobody to tell them that they have any rights, and besides, rights are very expensive luxuries anywhere, and cost as much to take care of as a carriage horse.

Now and then the people find out their rights, and light a barrel of petroleum with them, and are blamed: it is foolish, no doubt, and it is terrible, but the real blame lies with their masters, who leave them no other light than the petroleum glare. That they do not use their petroleum for anything except their household lamps is due to the patience and the docility of the people; it is not due to the embellished and filtered version of the Code Napoléon, nor to the administrators of it.

Santa Rosalia is a rambling place, straggling along one side of the green impetuous river; of course it possesses what it calls a piazza, and makes a sort of pretence at being a town; but the grass grows long in its stones all over the place, and its folks are as rustic as villagers can be. There were never very many people in the lowly borgo, but the few there were, at the time of which I write, dwelt in good harmony together.

There was Luigi Canterelli (always called Gigi) who dealt in all kinds of useful things from hammers to pins, from drugs to broad beans; there was Ferdinando Gambacorta (known only as Nando), who was plumber and cartwright and carpenter all in one; there was Leopoldo Franceschi (Poldo), who was locksmith, blacksmith, whitesmith, and farrier; there was Raffaelle Dando (Faello), who was the big butcher, and there was Alessandro Montauto (Sandro), who was the little one; there was Vincenzio Torriggiani (Cencio), who was the tailor of the community and might be seen sitting all day long cross-legged and hard at work on his threshold and for ever ready for a gossip; there was Filippo Rasselluccio (Lippo), who was the baker and also trafficked in grain and seeds; there was Giuseppe Lante (Beppo), who had a trattoria and wine shop, and would roast you a dozen thrushes or fry you a dozen artichokes against all the cooks in Christendom. There was Leonardo Mariani (Nardo), who kept a paint and oil and brush shop, and also kept the post-office after his own manner, which was to spread the letters out upon his counter and let them lie there till somebody should come in who would be going the way to which they were addressed, and would consent to take them thither. There was the apothecary of course, il dottore Guarino Squillace, who was paid by the commune about 20*l.* a year to look after its bodies; and there was Dom Lelio, the Vicar of San Giuseppe, who was paid about twenty shillings a month by the State to look after its souls; and there was the miller, Demetrio Pastorini, who dwelt on the river, and had handsome sons and daughters to the number of seven, and there were a great many other very poor people, nondescripts, getting their bread anyhow; and outside the village there were of course all the small gentry, and many *contadini* and *fattori*, who dashed through the place on fiery horses or in jingling break-neck *bagheri*, those bastard offspring of a cart and a gig.

Santa Rosalia had been made into the centre of a new commune some decades ago; but though wine had become ten times the old price, and taxes had become fifty times heavier, Santa Rosalia had not felt its new shoe pinch very terribly, for its syndic had been a very just and excellent person (as does sometimes actually happen), a certain Marchese Palmarola, as simple as Cincinnatus and as gentle as S. Frances. But unhappily for Santa Rosalia, Palmarola had died of tertian fever one hot summer time, and another and different person had been elected in his place, the Cavaliere Anselmo Durellazzo. The Marchese had seen to everything himself; had never signed a paper or a form without reading it, and enquiring into the case that required it; had let many foolish and cruel regulations be dead letters, and had never been known to be unjust to either rich or poor. Most people are unjust to one or the other. But then the Marchese had been a Catholic and a gentleman, and so had been silly enough to believe in such an antiquated thing as moral responsibility.

The Cavaliere Durellazzo had not these scruples; he had been a wax candle manufacturer on a large scale in a city, and though the Church had helped to make his fortune, he was much given to laughing at it; with his millions he had purchased estates in the commune of Vezzaja and Ghiralda, and the Giunta thought there was nobody better for a syndic; he thought so too. He was a fat, easy-going, sleepy man, and as soon as he came into office signed some hundreds of blank forms to save himself all trouble; he cared for nothing except playing dominoes and being bowed to by his peasantry. As he had passed all his life in bowing himself, it was a new sensation.

The commune under the Cavaliere Durellazzo soon got into disorder; complaints were made to the thirty, and the thirty made them to the seven, and the seven made them to the one. The Cavaliere Durellazzo looked around him, and bethought him of a remedy which should involve no trouble to himself. He summoned Messer Gaspardo Nellemane, who was then employed in the Municipality of the nearest city, and soon into the sunlight of Santa Rosalia there came a tall, trim, erect figure, clad in town-made clothes, who was commended to the respect of the commune in general as the new secretary.

Messer Gaspardo Nellemane was a man of some seven-and-twenty years; he was well made, and had a dark and rather handsome face, in which the Hebrew origin attributed to him displayed itself somewhat strongly. He was quite a grand personage in Santa Rosalia; he dressed in city fashion, and he had a great many rings, if he did not always wash his hands, and the way in which he smoked his cigar, wore his hat, and kicked a dog out of his path was quite that of a very fine gentleman.

Messer Nellemane had begun life in a little dusky den of pots and pans, and odds and ends of iron and brass, that we call *chincaglierie*, and there had tumbled about, a dusty child, amongst the rust and rubbish, till, seeing he was a sharp little boy, his old father sent him to school, and from school he went to a notary's office as clerk, and from there had mounted up into the Civil Service of Italy, until here he was, a great man, in Santa Rosalia, with twice as much as the apothecary, and four times as much as the vicar, as official salary, and bed and board beside, not to mention any such windfalls as might drop to him in the due course of a just administration.

Messer Gaspardo Nellemane lived in two little rooms, very bare of furniture, and was waited on by the man that swept out the Communal Palace, and ate white beans fried in oil, and salt fish, and had a bit of kid on highdays and holydays, just like any other unit of the modest public. But Messer Gaspardo, though he smoked two-centime cigars and drank a thin wine at a few pence a flask, was an ambitious man; he saw no reason why he should not become a deputy, and even a minister before he died, and indeed there was no reason whatever. He was only a clerk at fifty pounds a year; but he had a soul above all scruples, and a heart as hard as the millstone.

In station he was only a humble though energetic

official, carrying out the supreme will of the Giunta, just as young Bonaparte seemed a mere general carrying out the will of the Republic. But genius has its supremacy wherever it may dwell, and Messer Nellemane in real truth moved the Giunta as though they were automatic figures and he their central spring. The Giunta gathered round a council table every week, and believed they did business; but, in point of fact, they only looked through the spectacles that Messer Nellemane provided. Messer Nellemane saved them a great deal of trouble, and they were grateful.

There stood the Palazzo Communale in the midst of sunny Santa Rosalia, a square bald ugly building, dirty and naked and always dusty-looking, with its plaster cracking, and its paint peeling, and Santa Rosalia was told that this ugly building was their temple of liberty and equity; liberty public and private, equity that was no respecter of persons, but impartial and incorruptible; and inside the Palazzo Communale Messer Nellemane had it all his own way, and thence did rule the commune 'with suavity and moderation,' as he himself would say, when he would speak of his administration, as he took a *bibita* at evening in the doorway of the little humble caffè which was proud to house so great a man; a caffè where the Secretary and the Conciliator and the Chancellor sat and played cards, and drank little strong essences and syrups, and smoked a cigar together, most nights, in that perfect accord which characterised their public and their private career. They never quarrelled: not they: one held the sheep, another sheared it, and a third gathered the wool; if they had once quarrelled they might have let go of the sheep.

Messer Gaspardo Nellemane sometimes thought that he could very well have held and sheared and gathered all by himself, for he was clever, and his friends, the Conciliator and the Chancellor, were not distinguished for intellect.

The Conciliator was a fat bald man, who in remote days had been a priest, a cook, a taverner, a cheesemonger, and found all trades fail; he liked his glass and was generally half asleep: the Chancellor had been an apothecary's prentice once upon a time, and had got into trouble for mistaking the dog Latin on his pots and bottles, and giving the wrong drugs; he was small and thin and very timid, and had but one passion, artichokes in oil.

Messer Gaspardo Nellemane was of a different mould to his colleagues, whom he called so affectionately his dear Tonino and his beloved Maso; his was a master mind, and his own master the Syndic, the most worshipful Signor Cavaliere Durellazzo, never dared say a word of dispute or reproof to him, but, when he drove into Santa Rosalia once a week or once a month, nodded and blinked, and assented to everything, and muttered '*Va bene, va benissimo*' to all the acts and deeds, the elaborate judgments and obsequious explanations of his secretary. So Messer Gaspardo Nellemane ruled and reigned in Santa Rosalia in Selva, as a number of precisely similar people so rule and reign still, all over the land, in this year of grace 1880.

The public creates the bureaucracy and is eaten up by it; it is the old story of Saturn and his sons. Messer Gaspardo was a very insignificant atom of the European bureaucracy, it is true; but he was big enough to swallow the commune of Vezzaja and Ghiralda.

All the commune detested him, yet all the commune cringed to him. The commune had appointed the thirty, and the thirty had appointed the seven, and the seven had appointed the Syndic, Cavaliere Durellazzo, and the Cavaliere Durellazzo had appointed Messer Gaspardo; and when once this clever rider was upon the patient mule's back, nobody in all Vezzaja and Ghiralda was clever enough to get him off again.

Government, according to Messer Nellemane, and many greater public men have thought the same before him, was a delicate and elaborate machinery for getting everything out of the public that could be got; the public was a kid to be skinned, a grape to be squeezed, a sheep to be shorn; the public was to be managed, cajoled, bullied, put in the press, made wine of in a word; wine for the drinking of Messer Nellemane. Messer Nellemane was not a minister yet, but he thought as a minister.

He was only a clerk indeed, at a slender salary, and ate his fried tomatoes publicly in the little back room of the caffè; but he had the soul of a statesman. When a donkey kicks, beat it; when it dies, skin it; so only will it profit you; that was his opinion, and the public was the donkey of Messer Nellemane.

Messer Nellemane had blessed Santa-Rosalia for about three years and a half when the first of the incidents that I am about to narrate took place, and changed the fates of some very poor people; the sort of people that the world sometimes will deign to read about if Georges Sand or George Eliot write of them, but who, outside a story-book, are absolutely uninteresting and insignificant.

Messer Nellemane had been dining at three o'clock in the balmy afternoon of a lovely spring day, and was strolling along the left bank of the Rosa river: the bank where the houses were not.

Messer Nellemane this day was in a complacent frame of mind; he had been inspecting the roads with his friend Pierino Zaffi, who was the engineer of the commune; an engineer who knew too little even to be employed on a railway. Happily for him, however, he had gone to school with Messer Nellemane, and had in his boyish days lent Messer Nellemane little sums of money; so, when an engineer was wanted for the commune on the old one dying, Messer Nellemane had said, 'There is Pierino Zaffi, a man with capabilities to bore the Gran Sasso, and drain the Maggiore. It might be well if we could secure his services;' and the Syndic had said, '*Va bene, va benissimo.*' So Pierino Zaffi had also been put upon the civil list of Vezzaja and Ghiralda.

There was a very heavy tax for roads in the commune; everybody who paid fifty-francs-worth of rent had to contribute; the total amassed was considerable.

Now the roads were very bad in Vezzaja and Ghiralda, and Pierino Zaffi was there to make them better, and the big lump sum taken from the public for that purpose was there too. But for Pierino Zaffi to mend the roads, and for the money to be spent on them, would have been much too simple to be statesmanlike; they went quite another way to work, did these two school-friends. They put up the roads to auction; here are the roads to be mended; the roads will go to the lowest bidder; how much for the roads? Then a miller stepped forward and said he would take them in hand for 400 francs per annum; he was scouted. Then a stonemason said he would do them for 350; he, too, was put aside contemptuously. Then a contractor from the city said he was willing to offer 200; and he was dallied with coyingly because he was a contractor; and after much higgling, bidding, screaming, and disputing, the stonemason made a final offer of 140 francs per annum for the roads, and got them.

The stonemason's views as to the mending of roads were simple: he had all the flint that was chipped off, and all the rubbish that was shot, in his yard emptied at different places on the highways, and when he happened to possess neither chips nor rubbish he did nothing at all.

Goers to and fro upon the roads cursed the state of them; horses and mules fell into their holes, and wheels jolted to pieces over their ruts. The stonemason stolidly replied that if he did not keep the roads well the engineer could say he did not, and see to it. Then the engineer was summoned, and made an inspection, and breakfasted with the stonemason, and drank Vino Santo and was made comfortable in every way, and sent in a report which affirmed that it was impossible the roads could be better. 'There!' said the stonemason, and entrenched himself safely behind the report, while Messer Nellemane read the report to the Giunta, and the Syndic said, '*Va bene, va benissimo.*' And as for the roads, Messer Nellemane had looked at the green corn in the fields, and Messer Pierino had looked at the clouds in the sky, and both had declared themselves as to the state of the roads most satisfied, most gratified, nay, actually surprised with the excellence of them. Mules only broke their legs because they were obstinate, and wheels only came off because they were rotten; that was the fault of the mules and the wheels, clearly: the state of the roads was excellent.

That is how roads are managed in Vezzaja and Ghiralda. Municipal government is a blessing, and the greatest guarantee of freedom—so we are told.

Meanwhile, where did the rest of the public taxes for the roadkeeping go, when the stonemason's hundred and forty francs were deducted? This was a question nobody in Vezzaja and Ghiralda ever thought of asking. The patience of the taxpaying public all the world over is wonderful. It is probable that this donkey-like quality is what makes statesmen also all the world over, and especially chancellors of exchequers, so contemptuous of the public. They treat it as Sganarelle treats his wife.

Messer Nellemane had been with Messer Pierino on one of these tours of inspection and had come back in a good humour; the Vino Santo had been admirable, and the thrushes and the hare-with-herbs had been done to a turn. In a genial frame of mind, therefore, Messer Gaspardo strolled homeward by that pretty river, the Rosa, which is a bright stream, green as a lizard's back, rough and roaring in winter times of flood, clear and shallow in summer seasons, with broad stretches of pale yellow sand.

The Rosa is an historic river, though a narrow one; who will may read in ancient chronicles of holy pilgrimages made along its banks, and unholy war waged upon its shores, of Guelf and Ghibelline fording its waters, and of Spaniard and German engulfed in its flood.

But of these old tales Messer Nellemane thought not; for the past he had a boundless scorn; how stupid were those barons and troopers of middle ages who could only roast a Jew's feet, or use the thumbscrew to an usurer! how superior for the same ends were taxes, tribunals, and the law! Messer Gaspardo Nellemane was, like many other modern philosophers, quite convinced there had never been any times so good as the present.

He sauntered along, his Cavour cigar in his mouth; the sun was going towards the west, the Lombardy poplars fringing the river-banks shook in a slight breeze; elsewhere it was dusty and unpleasant, but by the river there were coolness, shadow, and no dust.

Suddenly the eyes of Messer Nellemane lighted on—a contravention. His eye brightened at the sight as a warhorse's at the panoply of troops. What he saw was an old man cutting osiers on the margin of the now shallow Rosa; near him a girl was beating linen in the water, and a youth a little way off was sifting the river shingle.

The old man, Filippo Mazzetti, always called Pippo, was a basket-maker and mender of rush chairs, and weaver of the wickerwork of wine and oil flasks. He was certainly very poor as the great world counts poverty, but he was as happy for all that as a cricket in the corn. He had a little house of his own, his very own, as the children say, that hung over a bend in the water, and he always managed to have a pound or two of meat on Sundays, and his canes and osiers could be had merely for the gathering.

The maiden beside him was the daughter of his

dead son; she was the pride of his soul and the apple of his eye. She was called Viola, for that name of Shakespeare's shy, bold, sweet heroine is one common amongst the country people here, and she was as like the Sibilla Persica[1] as a human face can be like an immortal thought. She had a very noble pensive face, and when she went to cut osiers and willows with her father, and bore the green bundle of the reeds, or a red sheaf of maple wands, upon her head, she was as full of grace and unconscious grandeur as though she had been a daughter of Cæsars.

She could not read a line, and her feet were usually bare, and she was hard at work from sunrise to sunset; but she had the old Hera-like beauty, the antique sculptural calm. Her grandfather had kept her strictly, and she had never stirred out without him; a little shrivelled old man, very small and very sunburnt, who looked beside her like a withered bough beside an amaryllis. She was devoted to him, and he to her, and here in Santa Rosalia their innocent lives had passed quite peaceably and painlessly until this spring day, as he went by the river, Messer Nellemane by ill fortune saw her washing linen there, Pippo cutting reeds the while, and the miller's eldest son, Carmelo Pastorini, knee-deep in the water, shovelling up and sifting shingle.

Messer Gaspardo Nellemane stopped, espying, as I have said, that thing whose sight was beatitude and yet exasperation to him—a contravention. He had made a code of little by-laws, all brand-new and of his own invention; he thought administration should be persecution; if it did not perpetually

[1] Of Guercino.

C

assert itself, who would respect it? He had made everything punishable that could be possibly distorted into requiring punishment.

Every commune has the right to make its own by-laws, and Messer Gaspardo had framed about three hundred and ninety, and the Giuntà sleepily and indifferently had assented to them, and the worshipful Syndic, Cavaliere Durellazzo, had looked them over and said, ' *Va bene, va benissimo,*' and so in Santa Rosalia all the secretary's regulations had been adopted and become law. Quite recently he had incorporated into these regulations the law that nobody must cut canes or reeds in the Rosa without permission of, and payment to, the commune. *L'État c'est moi*, and its pocket is mine too, was always in the thoughts of Messer Nellemane.

So he went down to the edge of the stream, and said, quite affectionately to old Pippo, because the maiden was so handsome, ' My dear friend, what you are doing there is against the law, unless indeed you have paid for a permit, and I think you have not. Can you show me your licence?'

Old Pippo, who was rather deaf and a little surly-tempered, grunted, and went on cutting. Messer Nellemane spoke a little more sharply.

' My friend, do you hear? It is expressly forbidden by the regulations of the municipal police to do what you are doing. There is a fine for the first offence, and a very heavy penalty if it be repeated——'

' Four hundred years and more my fathers have cut reeds in the Rosa,' said Pippo, looking up at last and sticking his pipe in his trouser band.

' We do not accept degraded precedents as any

justification for infraction of the laws of the commune,' said Messer Gaspardo, who loved very long words, for they proved that he was an educated man and did not speak like the vulgar.

'Eh?' said Pippo, who was easily frightened and yet timidly disposed to stand up for a right that was like an heirloom, only the long words worried and puzzled him so that he thought he must have done murder, or sinned against the Holy Ghost, without knowing it. '*Scusi tanto, Signore*,' he said in his confusion. 'But everybody gathers the reeds; my father and grandfather—and what shall I do for my baskets?'

'Petition for a permit, and if it be accorded you, pay for it,' said Messer Nellemane, sharply. 'If you cut them after this, you will be summoned and fined.'

Pippo scratched his head in bewilderment. Young Carmelo, knee-deep in the water washing his shingle, looked at Viola washing her father's shirt and saw she was trembling and staring with alarmed distended eyes up in the face of the great man.

'It is an old right,' said Carmelo, boldly shouting to the clerk of the commune. 'It is a right of the people, like these shingles here; the river is common to us all.'

'The people have no rights when the majesty of the law abrogates and abolishes them,' replied Messer Nellemane with dignity, which is perhaps the truest word he ever spoke, and wrote in the note-book which he always carried: 'Carmelo of the Casata Pastorini appears to be of a contumacious and disputative character; *mem*: to be watched.' He was about to utter words more severe, when he chanced to look down and see the beauty of Viola's upraised face. Messer Gaspardo Nellemane was human in all his greatness; he was dazzled for a moment, and weakened by the lustre of her humid and frightened eyes: he knew that she was old Pippo's granddaughter, but he had never noticed her before.

He changed the intended phrase into a milder one.

'You are warned, Mazzetti, and warned by *me*,' he said, with a charitable condescension in his tone. 'As you were in ignorance of the municipal regulations, I will not report you this time, but beware of another infringement on the law: see Article 6 of Rule XIV. of the Communal Code of Vezzaja and Ghiralda. *Buon' sera, buon' riposo.*'

Then he went on his way along the river bank with benignity.

'May I carry them in, think you?' said old Pippo in doubt and fear, fondly regarding his cut rushes.

'I would not care for him and his laws,' said young Carmelo, plunging his arms down into the shingle with a contemptuous laugh on his bright fresh face. 'He was made yesterday, and the river was here before any of us, and is meant for us.'

'That is all very well, Carmelo,' said Viola, timidly. 'But that gentleman has all his own way, and he has three guards at his beck and call, and with a few fines they ruin you: look at poor Nanni.'

Giovanni, the cobbler, who had sat at his stall in the open air, as his father had done before him all his life, had been smitten hip and thigh by Article 20 of the new regulations that had come in with the clerkship of Messer Nellemane which forbade anybody to sit outside on the pavement and encumber it. As old Giovanni was an obstinate and obtuse old man, and persisted in believing the stones before his door were his own, and persisted also in cumbering them very much with his board and his chair and his tools, the commune had summoned him over and over again, and finally added up his fines for contumacy and contravention to such a big total that Nanni, who made about a franc a day and lived on it, could no more pay the sum than he could have built St. Peter's.

So that the usher of the commune visited him and finally sold up his poor pots and pans and sticks of furniture, and the foolish old fellow was so hurt by this that he smoked himself to death with his last pinch of charcoal, and was found stiff and stark on his bare floor, for of bed and bedding they had left him naught.

Nanni had been a merry kindly old soul, and his death had been a shock to the people of his village, for he had made or mended the Sunday shoes of the place for half a century.

'I do remember Nanni,' said the young man, with a dark frown upon his face. 'These newfangled laws killed him; and as for the " gentleman," as you call him, if any one thrashed him they would do a good work.'

'Oh hush!' said Viola, looking affrighted after the figure of Messer Gaspardo as it passed along the opposite bank.

'Had I best carry them in or leave them?' said Pippo in the same perplexity, looking wistfully up from his green bundles.

The miller's son let fall his shingles back into the water, and with a stride or two through the clear stream reached the bundles, hoisted them on his shoulders, and went away with them to Pippo's house, a score of roods' distance down the river. Messer Gaspardo, who had glanced back, saw the action; he noted it in his note-book and walked onward.

The river was all golden and green in the late afternoon; here and there was the red flame of a knot of tulips; a lovely silence and radiance were over all the scene as the sun sunk to its setting. Messer Gaspardo went on down the bank of the Rosa, and looked very dark and very grim against the shining light of the evening skies.

Viola gazed after him and felt afraid, terribly afraid; she wished he had not seen Carmelo Pastorini take the osiers on his back. The young man indeed was indifferent; he was very young and bright and brave; he had drawn a lucky number and so been free with only forty days in the army, and able to stay at home with his father at the little watermill on the Rosa; he feared nothing. But Pippo and Viola feared everything, yet knew not what they feared: it is a ghostly burden of dread, that which the honest poor carry with them all through their toiling hungry days, the vague oppressive dread of this law which is always acting the spy on them, always dogging their steps, always emptying their pockets.

The poor can understand criminal law and its justice and its necessity easily enough and respect its severities; but they cannot understand the petty tyrannies of civil law, and it wears their lives out, and breaks their spirits. When it does not break their spirits, it curdles their blood and they become socialists, nihilists, internationalists, anything that will promise them riddance of their spectre and give them vengeance.

We in Italy are all of us afraid of socialism, we who have anything to lose; and yet we let the syndics with their secretaries, conciliators, and chancellors sow it broadcast in dragon's teeth of petty injustices, and petty cruelties, that soon or late will spring up armed men, hydra-headed and torch in hand!

## CHAPTER II.

MEANWHILE Messer Gaspardo went homeward to his rooms in the Municipio and sent for Bindo. Bindo Terri was one of the rural guards that had been put on the roll of the civic power of Vezzaja and Ghiralda to see to the due enforcement and carrying out of the three hundred and ninety-six new rules, with their various articles of which the Giunta was the putative, but Messer Nellemane was the actual, father. Bindo was a great scamp who was now sedulously bent on proving the wisdom of the adage, set a thief to catch a thief; he had been a blackguard all his youth; but as he loafed about in Santa Rosalia, snaring birds and running errands, Messer Nellemane, with the shrewd eye that was so useful to him, had discerned in this loafer the making of an officer of the State; and so strongly recommended Bindo to his master, Durellazzo, that the Syndic had said, '*Va bene, va benissimo,*' when it was proposed to clothe vagabond Bindo in hodden grey, with a belt and a short sword, and a feather in his hat, and make a rural guard of him in the interests of the commune; the zeal of Bindo being stimulated to boiling-point by the fact that he was promised half of every fine that he could impose upon the violators of the new code of Vezzaja and Ghiralda.

This zealous functionary Messer Gaspardo now called to him and said:

'What character does the eldest son of the miller Pastorini bear?'

Bindo, who more than once in years before his promotion had had a drubbing from the Pastorini for stealing corn, replied promptly:

'He is a savage character, disrespectful to authority, and masterful.'

'A dangerous character? I thought as much. Has he ever been in trouble?'

Bindo shook his head sorrowfully; the Pastorini, father and sons, were quiet, God-fearing, sturdy, honest fellows; just the people to vex and disappoint beyond measure a guardian of morals and of manners, who was to have half the fines he could manage to impose.

'That mill of theirs—does it profit them?'

'*Altro, signore!* There is nobody else to grind anything for five miles down the river.'

'And it belongs to them?'

'It has belonged to Pastorini hundreds of years.'

'With that *boschetto* beside it?'

'Exactly, illustrissimo.'

'You may go, my dear Bindo,' said his superior, who liked to be called illustrissimo. 'But keep your eye upon Carmelo Pastorini, for he seems to me a sullen unsympathetic rebellious young man, and in these days of socialism one never knows.'

Bindo pulled his curly forelock respectfully and withdrew, leaving behind him a list of that day's contraventions of Messer Nellemane's code, which comprised and forbade nearly every action that a man, or a child, or a dog, or a horse, or an ass, or a goat, or a cow, or a duck, or a hen, could be likely to perform upon a public highway; and since it treated as high treason nearly every primitive pleasure and habit and custom that this rustic world had ever been wont to indulge in, it was not very difficult for a vigilant officer like Bindo, always walking about with his eyes and his ears wide open, to furnish his employer with a list of transgressions as long as the list of Don Giovanni's amours.

Bindo Terri preferred the ways of virtue to the ways of vagabondage; instead of being put in prison he put in other people, which combined the charm of variety with the fascination of power. It was a more lucrative path too; if people did not wish their lives molested, their habits interfered with, and their dogs poisoned, they slipped some francs at intervals into Bindo's hand; and those butchers, and bakers, and cattle-dealers, and corn-factors who wanted to cheat the State of its revenues, and not pay fines on their sales, became a very considerable source of income to him, for he knew admirably when, and (for a consideration) how, to shut his far-reaching eye with a wink.

When you have not quite 20*l.* a year as your official income, it is understood that you must supply the vacuum left somehow. When the commune paid Bindo five hundred francs a year for his invaluable services, and gave him half the fines, the Giunta said virtually to him, 'Rob, oppress, be bribed, get your bread out of the public;' and he did get, not only his bread, but his wine, and his cigars and his sweethearts.

Very naturally he took into his especial hatred all honest folks, and folks careful to pay the taxes and obey the laws; they were quite unprofitable to him.

As Messer Gaspardo Nellemane did not make his code to render people virtuous or comfortable by its regulations, but to fill the municipal money-box by its infractions, so his myrmidon, the wily Bindo, did not walk about with his eyes open in hopes of seeing the law observed, but in hopes of seeing it broken. The big butcher on the piazza carried his dead bullocks away to the distant city without paying a farthing duty upon them, because he was wise enough to have a complete understanding with Bindo; whereas the little butcher by the turn of the river never would have any such understanding, persisting in saying stupidly that Bindo, in his unregenerate and unofficial days, had stolen tripe and pork chops off his stall a hundred times; whereby naturally his fines and his payments for every head of cattle, swine, or kids, fell heavily upon him.

What will you? Corruption is the natural law of all official life, all the world over, and why should Bindo be a solitary exception to the universal rule?

'Via!' said Bindo, with his tongue in his cheek and his feathered hat on one side, whenever anybody hinted to him that his hands were not so clean as was desirable in a guardian of the public morality and decorum.

Now Bindo had always hated the whole family of the Pastorini; in their little mill on the water with its great black wheels churning below, and its tall green poplars rising above, they had always dwelt harmlessly, honestly, and in peace with heaven and their neighbours. They paid their imposts regularly; cheated no one; bided at home, and were well liked by all; the sons working hard and rarely being seen inside a wineshop; a family to be peculiarly abhorrent to an officer of the State who received half the fines imposed on noisy or disobedient people.

Therefore the heart of Bindo Terri bounded within him when he heard these few pregnant words from his chief. He was a capable and ingenious youth, and of considerable powers of invention; in his mind's eye in an instant he saw Carmelo—Carmelo, clean of limb and clean of conscience, honest, frank, quiet, sober, everything, in a word, that was detestable,—brought before the tribunal and going from the tribunal to prison.

'Why not?' said Bindo; and his soul was joyful.

Meanwhile Messer Gaspardo sat down to the calm enjoyment of his list, lighting a long cigar.

It was a list that delighted his soul and fortified it; there were contraventions for keeping trees too low of branch, for letting children play upon the sacred steps of the communal palace, for letting dogs run loose, for letting plants stand upon window-sills, for emptying pails of water into the gutter, for having a chair and a chat on the pavement, for anything and everything that the enlightened regulations of Vezzaja and Ghiralda had forbidden.

'How perverse are the public!' thought Messer Nellemane, as he ran his eye over the papers. He wanted a model public; a public that doffed its hat to him, chained its dogs, never laughed or quarrelled, drilled its children like small police-sergeants, and respected his code as if it had come from heaven.

Yet he would have had but little enjoyment out of even this model public, could it have been created for him, for he would have had nobody to punish, and no fines to put in that municipal money-box which it was his profession to fill and his perquisite to empty. Like all other great men he was happiest in stormy waters, so he folded up the list with marvel at the people's perversity, and betook himself to the caffè of Nuova Italia, where he supped cheaply off a salad and some liver, and played dominoes afterwards with the Conciliatore Maso, who always made a point of losing the game to him. Any one who wished to be in Messer Gaspardo's good graces lost the game to him.

Santa Rosalia lies along the Rosa river, and its little humble houses open out in the centre on to a clear space, where the beautiful old church with its tapering campanile faces the hideous new communal palace; a broad space of dust and desolation stretching between the two and being called by courtesy the piazza. Pippo and other old men, and even younger ones, by remembrance of their childhood, could call to mind the time when the piazza had been shaded by broad plane trees and limes, and in the centre of it had stood a very old and large stone fountain, the delight of the people and the dogs, the horses and cattle that drank and the babies that played at it.

But an earlier Giunta, the first-born of Freedom, had cut down the trees and sold them; and Messer Nellemane coming, and finding the fountain a nuisance because every one gathered about it, and he did not think with Mr. Ruskin that the sight of women, loitering with their bronze pitchers round a fountain, at daybreak or twilight, in Italy, is one of the most poetic sights on earth, had it taken to pieces and carried away, and the water sent back into the river. The people groaned, mourned, and protested all they dared, but the Giunta willed it, and the Syndic said, ' *Va bene, va benissimo.*'

So the fountain became a thing of the past, and the labour for its destruction was entered for a considerable sum in the communal expenses under the heading of 'Works for the salubrity and decoration of Santa Rosalia.' An ugly waste ground, filled with rubble and rubbish, was all the people got in its place; and as for the old stones, some did say they were re-erected in a rich Russian's villa fifty miles away, Messer Gaspardo knowing the reason why. A gardener of the neighbourhood swore to his neighbours that he had seen them there, and that he had heard they were the carved work of some great ancient sculptor ; but Messer Nellemane said they had all been broken up to mend the roads, and had been of no value for aught else whatever, so the subject had dropped, as most inquiries into public wrongs or expenditure of public money do drop, and though Santa Rosalia mourned for its lost fountain it mourned altogether in vain, and the Giunta unanimously considered that the piazza looked very much better bare ; both trees and fountains begat humidity, they thought, and why should they not do in Rosalia just what was doing in Rome? As little dogs always imitate big ones, so villages love to copy great cities.

No one ever dared to name the stones to Messer Nellemane, who had given his word that they were broken up and under his feet and the cart-wheels, and nobody ever knew that he bought five thousand francs' worth of foreign scrip soon after they disappeared because these little purchases were made for him by a cousin who was a money changer in the town of Alessandria; a shrewd 'Ebreo,' with greasy clothes and sallow skin, who will in all probability end as a baron and a banker. This evening, however, when he had eaten his supper Messer Nellemane did not think of scrip or anything mundane; he thought of Viola Mazzetti.

Her grandfather's little stone house, called the Casa della Madonna on account of a blue and white china shrine set above its entrance, built in the thirteenth century, and strong and sturdy, though low and small, stood at the corner of the piazza sideways to the river, and with the unpaved road that served the borgo as a street alone separating it from the water. The door and the kitchen window turned to the piazza; and when Messer Nellemane sat on the opposite side of the square he could see the house very well.

Messer Nellemane, all the while he smoked, and read the gazette, and played at dominoes, kept his eye upon the cottage, and he could see the Rosa river also very clearly, and down it for a long way, and he saw young Carmelo come leaping along the opposite bank under the poplars and service trees, and wade lightly across the shallow, and leap ashore and run in without knocking through Pippo's open door.

And Messer Nellemane, who could not see through stone walls despite his omniscience, followed him in thought angrily, since the beauty of the maiden had allured his own fancy and desire.

While he pursued these discontented reflections and played dominoes alternately with his beloved friends, Maso and Tonino, and the clear autumn evening began to grow grey and tinged with sadness, Carmelo Pastorini whispered to Viola while old Pippo first smoked and then snored. Carmelo was a handsome fair lithe young fellow, wonderfully like the Faun of the capital, and just as admirably made; here and there amongst the populace one may see the old classic faces and figures almost unaltered, and men who have never stooped over desks and have always in childhood gone barefoot have much of the old perfect symmetry and ease of attitude, and stand well and nobly.

'How ill you march!' said one of his officers once to a Tuscan in his conscript days, and the Tuscan answered the officer, who was kind to him, 'Signor Capitano, how can any one walk well with a great strap across the breast and leather on the feet? If I might take off my boots and carry my knapsack on my head, then I would walk against any man:' and the first act of that youth's liberty when he had been set free was to kick his boots off into space.

Barefoot now, and decked in blue home-made linen, for the weather was warm, Carmelo leaned against the little window of the room and murmured to Viola, who was bending her beautiful dark face over her straw plaiting, but smiling a little, though seriously.

They were sweethearts in an innocent, calm fashion; they had neither of them anything in the world, but that did not trouble them; Carmelo could always work at his father's mill, and Viola had no fear of poverty. The spouse of St. Francis had always been her guest, and was no terror for her.

Men and maidens marry **improvidently enough** in this country, but most of them are happy in their marriages, and the children tumble up, round and blithe as little rabbits, and all goes well; or does go well, till the shadow of the Law falls like the shadow of death across the sunny thresholds.

These two were not to marry yet awhile, **nay**, they had scarcely spoken of it; the courtship was timid and reverent on Carmelo's part, rather than impassioned, for Viola had a saint's look about her, and saintly thoughts and ways, and old Pippo was a man not to be gainsayed in his own household, and he had said, 'adagiò, adagiò,' meaning that they were young and there was no great hurry. Demetrio Pastorini, the father, said the same, and so their lives went gently on in a sweet pastoral that was happier, and less troubled, than even triumphant passion.

This evening, however, in the twilight Carmelo waxed bolder.

'Why should we not marry as the others do!' he whispered, and Viola smiled ever so little, and old Pippo spoilt it all by waking up suddenly, and shouting: 'Not cut the osiers in the Rosa? Everybody's always cut them, for twice ten thousand years. Who's that new meddlesome fool with his rules and his rates and his rubbish?'

'Hush, grandfather!' said Viola, timidly, for she remembered the death of old Nanni, and from their window she could see across the river on to the piazza, and the desolate place where the fountain had been, and also could see Messer Gaspardo Nellemane playing dominoes on his green iron chair before the caffè with thin Tonino losing to him, and fat Maso looking on at the game. Messer **Nellemane** across the river also could see her; and when Carmelo had been sent away at eight o'clock, and they had eaten their bit of supper, and she had lighted a lamp for her grandfather to have a glimmer by which to finish a reed-bottomed chair wanted by the priest on the morrow, he could see still better the bent brown head of the girl, and studied it critically, as a virtuoso might have studied a canvas of candlelight effect of Ostade or Van Steen. It was almost as beguiling and delightful to him as the guard Bindo's list of misdeeds and misadventures.

Viola was beyond dispute the loveliest girl in the place. Those onyx-coloured eyes, those dreamy lids, those curved red lips, those elastic and symmetrical limbs, would have made her a beauty anywhere, at a court or in a studio, and had enough of physical exuberance, combined with maiden-like simplicity, to touch the inmost heart of a man who would, with all his will, have been a voluptuary had it not cost so much, and had he not loved his place still better than his passions. Still there was no harm in looking at her, he thought; and look he did, until her grandfather's piece of plaiting being done she put her light out, closed the shutter, and left only a little dark stone house facing the great man of the commune.

Then Messer Nellemane flung the end of his cigar away with a lordly air, pushed back his iron chair, and strolled homeward.

'One could marry her to Bindo,' thought this very prudent person, as he walked away through the white moonlight past the glancing Rosa water.

## CHAPTER III.

The next day was the last day of April, and in the remote villages above which the Apennines brood, as in those upon the mountains themselves, there still prevails the old gracious fashion of the *Calen di Maggio*: the 'bringing in the May,' as England called it when it was merry England, and not money-grubbing and machine-ground England, with its hedgerow timber felled, and its songbirds starved and mute.

In the cities and in the little towns the old custom has quite passed away, and even in many villages the wedding-night of April and May goes by without remembrance or celebration. But in the simpler and more remote country places 'Ben venga Maggio' is still said as Guido Calvacanti said it, and the time is one of harmless feasting and of tender song. In Santa Rosalia it still lingered thus, and on the memorable night the lads of the borgo went along the Rosa banks and out amongst the fields from house to house, bearing the May, and called themselves the Maggiaioli ; singing the ancient song :

> Or è di Maggio e fiorito è il limone,
> Noi salutiamo di casa il padrone,
> Or è di Maggio e gli è fiorito i rami,
> Salutiam le agrazze co' suoi dami.
> Or è di Maggio che fiorito è di fiori,
> Salutiam le ragazze co' suoi amori.[1]

---

[1] Lo! now the lemons are all in flower in May,
  Come too are we ; we give the house and host good-day.

·This year Carmelo carried the May, a green sapling hung with flowers and lemons, and his next brother, Cesarellino (little Cæsar), bore the traditional basket of nosegays to throw to the maidens. Other youngsters were with them, with red and yellow tulips in their hats, and gay-coloured shirts, and mandolines slung on their shoulders, and they went from door to door with their salutation and song, and in turn received wine and cakes garnished with red ribbons, and now and then money, which, making the sign of the cross, they put aside to be spent in prayers for the poor souls in purgatory.

Messer Nellemane, as he sat in the window of his room in the communal palace, saw the group of youths as they came along by the water, and he recognised the face of Carmelo, as the young man bore aloft the lemon-hung tree and shouted with a fresh and mellow voice the

Or è di Maggio che fiorito è di fiori,

and stopped before the little Casa della Madonna, where they tossed their flowers through the open window, and Viola, smiling, brought them out the sweet cakes. The brow of the spectator of this innocent pastime grew dark.

'What pagan folly!' he muttered as he saw. 'What childishness and benightedness in this age of reason!'

Surely it need not be allowed?

It could be put down under the head of disturb-

Now is the month of May, with blossoms on the boughs;<br>
We salute the maidens, salute their lovers' vows.<br>
Here is all the Maying, bud, and fruit, and flower,<br>
We salute the maidens, their love and all its power!

ance, or unauthorised festival, or public meeting without permission of the council.

The law has smitten almost all these innocent revellers to the dust; carnival is scarce more than a name; on Ognissanti indecent crowds push laughing and jostling over the dead; the Feast of St. John is suppressed, and replaced by the Feast of the Statute, and almost every procession of the Church is smothered by a dirty, jesting, brawling mob, impatient for fireworks and drink.

Messer Nellemane impatiently consulted his lawbooks and his own code, and found at least fifty-five different rules and regulations, any one of which would serve, and suffice to break down the leafy crown of the offending Maio.

Until ten o'clock of the night the peace of his evening was disturbed by the chanting of the old serenade, now near, now far, the vibration of the guitar, the sounds of laughter, the unpleasant knowledge that people were enjoying themselves without having applied for and paid for legal permission.

'Next year!' he muttered vengefully, as the singing died away and the village grew dark with night and slumber. Carmelo went to his bed drowsy and happy, with the Maio tree set up outside the mill-door in the starlight.

On the morrow was the weekly council of the Seven presided over by the One; and as Messer Nellemane was the mainspring and central lever, the brains and the heart and the nerves of this council-chamber, he was too much engrossed to give a thought to the little house with the china Madonna.

He had to exercise great tact at these meetings, for he was only a secretary, and was only supposed to take notes and read reports. But with an air of extreme deference and unimpeachable modesty he knew how to make his views adopted, and how in the presence of the Syndic to prompt him, and in his absence to replace him. Ostensibly the famous rules for the Polizia Igiena e Edilità of Santa Rosalia were a product of the minds of the Thirty, filtered through the Seven, and delivered as pure essence by the One, to the Prefect of the province, and ratified by him and by the Minister of the Interior. But actually these laws had all flowed from that fount of wisdom, the mind of Messer Nellemane. He had spent laborious days and wakeful nights in the gestation and production of them; they had cost him months of anxious thought; for when your problem is how to wring pence out of penniless pockets it requires meditation and deliberation; and Messer Nellemane being anxious not to leave a loophole unwatched by the law, passed as many vexed and studious hours as a mathematician or a physiologist. When accomplished, he had to see his work accredited as that of his masters: but this he bore patiently, knowing that most of the fruits of it would be his.

This day the council was long.

The Giunta consisted of two nobles, of two small gentry, of one lawyer, one doctor, and one usurer, the latter a rich person who had purchased a house on the Pomodoro road outside Santa Rosalia, one by name Simone Zauli. This day the usurer, who in power outweighed all his six colleagues, as he had the notes-of-hand or the mortgages of each of them in his pocket, was absent. In his stead the nobles were angry about the state of the roads, and had come in person to the meeting, a thing they did not do once in a twelvemonth. Their horses were hurt and their bodies were shaken by the state of the roads, and they appeared at the council irascible. It cost Messer Nellemane a whole morning of invention and adulation to appease them and bring them back to their old belief that his friend Pierino Zaffi was the first engineer in the world.

Having succeeded at last in doing this, by great ingenuity and infinite lying, the meeting broke up; the Cavaliere Durellazzo said, '*Va bene, va benissimo,*' which he always did, as if he were a cockatoo; and Messer Gaspardo Nellemane had far too many minutes to make, and entries to write, and letters to dispatch, to have any thought of Viola or Carmelo.

But the next morning he was free, and excused himself even from his habitual noonday attendance at the Palazzo Communale by alleging an errand to the city; under pretext of which he had himself shaved, oiled, and curled by the barber, and then, dressed in his best, wended his way to Pippo's house, having seen old Pippo wending his to the priest's with the rush chair.

The door stood open, and he entered with a polite '*Scusi, signorina mia.*'

Viola was washing lettuces and herbs.

Of course she was a poor, unlettered, and almost ragged girl, but she had beautiful arms, which were shown by her rolled-up sleeves; she had a beautiful bust, which her kerchief, loosely pinned, adorned; she had a lovely face, with a great cloud of raven hair; and even thus, seen at a tub with her lettuces, a painter would have fallen at her feet, and perhaps some great princes would too.

She coloured all over her face beholding Messer

Gaspardo Nellemane, dressed like a marquis, curled, perfumed, and gloved.

'*Scusi tanto, signorina mia,*' he said again, and wished her a good-day with many fine phrases. Viola laid down her lettuces, and pushed him a chair and stood before him, very shy, timid, and afraid.

'I called to speak to your father,' said Messer Nellemane, rejecting the chair with many flourishes. 'I wished to explain to him that this cutting of osiers in the river——'

'Ah!' said Viola, with a gasp; and she grew very pale, and her great eyes were like a frightened doe's. Her visitor hastened gallantly to explain farther; and added:

'Is in direct violation of our civic laws. But I came to say that Messer Filippo being so old a resident, and, having heard that his forefathers, as he said, always enjoyed that privilege, I think a point may be stretched in his favour and exception. I myself will see the Syndic on the matter, and—well, ahem! I will see that he is not troubled about this thing: indeed I will give him a permission myself if he will call for it, free of charge, any day at noon in the municipality.'

Viola murmured something quite unintelligible: but her eyes thanked the gracious tyrant who promised to spare her humble home, and he thought himself repaid. She was mute, indeed, and shy, even to stupidity; but Messer Nellemane was not ill-pleased at that; he deemed it a tribute of simplicity to his own greatness and attractions; and his bold, bright, black eyes, round like a bird's, fastened on her with such ardour that the maiden felt bewildered, and wished vaguely that her grandfather were at home.

Messer Nellemane, however, was in no haste to be gone; leaning on the back of the chair that he refused otherwise to occupy, he wove grandiloquent phrases and sugared flatteries into a medley such as had never astonished the ear of this simple maiden, and confused her sadly.

Carmelo never talked like that; and Viola saw with surprise, and a vague apprehension, that her guest had shut the door behind him on his entrance.

Messer Nellemane, nevertheless, did not quite declare his passion, but he paid her compliments that made her cheeks glow like a damask rose, and set her brain spinning; his hand touched hers, and pressed it, and he murmured, with his moustache brushing her wrist:

'Fear nothing for your grandfather, *carina*. With such a face as yours you would get him grace for far heavier transgressions than robbing the river of its reeds.'

At that moment a dog dashed in chasing the pig; the pig frightened the hen; the hen flew into the flour-bin; and Messer Nellemane's eloquence and courtship came to an undignified end, as Viola, grateful for the interruption, hurried to the harried sow, and drove it to its quarters in an inner closet. Messer Nellemane looked on with a troubled brow. A pig in a dwelling-house! It was Contravention of Art. 3 of Rule CCCL. of the Regulations!

The author of the rules for the Polizia Igiena, e Edilità of the commune could not fail to feel every fibre of his being morally offended and set up on edge like a porcupine's quills, and yet—he was in love. He bent hurriedly before Viola and the pig, and left the house in the confusion of public duty met and routed by personal inclination.

'If it were not for her—good heavens! they transgress every law!' he thought, as he put on his hat and walked to where the diligence waited, and, entering the shaky vehicle, rolled through the sea of olive foliage along the narrow roads towards the city which lay afar off in the sunshine, against the opal and pearl of the morning skies; its domes and towers gleaming in the golden mist like a New Jerusalem.

When Pippo returned, his granddaughter told him of the visit. With the suspiciousness that is so oddly grafted into these easily pleased and docile natures, Pippo stared and swore a little, and scratched his head, and said, 'What can he be a' wanting?'

Viola turned away because she felt her cheeks were hot; be a maiden ever so innocent, she feels the approach of a coarse passion, and trembles at it though unconsciously.

'Leave to cut the reeds? *Give me leave?*' cried the old man with great contempt. 'Lord! they'll talk of leave to let the grass grow, leave to let one's lungs breathe—leave to see, and speak, and cough, and laugh next! Lord! the whole world's crazed.'

Viola set his soup before him; hot water with bread in it, some garlic, and a little parsley.

'Will they let us drink our soup, I wonder?' grumbled the old man. 'Shall we have to pay a tax for that next? Don't you let that prying jack-in-office come spying here again. The saints above us! In my young days he'd have been knifed before he could have turned the place into a nest of wasps and snakes like this. Leave to cut the osiers! You'll have to ask leave to wear your own hair next!'

And he scalded himself with his broth in his haste and his wrath.

Viola went away inside their little back kitchen and cried a little, with a vague dread and pain upon her. She could not forget the bold admiration of Messer Gaspardo's black eyes, and she was afraid.

She did not say anything of her fears to her grandfather, nor to the young man Carmelo; she was of a reticent, prudent, serene nature, and she thought it could do no good to tell any one, but might produce danger and dissension.

Meanwhile her old grandfather, having scalded himself with his soup, cooled himself with a draught of watered wine, acid as vinegar, and, after giving himself his wonted midday sleep, went outside, taking some rushes to plait, and sat on the threshold with his chair on the pavement, disregardless of the municipal rules and the fate of law-breaking Nanni.

It was a lovely afternoon, and waned into a lovely evening in the village; the swallows were coming home, the shadows were lengthening, the sweet smell of the rosemary and the vine flowers was fresh on the wind. The people had ceased working, and stood and leaned against their doors, or out of their windows, and gossiped; all was as peaceful as a pastoral: only along the sunny dust a dark shadow went, and the people looked askance at it, and it took all mirth out of the jests, drove all tranquillity from the hearts; it was the shadow of the *oppressor rusticorum;* it was the figure of Bindo the guard, walking to and fro with a carabinier, and looking for contraventions.

To the rich it may seem nothing: this going of the guard to and fro, this system of inquisition and condemnation that comes up with the sun and never ceases with the fall of the merciful night. To the rich it is nothing; it scarcely ever touches them: they live behind their own gates, and if ever they are fined send their lawyers to pay the fine. But to the poor—with their threshold, their cradle, and their club, with their dogs and their babies tumbling together on the pavement, with their hard-gathered gains hidden under a brick or in a stocking, with all their innocent bewildered ignorance of the powers of the law, with all their timid patient helplessness under oppression, with all their unquestioning submission to great wrong in fear lest resistance should bring them wrongs still greater—to the poor this figure of the police-spy for ever in their midst, observing their coming and going, seizing on every industry and pittance, watching the lighting of their candles, the gambols of their children, the usage of their tools, the frolics of their dogs, the trailing of their house-creepers, all to one single end and object —'Contravention'—to the poor I say this figure of the tyrant of the tribunal darkens the light of the sun in this our Italy, hushes the laughter of the home and fills the leisure moment of the toilsome day with a weariness and carking care never to be thrown aside. The rich make these petty laws, and the parasites of the public offices carry them out; they are as thorns in flesh already bruised; they are as the gadflies' bite in wounds already open.

In vain do the poor suffer these things: no one cares.

When the Socialist burns or the Nihilist slays, then wise men wonder!

Blind and mad, no doubt, are the Socialists and the Nihilists, but as blind and as mad are the rulers of the people who treat the honest citizen like the criminal, and of the innocent acts and careless sports of his children and his beasts make whips to scourge him by his own hearthstone.

The law should be a majesty, solemn, awful, unerring; just, as man hopes that God is just; and from its throne it should stretch out a mighty hand to seize and grasp the guilty, and the guilty only. But when the law is only a petty, meddlesome, cruel, greedy spy, mingling in every household act and peering in at every window pane, then the poor who are guiltless would be justified if they spat in its face, and called it by its right name, a foul extortion.

Bindo lounged about in the village streets (taking care to have a carabinier and the carabinier's musket at his elbow) and looked out for all whom he might devour; were there a ladder leaning against a wall, a child at play on the bare piazza, a log of wood outside a door, a dog disputing with another dog, any trifle of the hundred and one trifles entered as cardinal sins on the books of Santa Rosalia—then was Bindo happy, and happy also Messer Gaspardo Nellemane.

Bindo used a wise discretion, it is true; and so did Messer Nellemane, as in the matter of the big and little butchers. Filth stank unrebuked before the pizzicheria door, because some good cheese and some toothsome *pasta* found its way thence to certain cupboards as a mere compliment of Easter; the apothecary's Spitz snarled on unchidden up and down the street, for that worthy knew well the panacea that lies in gilded pills; and the baker had his fuel in a heap before his door, and sold short weight, and adulterated his flour with ground peas and acorns, because the baker had been wise enough at Christmas to offer to Messer Nellemane some fine contraband tobacco and brandy (a present, he said, from France), and to Bindo had said, 'If you like a *fila* of white bread every morning you know you are always welcome; we are such old friends, I could not take your money.'

Of course, the pizzicheria man, and the apothecary, and the baker, all thought the commune of Vezzaja and Ghiralda admirably managed, or at least were bound to say so. They were the discreet, judicious, docile, reasonable people of the place. 'Why was not everybody the same?' thought Messer Nellemane and his colleagues and his myrmidons.

Now many of these people of Santa Rosalia were of ancient lineage and place; there were many families very poor, but who lived where their forefathers had done in centuries passed away. Pippo was one of these. In that house his forbears had dwelt for many generations, and there was a rivulet of water that passed through his wash-house and out at his door in which he himself had seen his great-grandfather soak the canes and osiers before him; his great-grandfather, who had been an old man when Murat's horsemen had been stabled in the church of San Giuseppe.

This spring rose somewhere in the earth of his

strip of herb and fruit garden, and had been allowed to run through the house and out of it and across the road to the river. Everybody always thought that it was the saints' blessing which had made the spring run there, just where there was a basket-maker and rush-plaiter always wanting to soak his willows and reeds. It never occurred to anybody that the little old house had been built over it for that use purposely.

This bright evening Bindo Terri, sauntering about with poisoned cates in his pocket for the dogs, and sharp eyes roaming everywhere in search of misdemeanours, caught sight of the water running merrily across the road, a narrow shallow brooklet, pleasant to see and carrying cleanliness with its presence. Water running out of a house and across a public roadway! Bindo was not sure whether it was a crime against the code, but he was quite sure that, if not, it ought to be. He opened his book of the Regulamenti Municipali, which he always carried with him carefully; and though he was not a very good scholar, he could spell through its clauses. He studied it now, travelling with his finger under each word, as the peasant-manner is in all countries. He found, as he expected, printed in Rule CCLVIII. of his beloved code, that it was forbidden to throw or let run any water on any public way. Bindo certainly had never read Shakespeare and never heard of him, but he said to himself, ' 'Twill serve.'

Pippo was sitting weaving in the door-way.

'Stop that water,' said zealous Bindo.

'Eh?' said the old man, in amaze.

'You must stop that water; water must not run across a highway,' said Bindo with stern authority. Pippo stared the more.

'God set it running there, and I doubt He won't stop it for you, jackanapes,' said the old fellow to the young one.

'You must cover it in, or drain it,' said Bindo, getting into a high official rage. 'It is against the law to have water in the public road. One has to step into it or step across it. You must cover it or drain it, or I shall report you.'

'Youngster,' said peaceable Pippo, very patiently, 'that water has been running as many years as the world is old; my father's fathers let it run, and thanked heaven for it, and so do I. Go your ways, Bindo Terri, and don't you come teaching a man sixty-six years old.'

For a guard to be called youngster! The insult made Bindo livid, and, had he dared, he would have crammed one of his poisoned *polpetti* down the throat of the offender.

He muttered some unintelligible words, at which old Pippo irreverently whistled, and he went on up the little street, if street it could be called, since it had no pavement, but only a path of cobble stones, and on one side of it was the grey-green Rosa.

'Dear Lady and all the saints!' cried Pippo to his neighbour; 'that young popinjay is saying now that water mustn't run as God set it running! I suppose our heads mayn't wag on our shoulders next!'

'Have you anything to show that the water *may* run?' said the neighbour nervously. He was the cooper Cecco (Francesco Zagazzi), a timid, meagre man, who had just had to pay a fine because his dog had sat outside the door instead of inside it, the dog being a terrier so small as scarcely to be discerned without a magnifying glass.

'Lord's sake, Ceccino,' said Pippo, fairly in a rage. 'The water's run three hundred years if one. Do you think the Almighty asked Bindo Terri's leave before he set the world a-going?'

The neighbour spat with anxious face into the dust. 'Almighty made dogs with four legs and didn't glue them down on their behinds,' he said wistfully. 'But according to Bindo Terri——'

'Bindo Terri have an apoplexy smite him!' shouted Pippo, which is the Italian way of saying 'you be d——d;' and he bundled together his osiers and withes and went in and screamed to Viola, 'Child, do you hear this? They're calling on me to stop the water! The Almighty's own stream, set a-bubbling in the beginning of the world, is to be stopped! That's a sight worse than telling me not to cut osiers!'

Viola grew pale.

'Bindo must have been joking, grandfather.'

'Lord knows!' said Pippo with a gasp. 'The world's topsy-turvy and the scum's all atop, when Bindo Terri can go about cheeking and trouncing a man of my years.'

'You must speak him fair, grandfather,' said the girl, uneasily.

'Nay, nay, that I'll never do,' said the little old man. 'I'll break his head. Stop that stream of water? Stop the sun a-shining, stop the wind a-blowing, stop the moon a-rolling! Why they're daft.'

'No, they aren't daft,' said the neighbour who had been fined for his terrier, and he shook the ashes out of his pipe very sadly. 'They're not daft; they're very sharp; they are too sharp for us, and that's the fact. Haven't you any bit of paper that'd show you might have the water?'

'Bit of paper? Bit of paper?' said Pippo, with a sort of ferocity. 'It ran for my father, and it ran for my grandfather, and it ran for my great-grandfather, and that's enough for me. Bit of paper? Who talks of a bit of paper? The brook is mine.'

'Perhaps they will forget all about it,' said Viola, with an effort at consolation.

'Bit of paper?' echoed Pippo, unheeding. 'Do you want a bit of paper to let the church stand in the square? Do you want a bit of paper to let the stars go on their courses? Bit of paper? The water runs through the house and out again, and it's a free thing, a free thing.'

The neighbour shook his head.

'If you haven't got a bit of paper——'

All the world to him was made up of bits of paper, he had been so often summoned and fined; happy people had bits of paper that released them from everything; unhappy people had bits of paper that condemned them for everything; to this much harassed man the world was chaos, and only this one idea was to be grasped out of its confusion. Pippo told him fiercely that his mother had been a female ass, and his father a galley-slave; but the neighbour bore the insult meekly, and went into his own door saying, 'that they never would let him alone about that water unless indeed he had a bit of paper——'

The populace, as I have said, can very well understand the law that punishes it when it thieves, when it slays, when it forges, when it fires; it can understand its chastisement well enough, and does not question the justice of it. But the law that punishes it for sitting in the sun, for running with a dog, for letting its child whip a top, for stopping its tired horse to rest in the shade of a wall, for letting its starved goat crop a bit of wayside grass that is nobody's and so is everybody's property, this it does not understand; at this it grows stupid and sullen as poor puppies do when cruel keepers beat them, and thus the guards get their fines, and the galleys their captives, and the graveyards their nameless tombs.

Bindo Terri went on into the piazza, and as the carabinier, who was no friend to him, told him somewhat roughly that he himself must loiter no more but go and look round the outlying country for the thieves that everywhere are ready to rob hen-roosts and granaries, the rural guard was disinclined to adventure his person alone amongst the populace, and went into the smaller Caffè of Nuova Italia, and called for wine and tobacco, and sat down and played cards with some kindred spirits.

'Diamine!' said Gigi Canterelli (he who was the grocer, and dealt beside in drugs and paints, and also had a sort of trattoria in his back-parlour), standing on the sill of the shop and speaking in a low tone as the figure of Bindo, deserted by the carabinier, was seen disappearing through the Caffè doors. 'Diamine! many's the time I've kicked and cuffed that rascal when he was but a *monellino*, for stealing plums and treacle, and knives and string. The saints bless us! And now he takes a turn at us all and does not forget old grudges! The other week or two past, ay, what did he do, think you?' added Gigi, turning to a young soldier just come off his term of service, who had been buying some gunpowder of him. 'The law bids me stick a light outside my door of a night (the Lord knows why—for there aren't a child twenty miles round that couldn't find me blindfold), but, however, there's the law, and I am not saying anything against it; I suppose the wiseacres made it for some good reason or another, and every night of my life I've lit that lamp since the order about it came in when we were all made free. But that night, it maybe a month ago, there was such a lot of folk in my shop, and they were all talking about that murder of the goldsmith in the city, and what with one thing and another, having nigh a score to serve at once (and one said the man had been murdered with a knife, and the other said he was shot, and another would have it he was strangled, and another said no, he had been brained with a hammer), I clean forgot the lamp—first time in fifteen years! I know the time because that order about lamps came in just the year after we got our liberty. Well, I forgot to light the lamp. Next morning comes that upstart, Bindo Terri, to me: says he, "What is your name?" "I should think you know it," I say; and I think to myself your breeches have felt my switch times enough when you were a pickle. "Don't answer me," says the upstart, as bold as brass. "What is your name?" "Luigi Canterelli," I say to him, feeling like a fool seventy years old, I, and having smacked that rogue often for robbing me! "Luigi Canterelli," says he, as though he were the Pretore in his black cap; and writes it down! Sure as fate, upon the morrow a summons comes to me—"contravention"—and bidding me go up before the Conciliatore, and the hue and cry out after me if I do not, and the pains of the Upper Court threatened! Then when I go, there is the blackguard himself witness that my shop was black when the moon came up, and twenty-seven francs in all are run up against me: and if I had said a word of the treacle and the string and the pocket-knife of the old time, the jackanapes would have been down on me for disrespect to an officer of the law. Oh! Lord save us!'

Gigi spat solemnly into the dust and filled his pipe, which had gone out in his oratory.

'We're all fools,' the young ex-conscript said gloomily. 'What have I had? Black bread, and ne'er enough of that, and set freezing in a cotton jacket up in Milan, in March, because the fellows down in Sicily had put on cotton jackets and so must we; though Sicily's as hot as hell, they say, and Milan's just an ice-house; and I all the while was sore needed at home here, and father has had to pay a labourer all three summers because I was taken away!—ugh!'

A friend nudged his elbow; Messer Nellemane in high silk hat and city-cut coat was sauntering by; Messer Nellemane looked the young soldier in the eyes.

'You are no patriot, my lad,' he said severely. 'I fear you have been but an indifferent soldier. You were a clod; the government made you a man. Be grateful.'

The young man coloured; he was wounded and ashamed; he was a peasant who had been taken by the conscription just as a young bullock is picked out for the shambles, and he had never understood why very well; his heart had been always with his fields, his homestead, his vines, his sweetheart; he had hated the barrack life, the dusty aimless marches, the drilling and the bullying, the weight of the knapsack and the roar of the guns; he had been a youth ere the government had made him a machine : he had not actively or outwardly rebelled, but he had hated it all, and he had come back to his native place, a harder, a crueller, and a moodier lad than he had left it; and when he thrummed his old mandoline by the farmhouse door, it had no longer any music for him; it seemed to him as if the beating of the drums had got into his ears and deafened him—and Messer Nellemane told him to be grateful. He looked down, shuffled his feet, doffed his hat, and was silent.

Messer Nellemane spoke with the serenity of one who never had served. Fortune, which took pleasure in favouring him, had made his mother a widow, when the time had come for him to enter his name, and he had been an only son, and so exempt from all military service.

'Never you mind; you're better than he is any day, the cursed Jew quill-driver,' muttered old Gigi to the young soldier; but the lad scowled and lounged away down the river-side moodily.

If the enemy had come into his country he would have held his own hamlet against them to the last gasp; but to be drafted off to Milan, to wear a fool's jacket and eat black bread while the fields were half tilled, and the old people sore driven, and the girl of his heart got married to some other man—no, he was not a patriot if, to be one, he must have been a contented conscript.

Yet he had ducked a Frenchman in the Mincio for calling Italians cowards. Messer Nellemane might not have done so much; unless, indeed, a

Minister had been looking on, and the valour would have been likely to bring him promotion.

The next morning Bindo Terri, amongst other contraventions, presented on his list the case of old Filippo and the running water. Messer Gaspardo drew his pen through it.

'Wait awhile,' he said to his zealous servitor. 'Of course no water must run across the road. You are quite right; it is a nuisance, and expressly forbidden; but you have spoken to Mazzetti, and we will give him time. He is an old inhabitant, and should be dealt with gently. We must warn, counsel, recommend, at first; and use our power afterwards if the person be refractory and obstinate. We must not be too harsh.'

Bindo Terri stared, disappointed and almost inclined to be rude to his chief patron. He could insist on his list of offenders being dealt with according to the regulations if he chose. But in his heart he was sorely afraid of Messer Gaspardo, who was so good to him; so he grumbled a little under his breath, and consoled himself with going out of the municipality and buying some bullock's liver to cook at home with phosphorus to make up into balls to fling about over the country roads to destroy all dogs that might be trotting innocently on their way to their homes, or their fellow-dogs, or sitting at their master's gates to guard his fields and vineyards. He had no right to throw it in the daytime, even the regulations did not allow that; but there was nothing to prevent him doing so; and if, as now and then happened, a sheep passing amidst a flock touched the foul thing in the dust, and was taken with what its shepherd thought a fit, the amusement to Bindo was complete when he watched from behind a hedge the beast's agony and the shepherd's dismay.

Messer Nellemane, although he drew rein to his myrmidon's zeal, in heart approved of it, of course. A spring of water bubbling across a public pathway was to him a thing of horror: was what a stole and rochet are to a stern Protestant, or a shot fox is to an Englishman; and there indisputably the little spring was, wimpering out from Pippo's garden door, and making a little silver thread in the dust. It was just one of those lawless, easy-going, illegitimate things, births of ancient customs and indolent privileges, which it was the scope of all the Regulations to reach, sweep away, and utterly destroy.

In truth, the water outside Pippo's gate made so slight a show as it ran to the river, that in passing over it, it had never struck the eyes of Messer Nellemane; he had seen it, but he had thought it the leak of a pipe or the accident of the hour. Now, however, it assumed to him all the awful blackness, all the unspeakable insolence, of a contravention. The Inquisitors are dead, but their souls live again in the Impiegati.[1]

For the present, however, he stifled his feelings, and only kept the water in memory, to use if need be; just for all the world as Torquemada would have kept the torture; and he continued his courtship, stealthily, so that Santa Rosalia might know nothing of it, but boldly, so far as that he dispensed with all hesitating preliminaries and plunged *in medias res*, with all the disregard of delicacy that became a great man condescending to notice a poor

[1] Clerks of the civil service or of any public works.

maiden. He did not, however, to his surprise, make much way in the maiden's good graces. He could never manage to see her alone; old Pippo was almost sure to be there, till Messer Nellemane longed to throttle him with his own reeds; or, if he were absent, there was the next-door neighbour, the cooper's wife with her tribe of children, or some of the Pastorini girls, or Viola's great-aunt by the mother's side, a little withered rosy-cheeked old apple of a woman, who called him Excellenza and opened her little black eyes wide at seeing such a grand personage come to the cottage.

Nobody was ever alone in Santa Rosalia; all doors were open, and all work was done to a chorus of chattering voices. Gossip is the very staff of life to all Italian communities, and the scanty bread and the watered wine are made up for by the delight of endless talk. The talk is of Lippo's cow that has calved, of Tina's baby that has cut its teeth, of Dina's girl that is to marry at Pasqua; of the vicar's new surplice, of the fattoressa's new gown, of the chances of oil being cheap and of flour being dear, of all sorts of little odds and ends of local tittle-tattle that are to them as the scandals of the Jockey Club, the combinations of Worth, the actions of the Porte, or the speeches of Prince Bismarck, are to us.

Viola had never been alone in all her life; her grandfather thought no woman ever should be; but her new admirer fancied that all these people round her were precautions taken against himself, and waxed very angry accordingly.

He did not want all the neighbourhood to talk of his courtship of this poor old man's granddaughter, and he knew very well that if you only fling an acorn in the dust one day people, the next, will swear to a grove of oaks against you.

The Italian tongue chatters like a magpie's; if they did not let the steam off thus they would be less easily ruled than they are; but no great talker ever did any great thing, yet, in this world.

Messer Gaspardo Nellemane was by no means an immoral man; he was rather cold of temperament, and being a wise person he saw how often a little naughty story when it gets afloat about a public career is to it as fatal as the rift in the lute. He had a wholesome horror of ever being compromised by foolish frivolities; he was an ambitious man, and these wayside dallyings had but little temptation for him. Nevertheless, Messer Nellemane was not a saint, and the beauty of Viola, granddaughter of Pippo, was seductive to him.

Marry her? No; he did not mean to marry; not until he should get some better post than this of Santa Rosalia, and be able to discover some heiress of a wax-candle-maker, or a *strozzino*, or an oil merchant, whose money would help to make him a deputy, since he fully intended some day to jump from the office-stool of the municipality to the benches of Montecitorio. No; he had no thought of marrying Viola, but she was very handsome, very beautiful, and there was docile Bindo Terri ready to take anything off his hands, from a frayed coat to a tarnished love. Bindo Terri would marry her—for a consideration.

Messer Gaspardo, though only a clerk, had all the ideas of a gentleman.

As it chanced Corpus Domini fell late in May that year, and of course there were to be processions all over the country, and every girl, however penniless she might be, would find a white or a blue frock, and perhaps a bit of tulle for a veil, and would walk with the Host as it was borne under an umbrella between the mulberry trees that lined the dusty roads and through the gardens of the neighbouring villas.

Viola was very poor, and her clothes, though clean, were always sorely patched and frayed; so Messer Gaspardo thought it good policy to go down into the city himself and choose a most delicate print of the Madonna's own azure, and a wreath of white roses and some shoes, shoes with bright silvered-looking buckles, just such as the ladies wore; and making all these up into a parcel when he got home, he left them himself on the table of old Pippo's cottage when Pippo and his daughter were absent.

On the roll of print he had pinned a card,— '*Con ossequie teneri alla più bella del mondo: dal suo devoto.*—G. N.'

He knew the right road to the female heart. Viola chanced to see the parcel when alone; her grandfather being outside smoking a pipe with a neighbour. She coloured very much, and then grew very pale. She could just spell out the words on the card. She hastened up the steep stone staircase to her own little miserable room and hid the packet under the sheet on her bed. She had only just caught a glimpse of the blue print, and the white wreath, and the buckles; and they had made her tremble as though she had seen the face of a ghost.

She was keen in all her simplicity as her people almost always are, and she had that doubt which always underlies their sanguine temper  If Carmelo saw these things he would be capable of flinging them at their giver's head and saying perilous words in the very palace of the municipality itself.

Even her old grandfather——

Her heart sank like a stone in the deep sea as she thought of the forbidden rushes and the running water at the threshold.

'If I spoke him fair?' she said to herself with her country-folk's belief in fair words as a panacea for all evils and ills, and a talisman against all peril and enmity.

'May I go and see the aunt 'Nunziatina this evening?' she asked of Pippo. Her great-aunt lived at the other end of Santa Rosalia; the same little apple-cheeked old woman who had stared at Messer Nellemane; she was poor, nay, she was penniless; she shared a room with three others and lived frankly on alms; very honest begging it was; she went round from house to house with a big basket, and got bread and broken meats, and a little money, and now and then a flask of wine, and then she sang her Jubilate. Everybody knew and liked her in this place where she had lived all her life, and knew very well that she had not a soldo in the world; her husband had been a day-labourer, and when he had chopped his hand off, in cutting a hedge of oakscrub and myrtle, and had died of mortification, the old Annunziata had been left destitute.

The Government, which forbids begging, and lands those who do beg in prisons, has as yet provided no poor-law; so eighty-year-old 'Nunziatina had no choice but to trot round with her basket, or to die silently of hunger. Many do the latter—and nobody cares.

Want seems sadder in this light and lovely land, where life requires so little to make it happy and to fill its needs, than it does in the dark grim North, where fog hides the suffering multitudes and cold is the tyrant of all. Here, give but a little bread, a little oil and wine, and life can sparkle on cheerily as the firefly burns in the cornfields; but, alas! even that little, thousands and tens of thousands have not, and so perish.

Messer Nellemane, and his kind, know the reason why.

'May I go and see 'Nunziatina?' said Viola, and her grandfather nodded assent; she went and got the parcel from under her bed and went out with it.

'What have you there?' said Pippo.

'The cloth I have spun; auntie can sell it better than I,' said Viola, thinking nought of a little fib for peace' sake, though she coloured as she spoke, for she was of a straightforward and truthful nature.

The old man ambled by her side on his little lean shrivelled shanks, for he never let the girl go through the village alone.

Arrived at the dwelling of Annunziata, he let his granddaughter go upstairs, while he stayed below, chatting with the carpenter who owned the cottage, and dwelt in the ground-floor of it, and let the rest to lodgers.

The cottage stood on a bit of waste land by a bend in the river; some poplars made a pleasant murmur near; some geese and goats strayed about on the worn grass.

'The Giunta cuts the trees down come Ognissanti,' said the carpenter with a groan.

'By Bacchus!' cried Pippo, who never tasted any wine better than vinegar.

'They'll cut our toe-nails off next,' sighed the carpenter.

'They would if they could get a centime a toe!' assented Pippo, and told his grievance as to the rushes and the stream.

Meanwhile, Viola upstairs told her story to her grand-aunt; a little old square figure with a straw hat on, and a very short skirt, and old leather boots like a ploughman's, and a cheerful sunburnt, ugly, pleasant face.

'Dear our Lady! but it is beautiful stuff for a gown!' cried the old woman, fingering the blue print as reverentially as if it had been the holy wafer. 'Eh, eh! I opened my eyes at him the other day! I thought, thought I, "Yon master comes not for naught!"'

'But I cannot keep it,' said Viola, with a flush on her cheeks and a little tone of inquiry in the words.

The old woman said at once: 'No, my joy; you would do ill to keep it.'

They had been all of them very upright and unstained folks in both these families from which Viola Mazzetti sprang, and their women had always been honest and chaste.

'Maybe, though, he means it in all honour?' said 'Nunziatina doubtingly, and thinking to herself: 'She is so handsome, the child; why not?—and after all, though a great man here, he was a tinker's son, they say; and when all is told he is but a clerk.'

Viola shook her head, and her cheeks grew red. The maidens of the poor soon learn what evil means.

'No, no; he is a bad man,' she said with a slight shudder. 'And besides, if he did mean well, I must keep faith with Carmelo.'

'The lad has spoken out, then?'

'Yes; we shall marry when the fathers say we can.'

'That is another thing,' said the old woman. 'Now what is it you want me to do, my dear; for there is something, I can see?'

'I thought this,' said Viola. 'I thought, I cannot go to Messer Gaspardo; that would never do; I never scarce stir by myself, and grandfather would be furious; and besides, I want him to know nothing, and Carmelo nothing either; so I thought, if you would take the parcel back to Messer Gaspardo, and thank him, and speak him fair, and tell him I am betrothed, I thought that might be the best way? You can see him any day, they say, at the communal palace; and we must try not to offend him, because he can hurt people so much, and he is already angry at things grandfather has done.'

The old woman chuckled a little, for she was a merry soul, though she was eighty-four and had not a penny on earth, and when she should die would be buried in a deal box by the parish.

'A pretty figure am I for a palace!' she said with a laugh as bright as a robin's song. 'But let us talk it over, my dearly beloved, and may the dear saints counsel us!'

They did talk it over, turning the matter inside out, and in every possible light, as Italians like to do on all occasions; the girl was harassed and oppressed by this love-gift; the old woman was rather flattered and amused.

'Pray speak him fair,' Viola begged of her ambassadress as old Pippo called to her to go down. 'Pray be humble and pretty of language to him, because he can do father so much harm!'

'Pooh, he can't eat us,' said the old woman, who had a spirit of her own. 'And he won't be the first man, my dear, that has found himself forestalled by a better than himself with a handsome maiden!'

Viola could neither smile nor blush.

'He can do everybody so much harm!' she said anxiously with a sigh. The dread of Gaspardo Nellemane was like a hand of lead upon her, 'Do speak him fair, dear, pray do!'

'Never fear,' said the old soul merrily. 'He can't do me any mischief, my child. Who has nothing loses nothing. Does not the proverb say so? Why should you be angry with the young man? He means no harm, I will warrant.'

'Viola! come down, I say! Your tongue will reach to the town and go twice round the cathedral!' roared Pippo impatiently from below; and the girl went down the cottage stairs heavy of heart, and wondering how her grand-aunt's errand would speed. She could not shake off the memory of Messer Gaspardo's bold black eyes.

But at the cottage-door they met Carmelo driving a cart of his father's home, empty, having taken sacks of flour to a neighbouring hamlet; and she and her grandfather got up into the cart behind the good old grey horse Bigio with its jingling bells, and so sped cheerfully past the poplars and along the river; and in the gaze of her lover's honest beaming eyes she was half though not wholly cured of her fears, and repaid a hundredfold for the loss of the dress and the rose-wreath and the shoes with the shining buckles.

In the forenoon 'Nunziatina took the parcel in her alms-basket and trotted with her stick to help her through Santa Rosalia to the municipal building, and then boldly asked for Messer Nellemane. She was a bright-hearted, high-couraged, old woman, and had that sturdy independence which is still extant among the old people who are too old to be able to learn to cringe before the national curse of municipal law.

She cared naught for all the greatness of Messer Gaspardo, and fought valiantly with Tonino and Maso and Bindo, all of whom tried to shut their doors on her, and at last, in sheer despite of them, she stumped up the stone stairs in her hobnailed boots that were three times too large for her, and at ten of the clock precisely stood in the august presence.

Messer Gaspardo welcomed her quite charmingly; he knew she was the grand-aunt of Viola Mazzetti. He was seated in state, ready to receive anybody, as was his wont from ten to twelve, with a long writing-table before him, covered with papers, and the green blinds shut against the sun, and maps of the district and books of the Penal Code and the Civil Code around him; and really he might almost have been taken for the Prefect of the Province, so grave and majestic an embodiment of the Law did he look.

'I am glad to find your excellency all alone,' said the bright little old woman, laying down the big parcel on the writing-table, for she thought to herself, 'I am told to speak him fair, and nothing will please him like a grand title, that makes me look like an ass to use it.'

'All the country is always talking of all it owes to your illustrious self' (and that is true, she thought, because every living soul is always cursing and abusing him from morning till night), 'and never should I have ventured, a poor old beggar as I am, to intrude upon you, only that I have to speak to you about my sister's granddaughter——'

'Speak on,' said the secretary, but his eye grew annoyed and startled; this was by no means what he wished; to have his admiration of Viola made a subject of discussion in her family was the last thing that consorted with his desires or designs. 'The girl has been boasting already,' he thought angrily, and gave a malediction to the vanity of woman.

'You admire Viola, they tell me, and so indeed it seems, since you send such fine presents, *signore mio*,' continued the crafty 'Nunziatina, and waited for him to reply.

Messer Gaspardo gnawed his moustachios irritably.

'Every one admires a beautiful girl,' he said at last, with an uneasy laugh. 'You must not conclude too much from that——'

'No, no, sir, not I,' said the old woman very cheerfully, but her little sunken still bright brown eyes plunged their regard into his and read him, down to the secrets of his innermost soul. 'Gentlemen like you have a kindly way of paying compliments that mean nothing; oh, nothing at all; and my Viola is a girl of a great deal too much sense to have put meaning into anything you said or did.

F

Only as she is very grateful to you for such courtesy, and could not come very well to say so, she bade me speak for her; and do you be very sure, sir, that none the less thankful is she, though her feeling as to what is right makes her send your pretty things back by me, sir.'

Therewith 'Nunziatina took out of her basket all the gifts that had represented with Messer Nellemane the pearls of Faust, and laid them very respectfully down on his table.

Messer Nellemane grew of a sickly colour. He was pallid with rage. He half rose from his seat.

'What, woman!' he stammered; 'what? Are you mad? Do you dare to insult *me*?'

'No, no, sir; never a thought of it,' said wily Annunziata; 'no more of it than you had in buying those pretty things for the child to wear on Corpus Domini; a kindly thought, just like a gentleman——'

'Why then—why——' still stammered Messer Gaspardo, still aghast with wrath and wonder.

'Why, sir?'—the little old woman drew herself up quite straight, with both her hands on her elm-stick—'why, sir, because it is not meet for maidens, and motherless maidens, to take gifts from those too much above them to mean honest marriage, or have any thought except a foolish sport that may divert the man but does destroy the woman. City girls, I know, are ready for that sort of play, but our girls are not. That is all I wanted just to say, and thank you kindly, Signore Gaspardo; for I am quite sure you had no thought of harming Viola. And now let me take away the inconvenience of myself, and bid you a very good day.'

With that Italian phrase of peasant farewell which here was no figure of speech, for she was indeed the greatest discomfort to him that had ever fallen across his prosperous career, the little old woman in her straw hat and her short petticoats bowed to him, with that grace which oftentimes even the humblest and the very aged keep in this land where Art once ruled supreme, and trotted out of his room and down the stone stairs with a little tranquil chuckle.

She had said nothing of Viola's betrothal; the Italian courtesy and caution alike lay down as a fixed rule for rich and poor, that you should never say a disagreeable thing under any pretext or pressure.

'He will learn it soon enough,' she thought, 'and he is a bad man, and a dangerous; the devil dwells under his eyelids.'

To her granddaughter, however, she only said cheerfully, 'I put it to him politely, my dear, and thanked him; and I hope you will hear no more of his nonsense.'

For she reasoned with herself, Of what use was it to tell the child her own fears? She thought it would be of more use to buy a real wax candle, instead of a bit of kid, the first time anybody should give her some coppers, and burn it before the Madonna up in the old oak-tree of the church of San Romualdo upon the slopes behind her dwelling-place; a shrine which had been set in the trunk of that old tree no one well knew how many hundreds of years before, and at which were wrought still many marvellous cures, and many infinite kindnesses of the Holy Virgin to true believers. The candle that very week she did buy with the first money she got on her rounds, and it twinkled its life out in the hot May day until at night the little white moths burned themselves up in it by scores, and it dwindled into darkness as the stars began to gleam and the nightingales to sing.

But whilst her holy candle burned under the holy ilex trees, the fires of an unholy rage burned in the breast of Messer Nellemane. He felt he had been checkmated, and checkmated by a little old trot in a ragged petticoat who, he felt, had been jeering at him with her *illustrissimo*. His own grandmother, indeed, still living in the township of his birth, was not one whit less ragged or impecunious than was 'Nunziatina. But he always strove to forget his grandmother as he strove to forget his father's old iron and rusty brass, for it was not meet for a man on the highway to a political party and a ministerial greatness to cumber himself with these remembrances. He sent his mother, indeed, now and then a banknote in a registered letter, but it was always on the understanding that she never of her own accord recalled her existence to him.

A retentive memory is of great use to a man, no doubt; but the talent of oblivion is on the whole more useful.

The fire of his rage consumed him, and he was the more angry because at the moment he knew not how to smite those who mocked at him.

An hour or two later, however, he carelessly said to Bindo Terri:

'That old woman who came to bring me a petition to-day—she is a professional mendicant?'

Bindo watched his chief's face anxiously to get his cue, but could read nothing.

'La 'Nunziatina?' he said, hesitatingly. 'No, Signore, I would not call her that; everybody knows her; she has been always like this; she goes from house to house, and out to all the villas in turn——'

An angry glisten of Messer Gaspardo's eyes told his faithful servitor that he had gone on the wrong tack: he hastened to make amends.

'A beggar, of course, she is,' he added. 'I think she has been one twenty years. I remember her as long as I remember anything, and she always lived by charity. A lady did get her awhile ago permission to get taken in at Montesacro; but the old cranky, crazy creature said she could not live shut up: if she could not walk her dozen miles a day she would die—so she said. Yes: to be sure, *illustrissimo*, she is a beggar.'

'A vagrant!'

Messer Nellemane shrugged his shoulders and sighed over the degeneracy of a public which would still continue to find patrons to support and pamper mendicancy. He fell into deep meditation. In the 395 Regulations framed for the Polizia, Igiena, and Edilità of the commune there was one terrible void: there was nothing at all said about beggars.

'They can find means to maintain all these creatures, and yet they declare they cannot support the imperial and local taxes!' he said aloud to his subordinate; by his 'they' meaning the landowners of the district, men of long descent, patrician appearance, and courtly manner, whose rank was the bitter envy of Messer Nellemane, whilst their poverty was the object of his equally bitter scorn.

Bindo Terri sighed too, and put up his hands to express his own equal regret and horror. Himself, he knew very well that most of the people who gave alms to Annunziata were people of the poorest sort; peasants or homely folk, such as masons, carpenters, smiths, and the like; but he saw that it would not suit his chief's mood then to say so.

'There is nothing about beggars in it?' he said questioningly, turning over the leaves of his beloved and revered Regulations.

'Not as yet,' said Messer Nellemane. 'The good Cavaliere Durellazzo is, perhaps, too lenient to the vagrant classes.'

The good Cavaliere Durellazzo was just then sitting in a straw chair, with a wide straw hat on, smoking a cigar made, for the most part, of straw, on the sands of a summer resort on the Mediterranean, and no more troubled himself about his commune when away, than he did when at home in it.

## CHAPTER IV.

That very night, as ill luck would have it, Messer Nellemane went sauntering down the green banks of the Rosa, for the pleasure of surveying a grim piece of work he had done the year before. An old convent, once of an Olivetine Congregation, crowned a hill that rose up from the Rosa; it had been a beautiful hill, clothed for centuries with forest greenery, in which many a tall cypress, hundreds of years old, and of great height and girth, towered majestic, whilst the bronze-hued ilex oak, and the silver poplar, and the chestnut, and the acacia, all grew in amity together, sheltering in spring time millions of primroses, and of many another wee wood-flower.

Santa Rosalia is in a lovely pastoral country; the country that seems to thrill with Theocritus' singing, as it throbs with the little tambourine of the cicala; a country running over with beautiful greenery, and with climbing creepers hanging everywhere, from the vine on the maples to the china rose hedges, and with the deep blue shadows and the sun-flushed whiteness of the distant mountains lending to it in the golden distance that solemnity and ethereal charm which, without mountains somewhere within sight, no country ever has. But since the advent of freedom it is scarred and wounded; great scar patches stretch here and there where woods have been felled by the avarice illumined in the souls of landowners; hundreds and thousands of bare poles stand stark and stiff against the river light, which have been glorious pyramids of leaf, shedding welcome shadows on the river path; and many a bold round hill like the *ballons* of the Vosges, once rich of grass as they, now shorn of forest and even of undergrowth, lift a bare stony front to the lovely sunlight, and never more will root of tree, or seed of flower, or of fern, find bed there.

Such is Progress.

This convent of Francesca Romana had been 'appropriated' in the sacred name of liberty, and the nuns had been all sent here and there, back to their families if they had any, and out to weary loneliness if they had not, and the dowers they had given the Church had gone to the coffers of the Government, and enriched contractors, and engineers, and ministers.

The old home of these Olivetine Sisters itself was despoiled, much as it would have been by an invading army that was allowed loot. Its crucifixes, its ivories, its carvings were sold by the State to curiosity dealers, and its frescoes, by Sodoma and the Carracci, were cut off the walls and disposed of to a foreign nation.

All this had been done before Messer Nellemane's time, although done by men so closely like to Messer Nellemane that they might have been his elder brothers.

The deserted building, when he had come into the village, had stood on the hill like a wrecked city; majestic still, since its old walls, all faced with marbles and porphyry, would have yielded to nought save cannon; and its tall bell-tower, exquisite in its slenderness and symmetry, and its ivory-like whiteness, had still pointed heavenward from its green throne, though its bells had been torn down and melted to help make a bronze statue of one of Messer Nellemane's elder brothers away in the city, where it was called the Monument of a Soldier of Liberty, and had Fame and Peace seated together at its base.

The building was an empty shell, and while the Government were always meaning to turn it into an institute, a barrack, a powder magazine, or a laboratory, the years had slipped away, and damp and drought alternately were changing it into a ruin. But the forest beauty about it was still untouched when Santa Rosalia first beheld Messer Nellemane; and when he had been a little time upon that office stool of which he intended to make a starting-point to a future ministry of State, he cast his eyes upon this shattered temple of superstition. To his amazement the timber on the hillside had been all left standing.

All those instincts which always made him feel it was his destiny some day to become a minister of finance, or of the interior, rose up in his breast.

What waste of the public purse! And what a commission awaiting for somebody! Messer Nellemane, of all things this world held, loved best a job. The official mind always loves a job. Moreover, he detested trees, as he detested dogs. As dogs were only endurable when chained up, so, to him, trees were only tolerable when sawn into lengths and neatly planed.

The official mind, with which he had been created, viewed with abhorrence the unministerial and improvident existence permitted to that once sacred wood, whilst the convent it surrounded had been dealt with as free thought can always deal with such monuments of superstition.

Messer Nellemane made a humble suggestion on the matter to Cavaliere Durellazzo; the Syndic made a communication to the Giunta; the Prefect of the province was seen and whispered with; the Prefect went down to Rome and whispered with the Minister of Public Works, who was his friend. It was suddenly discovered that there was a great need of oak wood in the dockyards, though they were building ships of nothing but iron; soon it was decreed that the trees which had sheltered and graced the bigotry of the past should fall to help fill the treasuries of the present.

The Ministry entrusted the direction of the sale to the Prefect; the Prefect entrusted it to the Syndic of Vezzaja and Ghiralda, the prefectorial commission being a thing understood; of course, no one speaks of such matters. The Syndic entrusted it in turn to his secretary, the syndical commission being, of course, equally understood; and the Giunta also being understood, without words, to have each of them an interest in the ultimate proceeds.

But it may be taken for granted that, when the various commissions, first of the big Ministers down in Rome, and then of the big Prefect down in the adjacent city, and then of all the lesser personages concerned, not omitting Messer Nellemane himself, who took all the trouble of it under the rose, were all shaved off the sum total brought by the sale of that wood to the State, the nation never bought timber dearer for its dockyards.

However, everybody was very pleased except a few artists who tried to make a noise about it, as those troublesome beings always do, and the people of the commune in general, who were not consulted and did not count.

The particulars of the sale were amongst those official things which never issue out of pigeon-holes, and concerning which blue books, green books, yellow books, all books parliamentary, are silent in all countries.

The trees fell; the giants of centuries crashed down under axes or under fire; the hares, the birds, the myriads of innocent pretty, forest life that had lived under them so long, fled away or were ruthlessly destroyed; cartloads of timber went to burn in the furnaces of public works or rot away in shipyards; and Messer Nellemane bought privately, through his trusty cousin, some foreign scrip; indeed everybody concerned in the sale bought something.

The convent stood bare and drear upon its desolated hillside, and above the river rose a great slope, naked, scarred, frightful, with charred holes yawning where the primrose tufts and the blue irises had blossomed in that same springtide.

Messer Nellemane looked up at it now, and felt it had been a work worthy of him, and one fully in the spirit of the age.

It was really quite equal to the pulling down of Tell's chapel and of Milton's house; to the destruction of the walls of Augsburg and the towers of Nurnberg; to the levelling of the Spanish Houses of Brussels and of the gates and the bastions of Gall, of the Grand Châtelet of Paris and of the Tabard Inn of old London; he felt that it might take its place proudly amidst all the greatest destruction wrought by Progress and Economy in this noblest and most æsthetic century, by means of its chiefs and executants, the Municipalities.

In the old time architects and artists had wrought here diligently, reverentially, lovingly, in the name of God and of the arts; but Messer Nellemane, though he had never heard of Sainte Beuve, would have quite agreed with him, that ' *Dieu, ce n'est pas français,*' and for his own part would have been as ready to affirm that Art was no longer in the Italian dictionary.

In the old time European municipalities thought that they existed for the ends of patriotism and the glory of their cities; they built for the honour of God and the love of their country. But nowadays all that is changed; a municipality is only a selection of persons intent on their own interests; the motto of each is 'my policy's myself'; whether old walls are pulled down or new ones put up, gold comes off the mortar for the town-councilmen, the contractors, and the commissioners, and they can never understand why every one is not as satisfied as they are. Whether the question be one of demolition or construction, all they look for is what it will bring.

Whether trees fall in Kensington Gardens or the Cascine, whether old churches are pulled down in Rome or in Paris, whether new streets make hideous Venice or Vienna, whether gardens are chopped to pieces on the Pincio or in the Bois, there is always somebody who pockets something *sub rosâ*, and instead of Jacques Cœur or the Fugger, or William of Wykham, or Alan Walsingham, we have officers of Public Works as avaricious as Harpagon, as dull as Prudhomme, and more ruthless than Attila.

They are always amazed that you are not contented.

If you want a handsome structure, can you not make a large glass frame for a market or an exhibition, or raise a fine sugar-white gimcrack in plaster and stucco, that you can call a war office, a church, a college, or a palace at your pleasure ?

The bureaucratic and the municipalic mind cannot comprehend any higher joy than destroying, reconstructing, and pocketing the proceeds of both operations.

Our friend Messer Nellemane had been born with the bureaucratic and municipalic organs both largely developed in his brain, and within his narrow confines he contrived to compass vast things, and his heart was always comforted as he looked up at the bald gneiss and sand where the convent oaks once had stood ; but, as woe would have it, taking this night his favourite stroll past ruined Santa Francesca, he saw two shadows in the evening light, and all his comfort fled. The shadows were far below him, and were entwined one with another, like two young acacias that have grown up and leaned together; they were moving slowly over the long grass under the lines of the silver poplars by the watermill.

His heart gave a leap of rage, and his ruddy face grew livid.

He recognised in the happy murmuring lovers under the trees, Viola and young Carmelo. His passion was stung to the quick, and his pride and his vanity were wounded yet more deeply. 'She rejects *me*!' he thought, and no emperor flouted by a peasant maid, and seeing a rustic lout preferred, could have felt himself more grossly and with greater ingratitude insulted.

True, the old shop of rusty iron was not so much above the mill as an origin; but then Messer Nellemane was now a servant of the State, nay, rather, an integral piece of the State itself, as a cogwheel is a piece of the great machine it helps to work; and he thought himself a very great personage.

He walked now above the river on the bare ridge beneath Santa Francesca, and saw the lovers strolling below, through the poplar wood, with the big white dog of the mill, Toppa, strolling as well in front of them, and all his soul burned within him with rage and jealous chagrin.

He could see the brown wheel churning in the water; he could see the flour sacks leaning against the fence under the hedge of elders; he could see the jay in its cage amongst a passion flower that covered all the house wall; he could see the snowy head of the old miller himself, leaning out of a little square window, and calling orders to the boy who was waiting with the mule-cart at the gate; and he could see the lovers loitering in the sunset warmth by the river; lovers, who thought to live all their days out there peacefully under that same roof, and leave their children to come there after them, and get their bread by the same old wooden wheels churning the same green waters where the green leaves grew.

He stood on the heights above, and looked down on the tranquil little scene;—with a curse.

## CHAPTER V.

Two or three days later was Corpus Domini; it fell on the last day of May.

Viola would not have been a daughter of Eve had she not thought longingly, on the eventide before this great feast, of Messer Nellemane's blue gown and white wreath. What would not the other girls have said if they could but have seen her in that beautiful dress, and with the buckles shining on her feet!

She never wished that she had kept them, but she often did wish that they could have been the gift of her grandfather, or of Carmelo.

The procession was the great day of the year in Santa Rosalia, as in every other village and little borgo round. Messer Nellemane, who was a *libero pensiero*, yearned to have it suppressed; he thought it degrading and idiotic. Like a true Liberal thinker, he was of opinion that as there should be no distinctions for the rich, so there should be no diversions for the poor. He would have forbidden banners, music, colours, lights, public services, and gatherings of all sorts, except for Liberal purposes, under threat of heavy pains and penalties, but he had no power; the Government has not quite made up its mind as yet to do away with any time-honoured custom, and he, without the Government, was helpless, for this was an imperial matter.

So all day long, every Fête Dieu, the tolling and chiming of bells, the aspect of villagers clad in their festal array, the sounds of chanting, the scent of incense, the sight of banners, pursued him, and made him irritable and unhappy; so unhappy that even the number of contraventions, generally to be gleaned on a day when people were too merry and too engrossed to chain up their dogs and shut up their children, could not altogether console him. Besides, even Bindo was so carried away by the influence of long habit that he was himself not so watchful as usual on this day, when the girls were all looking their best in their white or blue gowns, and most houses had open doors and a full table, and at nightfall there were dancing and illuminations in the piazza.

This summer the procession was especially hateful and foolish in Messer Gaspardo's sight; was more than ever loathsome to him, since Viola Mazzetti did not wear his gown, and his garland, and his shoe-buckles, but came out in her humble grey skirt and bodice, that were to her loveliness like the dark leaves to the mangolia flower, and had never as much even as a silver pin set in her hair.

Old Pastorini, too, was the *capo* of the feast, and managed everything, and in the village band Carmelo beat the drum; beat it indeed with more zeal than discretion, so that it could always be heard high above every other instrument at every moment, but was very much praised, and looked very handsome and bright as he did so.

Messer Nellemane found all this too much for him, so he rose early on this day, and went on business over to the great city, twelve miles away under the mountains, and let Santa Rosalia have its fooling since he had no power to stop it.

And Santa Rosalia had it; very peacefully and piously at first, and then very good-naturedly and gaily, mingling the sacred and the profane in an innocent jumble, singing the *O Salutaris* one moment devoutly as they followed the Host, and the next, humming waltz music merrily as they jumped round in the dance.

Italian merrymaking is no longer pretty; the sense of colour and of harmony is gone out of our people, whose forefathers were models of Leonardo and Raffaelle, and whose own limbs, too, have still so often the mould of the Faun and the Discobolus. Their merrymaking has nothing of the grace and brightness of French fairs, nor even of the picturesqueness and colour of the German feast and frolics; even in Carnival, though there are gaiety and grotesqueness, there are little grace and little good colouring. Yet the people enjoy themselves; enjoy themselves for the most part very harmlessly, and very merrily, when they forget their tax-papers, their empty stomachs, and their bankrupt shops.

The village enjoyed itself this day of the Feast

of God, though its piazza was very dusty, and its band very out of tune, and its food and its drink as thoroughly bad as they could be. But it was Corpus Domini, and every one was happy; and when the long procession had said its last prayer the *trescone* began in the square, and every house was hung with crescets of light.

Messer Nellemane, being compelled to return by the last diligence that ran to Santa Rosalia from the town to which he had gone to escape from the ceremonies and festivities, found himself at ten of the night in a still crowded piazza as he descended from his rickety conveyance. The Municipality was black as crape; that he could ordain; but every other house round the place was twinkling with the flame of lighted oil in little iron sconces; the very same sconces that had been used in the Cinque Cento to celebrate feasts and frays and saints' days.

The lights were blazing brightly; the music was sounding jocundly, the youths and the maidens were going round and round, laughing and chattering as they jumped. The drum stood on a pavement with the honest dog of the mill guarding it, and Carmelo was dancing with Viola, while old Pippo and the miller, sitting on two rush chairs beside the dog and drum, looked on smiling and beating the time.

A shining sky was over them all; the river glistened in the strong moonlight; the air was heavy with the scent of the lilies and the stocks, the carnations and the roses in the gardens around. Santa Rosalia was *in festa,* and the two old men, warmed by a little more wine than usual, were saying one to another,

G

'They might as well wed at once? They will never be richer, and there is no time like youth.'

Messer Nellemane did not hear the words of the old men, but he saw the young dancers.

He went on sullenly, with his hat drawn down over his brows, pushing his way through the crowd without any of the somewhat pompous politeness of demeanour which marked him usually.

He slammed his door, and went to his bed, and shut his shutters to shut out the shining heavens, the fragrant air, the glittering little lights; but the laughter, and the music, and the joyous blithe-hearted murmur that rose up from the dancers below the shutters, he could not exclude; and he cursed them.

For the first time his *liberi pensieri* were distasteful to him and unsatisfactory; for atheism makes a curse a mere rattle of dry peas in a fool's bladder, as it makes a blessing a mere flutter of a breath. Messer Nellemane for the first time felt that the old religion had its advantages over agnosticism; it gave you a hell for your rivals and your enemies!

In the next week there came a little party up to the Municipality of Santa Rosalia. They were Pippo and his granddaughter and the two Pastorini, father and son. They were in festal attire; Pippo wore new dark blue hempen clothes, and had his jacket on one shoulder, and his shirt well ruffled up above his trouser-band; the miller was in his Sunday suit, all grey; Carmelo had a pink shirt and a blue necktie and a jay's-wing in the band of his wide-awake; and Viola had a gown of pale dove-coloured stuff that she had bought in the town of Pomodoro for her wedding, and had her dead mother's string of seed-pearls about her throat; her pale cheek was as red as a rose, and but for her grandfather's stout hold on her arm she would never have found feet to bear her up the flight of steps.

Bindo Terri, lounging in the entrance, saw the little group, and thrust his tongue into his cheek and spat on the stone. Pastorini the elder, who was the stoutest-hearted of the quartette, asked for the most worshipful the Syndic.

Bindo whistled.

The Chancellor, who was inside the door, and who was busy eating little black figs and whittling a stick, said the Most Worshipful was at the Bagni for his health, but there was in his stead and equal to himself for all intents and purposes of business the Most Estimable his secretary, Messer Gaspardo Nellemane.

Viola changed from her soft warmth of colour to a great pallor.

The miller said stoutly: 'Then his Most Estimable the secretary let us see. It is a matter that brooks no delay, eh, son of mine?'

Thereat Demetrio Pastorini laughed, and chuckled, and winked, being a merry man, and the Chancellor bade them go on up the stairs, and on the landing place, at a door to the right, they might enter, he said; then he returned to eating his figs and throwing the skins on the floor of this august place where children were forbidden to play.

They went on up the staircase, and at the door the elder Pastorini rapped with his staff.

'Enter!' said the voice of the high functionary of state within, and they entered and stood in the presence of Messer Nellemane.

A single gleam, like the glitter of a steel mirror in moonlight, lit up cruelly and fiercely the eyes of the rejected lover of Viola; he guessed their errand.

A moment more, and the evil light ceased to shine in his regard; he smiled a pleasant and condescending smile of patronage.

'Ser Filippo, good-day—Signorina mine, you look as fair as the morning. Signore Pastorini, what can I do for you? But I divine your errand—nay, before as an official I execute your business, let me as a friend wish you all happiness.'

The men were subdued, fascinated, deceived; they thought what a good comrade this tyrant of the community could be; the maiden alone was not blinded; she had seen the first, fell, fierce gleam of her village Faust's eyes, and it had stabbed her like a knife. The smile that had replaced it was no lovelier to her than would have been the hissing jaws of a swamp-snake.

Her heart was heavy, but she curtseyed and thanked him.

Messer Nellemane said some more polite words and well-turned assurances of friendship, and old Pippo thought, 'He'll never go against me for the rushes and the water now—after all this.'

Then the Syndic's secretary proceeded with the Syndic's work of registration and wore an unruffled brow.

The intended marriage of Pastorini Carmelo, aged twenty-two, and Mazzetti Viola, aged seventeen, was formally announced in print, and stuck up, for all the commune to see, behind a dirty glass in a dirtier frame with those admirably delicate and spiritual formularies which modern governments deem necessary for the hedging in of the divinity of love.

Then Viola took off her pearl-coloured gown and went to make some bread, and Carmelo tucked up his sleeves and went forth to work amongst the sacks till nightfall, and both knew that when the round moon should wane and grow a slender horn once more in the summer skies, the day of days would dawn for them.

## CHAPTER VI.

Soon after Corpus Domini the Rosa water became too low to turn the great wheel of the Pastorini's mill. This often happened in Santa Rosalia now that the woods of the convent and of other hills in the stream had been felled, and that farther up in the province, at the making of the new railway, whole forests of sweet chestnut and of pines had been destroyed; needlessly in most instances, only that so fine an occasion for the making of loot could not of course be missed by the army of contractors, landowners, and officials of public works.

'I never knew the like when I was young; there were always four feet of water even in the Leone month,'[1] said Demetrio Pastorini, scratching his head wofully as he gazed down on the sun-dried wheels and the shallows that showed all the pebbles and the sand, the water weeds and the little fishes.

---

[1] The month of August is always called in Italy the month of the Lion.

'Lord-a-mercy!' said Pippo, 'when we were young, things were let alone as God made them; now they're always messing and muddling, and thinking as how they could have built the world a deal better.'

'I suppose it's that,' said the miller sorrowfully. 'Never when I was young was Rosa dry. As fast as wheat was cut in midsummer, 'twas ground by us.'

'It's along of the meddling and muddling,' said Pippo. 'Why Lord! they do say that beyond Pomodoro on Tagliafico's ground they are threshing wheat with a kettle on wheels!'

Old Pastorini sighed: he was a better educated man than old Pippo, and he knew that into the quiet, sweet, pastoral lands there were coming the 'buzzing and muzzing' of those unsightly machines which are the best friends of socialism, being the gain of the proprietor, and the curse of the peasantry, everywhere throughout Europe.

He had never heard of Virgil and of Theocritus, but it hurt him to have these sylvan pictures spoiled; these pictures which are the same as those they saw and sang; the threshing barns with the piles of golden grain, and the flails flying to merry voices; the young horses trampling the wheat loose from its husk with bounding limbs and tossing manes; the great arched doorways, with the maidens sitting in a circle breaking the maize cone from its withered leaves, and telling old world's stories, and singing sweet *fiorellini* all the while; the hanging fields broken up in hill and vale with the dun-coloured oxen pushing their patient way through labyrinths of vine boughs and clouds of silvery olive leaf; the bright laborious day, with the sun-rays turning the sickle to a semi-circlet of silver, as the mice ran, and the crickets shouted, and the larks soared on high; the merry supper when the day was done, with the thrill and thrum of the mandolini, and the glisten of the unhoused fireflies, whose sanctuary had been broken when the bearded barley and the amber corn fell prone; all these things rose to his memory; they had made his youth and manhood glad and full of colour; they were here still for his sons a little while, but when his sons should be all men grown, then those things would have ceased to be, and even their very memory would have perished, most likely, while the smoke of the accursed engines would have sullied the pure blue sky, and the stench of their foul vapours would have poisoned the golden air.

He roused himself, and said wearily to Pippo, 'There is a tale I have heard somewhere of a man who sold his birthright for gold, and when the gold was in his hands, then it changed to withered leaves and brown moss; I was thinking, eh? that the world is much like that man.'

'Truly,' said Pippo, who did not very well understand. 'But what has the world to do with us? We have done well enough without it.'

The miller shook his head, and turned from the shallow waters.

'It is all "world" now: that is the worst of it. There is no country, or soon there will be none. Even Rosa water is running away, you see!'

Pippo went home to his daughter, and said: 'The end of all things is a'coming: Rosa is drying up; I do not see how you can marry if the mill stops. To be sure you could always live in this house, and Carmelo could always be a *bracciante*.'

Viola's eyes filled: she did not mind how poor Carmelo and she might be, but she thought it would be such a terrible shame to him to be a *bracciante*—a day labourer—everybody looks down on these, and nobody is one that can, by any means, avoid it.

Viola never contradicted her father; but she slipped away, and went inside San Giuseppe, which stood in the piazza, and prayed to that Bohemian S. John who is the patron of all running water, to set the Rosa flowing again, and the tears ran down her cheeks as she prayed.

Messer Nellemane met her straight, face to face, as she came out of the church and he out of the caffè: he took off his hat with the sweetest smile.

'When is the *giorno felice?*' he asked.

She murmured some unintelligible words, coloured hotly, and ran towards her own door, her little yellow dog Raggi, who had been in the church with her, scampering in front.

'A dog loose!' said Messer Nellemane to his myrmidon Bindo, who was near. Bindo muttered sheepishly that it was 'such a little one.'

'Little or large, what is the use of rules if they be not enforced?' said the superior, very sternly. 'A little dog may bite or go mad just as easily as a large one.'

'And that is true, signore,' said Bindo. 'And besides, they never pay any tax for this one.'

Messer Nellemane made a note of the fact, and the next day took the tax-gatherer to account for leniency and inattention.

When in the evening the great man sat on his usual green iron chair in front of the Nuova Italia with his comrades and colleagues, fat Maso and thin

Tonino, he saw the young Pastorini, Carmelo, with his two brothers, stop the mill-house mule before Pippo's house, and Viola come out to talk to them on the doorstep.

'There is the miller's cart,' said Messer Nellemane to his colleagues. 'By the way, I hear the mill has not worked for a month. The Rosa up there is so dry.'

'It never used to be dry. It used to be a very deep stream,' said the Chancellor. 'I cannot tell the reason of it, unless it be that drying up the Lago di Giglio has scorched this up too.'

Messer Nellemane gave him a glance of scorn: the Lily lake had been a beautiful piece of water which had been drained, as a speculation, by a rich man, and the draining had been called progress and patriotism, though it had destroyed great beauty of scenery, and been the ruin of some three hundred families of freshwater fishermen. All the syndics and their councils had admired the work exceedingly.

'It is very injurious for the interests of the province,' continued Messer Gaspardo, 'to be dependent thus on the caprices of a river. It would be a great thing if a steam-mill could be established.'

'*Ouf!*' said little Tonino, opening wide his eyes. 'And what would become of the Pastorini?'

'The interests of the few must always be subordinate to those of the many,' answered Messer Nellemane, with his usual excellence of phrase and opinion. 'It is quite absurd in these practical times for a whole commune to be dependent for its bread on the accident of a river being full of water. We must see what can be done in the matter. Of course,' he added, 'it would at the moment be very hard upon the miller and his family; but some one must always suffer for any great work, and the cause of progress is sacred.'

'Just so,' said Maso and Tonino in concert, being always convinced, if not enlightened, by the magnificent words of Messer Nellemane.

'There was some talk of such a mill before the Cavaliere went to the baths,' said their instructor, though he had never until that moment ever thought of such a thing. 'And, certainly, if the river continue to run dry like this, something must be done. The miller is not very well off as it is, I believe; and this is an improvident marriage that he is making for his son.'

'They won't have many beans in their pot,' giggled Maso, who was a vulgar man.

'Alas! no,' said Messer Nellemane, who was never vulgar, with an air of regret. 'It is these hasty and impecunious marriages that bring about the beggary of the nation. They ought to be forbidden by the law. The State forbids suicide; why not also forbid an ill-judged marriage?'

'What would the women say?' chuckled the vulgar Maso.

'They have no voice in politics,' said Messer Nellemane, coldly: he was a very literal man, and never saw a joke in anything. The land of Pasquin and of Polichinello has ceased to laugh.

'What a minister he would make!' said Maso admiringly to Tonino, when their great man had left them to go and read the 'Diritto,' which had come to him by the evening's post: the little girl of Nando running over with it obsequiously.

'Ah, he would indeed!' assented Tonino; but

there was no great warmth in the assent: Messer Nellemane always beat him at dominoes, and hurt him both in pride and pocket.

That night, as it chanced, old Annunziata was coming home alone along a path across the fields from one of the farmhouses in the hills. The *massaja* there had been very good to her, and had given her some eggs; not to eat, for Annunziata would have thought that wild extravagance indeed, except at Pasqua, but to sell for her own profit.

On this path, dark with twilight and the thick canopy of overhanging pines, the old woman was accosted by a drunken fellow—a smith from the forge above at Sestriano—who shook her, jeered at her, and carried away her basket of eggs. The poor old soul went bruised and weeping down towards Santa Rosalia; she had made a good fight for it with her oaken stick, but she had got blows in return, and had lost her eggs.

She met Carmelo Pastorini as she neared the village, and told him what that drunken lout, Pompéo of Sestriano, had done to her. Carmelo listened with all his bright face lit up in a radiance of wrath, and before she could stop him had dashed up the hill path, had overtaken the staggering scoundrel, and had rescued the basket, though the eggs were all smashed in the dispute for them.

But Carmelo thought that he would not tell her that: he had a little money of his own, allowed him by his father—very little—for his tobacco and his clothes: he had a franc left, and he strode farther up the hill, and bought a dozen eggs at the first farmhouse that would sell them. 'It will be only to go without a pipe for a week or two,' he thought; for he spent one centime a day on his tobacco.

Annunziata was home again in her chamber with the other old women by the time Carmelo reached Santa Rosalia, and she had to get out of bed and speak to him, as he threw a stone at her shutter.

'I have got back your eggs, 'Nunziatina,' he shouted to her. 'Let me down a bit of string, and you can draw up the basket.'

The old woman, laughing and crying with joy, did as he bade her, and the eggs were drawn slowly upward against the white wall in the silvery moonlight.

'Thou art a dear good lad,' she cried, 'and Viola is a lucky maiden.'

Carmelo laughed, and called back:

'Do not tell on the poor devil, mother. He was drunk——'

'Not I,' said Annunziata. 'I wouldn't put a poor toad in the lock-up for a bag of gold if he took it of me—not I.'

'Good night,' said Carmelo, and went away, humming to himself,

> Nel mezzo del mio petto è una ghirlanda,
> E ne l'ho scritto il nome di Viola,
> Quattr' angioli del ciel suonan la banda.[1]

But as not a mouse squeaks in its own hole without all the country-side chattering about it, this encounter with Pompéo of Sestriano got wind, and all the village was talking of it next day. The story

---

[1] Around my breast there is a garland,
And on it's writ the name of Viola,
And four angels of God make melody!

Every lover of course substitutes the name of his beloved.

ran here and there like a jack-o'-lanthorn in a swamp, and, of course, grew in the telling.

In consequence the carabiniers, at Messer Nellemane's instigation, visited Pompéo at his forge in Sestriano, and visited Carmelo at his father's mill, and great fuss and noise were made about it, and the two men and the old woman were summoned to the Municipality.

The old woman, trembling like a leaf for her very life, for she had never been called up by the police in all her years, made light of it, and said she 'was sure that 'Péo had but done it as a joke.'

'The law does not recognise jokes,' the law said to her by the august voice of Messer Nellemane, who was examining her.

Pompéo himself declared that he had no remembrance of anything at all; and most likely spoke genuinely, for he had been very much the worse for wine; and when he had awakened on the hillside at morning had not been able, in the least, to recollect how he had come there.

When Carmelo was examined he laughed outright.

''Péo was drunk,' he said, 'and I knocked him down to get Viola's aunt's basket away from him, but he heeled over as if he were made of straw and fell on the grass under the vines, and there I left him. I broke none of his bones, you see, and I hoped nobody would know anything.'

'The Law knows everything,' said Messer Nellemane, with a frown, 'and for concealing a theft there is a very heavy penalty, and the interests of public justice require———'

Annunziata, beholding the blanched, scared,

stupid face of the sottish smith, felt all her courage and her charity burn in her.

'Holy Mother! sir, most illustrious, I mean,' she cried in desperation, 'there wasn't a bit of harm of any sort done, and I am certain the poor fool took them from me not knowing; and he wouldn't hurt a hair of my head if he were sober; and the eggs were all safe and sound, and nobody could go against any one when the eggs were all got back; and as for me, not a soul would I put in prison if they cut the gown from off my waist; not I.'

'Woman!' thundered Messer Nellemane, losing his benignity before these atrocious principles, 'do you dare to insult the majesty of the Law? Abstract justice is alone fit to govern any human action. You have a duty to society——'

'*Me*, sir!' cried Annunziata, and muttered to herself, 'Well-a-day! one does live to come to something.'

'Which must be above all personal considerations. Let us examine for a moment to what your astounding, your inexcusable, laxity of principle would lead. You would actually establish the frightfully immoral fact that, if stolen goods were returned intact, the theft would be condoned, effaced, become as though it had not been! You ignore entirely the moral heinousness of the crime. You take the low and debasing view that the only thing of importance in a theft is the pecuniary loss it may inflict! Whether your goods were returned to you safe, or were destroyed, is altogether beyond the question. What moral teachers have you had, woman?'

Annunziata dimly comprehended that her morality was impugned, and her little black eyes blazed with righteous rage.

'I have been a decent person all my days, sir.' she said with a resentful fierceness in her voice. 'I was a good wife while my poor man lived, and since he died, thirty year or more ago, never have I done a thing he'd be ashamed to see.'

Messer Nellemane paid no attention to her whatever, but continued his dissertation, to which Carmelo listened with a merry grin upon his face, Pompéo stupidly with open mouth, and the Chancellor, the Conciliator, and Bindo Terri, with his colleagues, in attitudes expressive of righteous awe and overpowering admiration. Finally, Messer Nellemane unwillingly felt that no judge would sentence with any severity for an offence non-proven, and prosecuted against the aggrieved person's will; yet, reluctant to let them escape altogether, he decided after this unofficial examination that the Sestriano smith should be summoned to appear at Pomodoro, to be there judged for drunkenness and attempted theft, and that the miller's son should pay a fine of twenty francs for having taken the law into his own hands in lieu of summoning the police, an offence against the Code.

Carmelo made a wry face. Every farthing could be ill afforded by his father.

'Those are the dearest eggs that were ever laid, mother!' he whispered to Annunziata.

The old woman wrung her hands.

'And that poor soul to go to prison for me! Oh dear, oh dear! And the gentleman won't hear a word that I say!'

So that bright summer day was clouded over for them all.

'You will have to be witnesses at the trial of Pompéo,' said the guard Bindo, with keen relish, to them, as the old woman and Carmelo went down the municipal steps.

'Nay, I'll never say a word against him, poor creature. When the wine's in the wit's out,' said Annunziata.

'I'll say again what I said in there,' added Carmelo, 'and that's just the truth; he went over at a touch, like an owl in noonday. And as for you, Bindo, if you had against you all the witnesses that see you in the caffès, would you wear that fine popinjay's hat and jacket long, I wonder?'

Bindo growled and muttered something about his wish that Carmelo and all his people should be burnt.

'*Sia brucciato!*' remains a favourite imprecation in the language, having been transmitted no doubt from the day when heretics and Hebrews and all such sinners were sent to the stake.

Carmelo went onward, disregarding the storm he had raised, and singing at the top of his voice the *stornello*:

> Io benedico lo fiore d'amore,
> Rubato avete le perle al mare,
> Agli alberi le fronde, a me il core.[1]

What did Bindo's wrath or the punishment hanging over the drunken head of Pompéo of Sestriano matter to him? He was not more selfish than another, but he would not have been a youth and a lover if he had had room for any other thought long together than that of his approaching nuptials.

---

[1] I bless the flower of Love,
It has stolen the pearls from the sea,
It has stolen the leaves from the trees,
It has stolen the heart from me!

The papers of the marriage had been long enough behind the wire cage and the dusty glass of the communal palace, and the time had rolled on until now on the first day of July he would be wedded to Viola, and only forty-eight hours separated him from that morn. He ran along the village laughing and singing, with a fresh rose stuck behind his ear and a fresh ribbon round his hat, and reached the house with the white and blue Madonna, and went in and sat in the window-sill, looking down on the girl's hands as they plaited, whilst Pippo worked and smoked his pipe on the threshold.

'You were so good to 'Nunziatina,' said Viola, raising eyes to his that were wet with tears of pleasure.

'Che!' laughed Carmelo, swinging his shapely bare feet against the wall of the window. 'Won't she belong as much to me as to you? She shall never want a basket of eggs while I live.'

## CHAPTER VII.

MEANTIME Bindo slunk away across the square, fumbling at the revolver with which the commune had lately armed him on pretext of mad dogs, and meditating within himself on his vengeance. Suddenly a bright inspiration occurred to him.

The favourite mission of Bindo was to poison dogs. Messer Gaspardo hated dogs; they had an unfortunate way of smelling at him which made people laugh and remember the old saying that a dog can smell a rogue, and hurt his dignity in his own sight and that of others. Moreover, courage does not characterise the tyrant always; though Attila was brave, Messer Nellemane was not. He was afraid of dogs; and he had made it Article I. of Rule I. in his Regulations that a free dog was never to be seen in all the length and breadth of Vezzaja and Ghiralda.

But there will be always dogs loose, all Regulations to the contrary notwithstanding, for there is no population anywhere in which everybody is a poltroon. So, as loose dogs still trotted about the commune, and led their pretty, merry, brisk lives under his very eyes, in impertinent disregard of Article I., Rule I., Messer Nellemane had at once bethought himself of poisoning them. Phosphorus was cheap and deadly, so were rat-poisons, and when fried with liver as Bindo fried them, and thrown about in the dust of the highway, they stretched many a gallant hound low, and left many a puppy rigid and swollen after an agony more terrible than the hanged malefactor suffers; whilst for those that his poisoned *polpetti* did not slaughter he wore out the lives of the owners thereof with summonses without end and fines without mercy.

It grew to be the general belief in Vezzaja and Ghiralda that you had better stab a man than keep a dog, and you would pay less for doing it, too.

Carmelo, like most sons of the soil, was fond of his dog, a fine curly white fellow, strong and young like Carmelo himself, who was called Toppa because he scared away robbers. Toppa, by choice, kept close about the mill, and in that little *boschetto* of poplars which had belonged to the Pastorini longer than men could remember; for he was a good and dutiful dog, and knew that if he went roaming, thieves might break in and steal. Therefore Toppa rarely fell under the head of a contravention, since even the Article I., Rule I., could not assert that a man's dog must not be loose upon his own property.

Nevertheless, on Toppa the evil eye of Bindo had often fallen, for Bindo had been pinned by Toppa more than once in unregenerate days before becoming a functionary of the State; and moreover, Messer Nellemane had said, 'That dog at the mill looks dangerous; he barks when any one passes;' which hint sufficed for the guard now that to natural cruelty was united the thirst of personal animosity. At dawn, whilst the mists of earliest morning were still white on the river and the hills, he walked warily within sight of the little wood by the mill, intent alike on hurting Carmelo and pleasing his patron. Toppa was lying with his head between his paws on the grass on the bank; he kept wide awake all night from his strong principle, and now when the sun had risen, knew that he might slumber and dream in peace without peril to the homestead.

Nevertheless, when he heard a step fall upon the thick dust of the road, Toppa, although he was no longer sentry, performed a sentry's part and rose, and ran, and looked. He kept within his own boundary, as he had been taught to do, being a very faithful dog, and only looked; a cat may look at a king, says the old saw, but in Vezzaja and Ghiralda a dog must not look at a guard.

Bindo spoke not a word, but he threw something he held in his hand from the road where he stood into the grass beneath the poplars, near the dog.

Toppa was at no time very well fed—no dog is in this country—and he had not eaten since sunset. His nostrils smelled an odour savoury and sweet to them. The thing lay in his own grass, within a foot of him; he drew close to it and smelt it closer; it was a fried slice of liver rolled up in a tempting way. He ate it. Almost in an instant he staggered, strove to vomit, became convulsed, gasped, and gave a strangled, hollow moan, then turned round giddily, as men may when drunk, and fell prone on the dewy grass.

Bindo leapt to him, seized him by the skin of his throat and back, and dragged him into the highway; the dog was quivering, rolling, panting in agony as the poison burned and tore his entrails.

Leaving him there, Bindo slunk away. Toppa lay in the dust, mute in his death-throes; his snowy, curly body swelling and writhing, his bright brown eyes protruding, his tongue forced out, his limbs paralysed; suffering as men deem it too cruel to make murderers suffer. Within a stone's throw of his master and his friends, he could not raise a cry, he could not move a limb. The burning hellish poison had its way, tearing, consuming, killing him.

Presently the mists began to yield to the lovely light of the fuller day; and in the sunshine on the lonely road Toppa lay dead; foam on his lips, a little blood upon the dust that he had vomited even as he died.

His happy, harmless, honest life was done.

A few moments later Carmelo, who seldom forgot the dog, came out under the poplars to call him for a bit of bread. He called in vain. Knowing that

Toppa never wandered away, and was ever alert to answer his voice, he stepped across the strip of woodland, meaning to whistle down the road. His eye fell on the dead body in the dust. He threw himself on his knees beside it. One glance told him the truth; one instant he gave to grief, passionate as though he had seen a brother perish.

Then on to his feet he leapt; with a great shout to all the saints of heaven for justice, he ran fleet as a deer down the road to see who was in sight; the name of Bindo Terri sprang to his lips, and the figure he saw afar off flying in the dust was Bindo's.

Swift as the hurricane the young fellow tore in the wake of the guard, who now was spurred with a dire terror, and ran not knowing what he did. With one last bound, like that of the hound on to the wolf, Carmelo seized Bindo in his grasp.

'You have killed my dog!'

'I? No—no—no!'

'You have!' swore Carmelo, with an oath, and shook the slenderer form of the guard in his grip.

Bindo gathered up a desperate courage.

'I have not killed him, no. He may have picked up poison on the road—it is the law, the law allows it.'

Carmelo's hand closed on his throat.

Without a word the more, he dragged him to the edge of the road where some wood was lying for fencing, and with his other hand snatching a stave of oak, swung Bindo Terri backwards and forwards, striking him on the head, the arms, the shoulders, with the wood the while; men were at work in the vineyards beside the road; they screamed, and ran, and caught the arm of the young Pastorini, and, being five to one, wrenched him asunder from the trembling frame of Bindo, being willing enough to see harm wrought on the body of the guard, but afraid of the law if they looked on at the death of one of its myrmidons, and Carmelo, left alone, would have killed him in that rude justice which a righteous vengeance is.

The moment that the vine-dressers freed him, Bindo Terri staggered away, sick, bleeding, bruised, and nearly dead with fright. Carmelo struggled in vain in the hold of five strong men.

'He has killed Toppa!' he gasped, his eyes bloodshot, his muscles straining, his whole body writhing to be free.

'Ay, ay! has he done that?—and he merits death himself,' muttered the eldest of the peasants. 'But they will have the law on you, and worse, for touching him, the vile little villain, that the snakes must have spawned.'

'My dog! My dog!' moaned Carmelo, as his passion dissolved into an agony of grief, and his eyes filled with blinding tears, and dully and stupidly he went back to where the dead dog lay, and sat down by him in the dust, and wept.

The men stood around silent and sorrowful, but sorely afraid.

Bindo Terri was a poisoner and a scoundrel, but the arm and the shield of the law were over him, and made him sacred, as religions of old made sacred the snake and the toad.

The law here ordains that you cannot be arrested for anything you do, unless you be taken in the act, even though the deed be clearly proved against you. But there are sins so heinous as to be beyond this mercy, as the crimes in the Latin documents of the Vatican are beyond pardon, human or divine. Carmelo's was such a crime.

You may lay a sacrilegious finger on the Host with more ease than on the person of a municipal guard. Nay, there is more fuss when one is touched than when the King is shot at: if Passavanti had tried to assassinate a guard instead of a sovereign, he would not have been let off the scaffold so easily as he was. Therefore, when Bindo Terri picked himself up, staggered into the house of the elder guard, Angelo, which was within a rood of the millhouse, and there fell down, groaning aloud that he had been murdered by the devil Carmelo, the elder man flew, as one possessed, down the road to the picket of the carabiniers, and brought them to the spot to avenge a foul and inexcusable assault, whose end would be sooner or later death; and clamoured and roared and raved, while Bindo, dying Bindo, raved with him, and forced the gendarmes to go and seize the assassin. Law can stretch at either end when wanted.

The carabiniers, with their sabres and their white belts flashing in the sun, strode straightway, therefore, to the mill upon the Rosa and laid hands on the youth, who sat on the bench of his house under the trees with the dead dog at his feet, and his father and brothers and neighbours gathered around him in sad sympathy.

'But to-morrow is his marriage-day!' stammered the old father, half mad himself with rage and sorrow.

The carabiniers laughed a little grimly, and pulled Carmelo up roughly by his arms, and marched from the door, pushing him with them. In their hearts they sympathised with both the Pastorini, but it was not their place to say so.

'I did what I had a right to do,' muttered the lad firmly. 'He killed my dog: I beat him, the poisoner, the devil; I would have beaten him till he could not have stood: I had the right.'

'You had no right even to complain. Your dog was the offender; he was on the public road,' shrieked the elder rural guard Angelo, and shook off the miller and thrust Carmelo on between the gendarmes.

'I will go with you without force,' said the youth haughtily. 'I have no fear; I was in the right.'

And he walked on steadily, only turning and pausing once to say to his father, who followed him:

'Do not come; stay and bury Toppa. Bury him just there by the porch. He will know we pass in and out, and he will not feel alone. And tell Viola not to mind; it will go well with me; no judge will keep me for a moment when he hears how it all came about.'

The carabiniers behind his back looked at one another and raised their eyebrows satirically. They knew well how the Law would deal with this brave young fellow.

They took him through the village to the lock-up of the place.

Early though it was, every one was astir, and all had heard that Bindo Terri had been thrashed by the younger Pastorini; some had heard that Bindo was dead outright; not a soul regretted his fate if it were so; but not a soul either dared to say what they felt or stretch the hand of friendship to the prisoner.

Only old Gigi Canterelli stepped bravely out of his shop and cried to him, 'My lad, if you want a little money or a good word, remember I am here, and send for me.'

But no one else said a syllable.

Carmelo was thankful that as the way to the prison led through the centre of the piazza they did not pass the house of Pippo; he trusted that Viola would know nothing until his sister could reach her and soften the blow to her by tender modes of narration, as women know how to do one with another.

But sad mischance would have it that in the centre of the square he met old Pippo carrying three rush chairs on his back, which he let fall in the extremity of his amaze.

'God's mercy, lad, what hast been doing?' he called to his son-in-law of the morrow; and he began to tremble wofully. Carmelo trembled too, for the sorrow that he caused.

'Grandfather,' he said tenderly—it was the first time that he used the name—'do not be alarmed. Bindo Terri killed Toppa, and I have avenged him; that is all. The good judge will judge me innocent.'

'O Lord, O Lord!' groaned Pippo, all in a palsy of fear and sorrow; 'what matters of being innocent? If you touch a hair of the head of those slave-driving, venomous, viperous jackanapes it is all over with you, all over with you! And to-morrow your wedding-day, and my girl at home stitching the veil. O Lord, O Lord!'

The carabiniers hurried Carmelo onwards. 'A pestilent, seditious, foul-mouthed old tongue that fellow has,' said they to one another; and they thrust the young Pastorini with scant mercy into the place of detention; a square bare cell with a brick floor, damp and dirty, and a barred door and a little grated casement high up in the wall.

'But take me to the judge!' cried Carmelo; 'take me somewhere to be heard!'

'All in good time,' said the carabiniers, and banged the door to on him, and drew the bolts outside it.

Meanwhile, Viola, sitting in the doorway with the little brook running babbling over the stones in front of her, was stitching some orange-blossoms she had picked off a tree on to the veil she would wear on the morrow; she was singing in a soft low voice one of the love-songs of the country:

> Al piè d'un faggio in sull' erba fiorita
> Aspetto, aspetto, che giù cada il sole;
> Perche quando sarà l'aria imbrunita
> Appunto allor vedrò spuntar il sole,
> Levarsi quel bel sol che m'ha ferita,
> Che mi ha ferita e che guarir mi vuole.
> E questo sol, ch'io dico, è il mio bel damo,
> Che sempre io gli riprico io t'amo, io t'amo,
> E questo sole è il giovanettin bello
> Chi a Ferragosto mi darà l'annello.[1]

She was happy. The fear of her powerful tempter and enemy had passed away from her, and the future smiled at her with the eyes of love and faith. A life of labour, of poverty, of fatigue awaited her, but also a life of sunshine, of affection, of peace; to the first she was well used, the second seemed to her heaven.

[1] At foot of hill, amidst the flow'ring grass,
I wait, I wait, until the sun shall set;
Because, when all the air is dusk and dark,
Scarce will the drooping sun the night have met,
Than will arise that sun which wounded me,
Which wounded me, and now my cure will bring;

## CHAPTER VIII.

There was no court open that day at the Pretura, and the Pretura was seven miles away in another commune, Vezzaja and Ghiralda not being blessed with one, and for criminal matters and large debts being bound to betake themselves to the larger township of Pomodoro-Carciofi, though small civil causes were tried before the Conciliator in Santa Rosalia itself.

So the long hours rolled on, and Carmelo remained in the dirty cramped little den behind the barred door. His father and brothers and poor sad old Pippo came to visit him, and the Pastorini paid for him to be kept apart from any other malefactors, and Gigi Canterelli sent him a smoking dish to break his fast with, and a flask of wine. But Carmelo could scarce touch either, and had hardly a word to speak except over and over again he said,

'Is Toppa buried?—Viola is not angry that I avenged him?'

No other ideas save these seemed to be in his brain; he was dull, and yet fierce; quite changed from the gentle and grave, yet blithe and simple, lad that he had always been.

'God forbid I should say that you did wrong; who would not have struck a blow for the poor

---

    And this fair sun, I tell thee, is my love,
    To whom, in echo, 'Love, O Love!' I sing.
    And this fair sun is that most beauteous youth
    Who, August dawn'd, will bring to me the ring!

*Ferragosto* is literally—first of August.

dog?' said his father weeping. 'But oh, the pity of it, to see one of my honest sons in these thieves' den!'

For the Pastorini youths had never had a stain or slur upon their name, and for many a generation the men at the mill had been law-abiding, God-fearing, and most dutiful sons of the soil.

'I did right!' said Carmelo doggedly, and his brothers all echoed, 'Yes, you did right. But, alas! alas!——'

Meanwhile Messer Nellemane stood by the bedside of Bindo, who had taken to his bed at once, and groaned, and shivered, and vowed all his bones were broken, and the complaisant apothecary rolled him up in wadding soaked in almond oil, and pretended he might die. Messer Nellemane, tenderly regretful and benevolently compassionate, bent over the sufferer, and said in benignant tones:

'My poor, poor fellow! This is all your reward for a too zealous love of duty, and of course you never touched the dog at all; is it not so?'

Bindo opened wide his eyes, and almost grinned in his employer's face; then, recollecting himself, gasped as though his breath were failing him.

'Not I, Signore; he was stiff and stark, poor beast, when I came upon the road.'

'Precisely,' said Messer Nellemane. 'That will be put in evidence. The Pastorini have long borne you a grudge, you say, and took this excuse to pay it off on you. A shocking case! A most brutal assault!'

He shook his head as he spoke, above the bed of the victim, and the pliant apothecary shook his.

'Contusion of the vertebra,' he murmured, 'and

sympathetic action may supervene in the heart and lungs, and then——'

'Hush! he has youth on his side,' said Messer Nellemane tenderly, and stroked the curly head of the guard as he might have stroked a child or a puppy, had he not happened to hate both pups and children.

When he left the sick chamber, taking the parish doctor with him, the invalid sat up in bed and shouted to the old woman who waited on him.

'Give me my pipe and a beaker of that Vin Santo, and fry me some tripe and artichokes, and hand me the Book of Fate.'

The Book of Fate was the teller of dreams and foreteller of lucky numbers for the public lottery, and with this favourite literature, and his tobacco, and his wine, the murderer of Toppa passed a brave and merry day, even though he was supposed to be upon his death-bed, and was wrapped up in oil, and had begged to see the priest, and had all the sycophants of the place (which, to do Santa Rosalia justice, were not many), coming perpetually about his door, and asking whether he was out of danger.

At home Viola was passing the bright hours weeping and kneeling before her little clay figure of the Mother of the Poor.

Old 'Nunziatina was seated beside her, rocking herself to and fro on her elm staff.

'My candle was no good!' she moaned, 'and yet I spent all I had!'

## CHAPTER IX.

The long bright day and the short luminous night passed, and melted into dawn once more, and Carmelo saw the sunrise of his marriage morn glow on him from the iron bars of a prison cell. At eight of the morning the carabiniers put him in a little vehicle, and took him away to Pomodoro-Carciofi; making him sit between them, and looking very droll themselves in the little swinging springless cart, with their sabres sticking out on each side, and their cocked hats as stiff as Napoleon's upon the Vendôme column.

Pomodoro-Carciofi was a twin township, as Buda-Pest is a twin city; it was very small, very dusty, very ugly; there were a good many dyers in it, and the smell of the dye was in its atmosphere; it had a noble campanile and some fine frescoes of Luini's, but nobody ever came to look at them; it had also had an altar-piece of the Memmi's, but one fine day somebody had sold that, and it being everybody's, and so nobody's, business to punish the thief, it went unpunished, and a large oleograph was stuck up by the municipality in place of the Memmi, and the townsfolk liked it better because it had more colour in it.

The court of law was in a dull, grim, stone house that looked upon a blind wall at the back of the church that rejoiced in the oleograph; an ugly square room, which had been newly whitewashed, was the audience and judgment chamber; and here all criminal cases of the rural commune of Vezzaja and Ghiralda were tried and decided by the young attorney who administered the law to some ten thousand persons in all matters, from a fifty-franc debt to murder, arson, and theft, and who had for his salary about as much as one gives one's groom, and not half what one gives one's coachman.

The country is divided into districts; each district has its own Pretore, who unites in his one ill-paid person the onerous duties of county-court, civil, and criminal judge. In England the first of these offices is deemed worth as many hundreds a year as it gets pounds here. That, notwithstanding such treatment, the Preture-ship is sometimes filled by very excellent and upright men, is a credit to the legal fraternity of Italy; it is no thanks to the administration. A man has the peace, the purse, the virtue, the liberty, almost the life, of a whole community in his hands, and he is paid less than a groom or a gardener!—as a jewel in a toad's head is a just man in this office.

The country Pretore can be harassed by the King's Proctor, and his verdicts can be protested against in the city courts, but for the main part, and certainly over all the poor classes of his districts, he is unresisted and his decrees are inviolable. Aristides in so onerous a position could scarcely mete out perfect justice. I have known, as I say, admirable and excellent persons in this post, and I respect them deeply; but they are rare exceptions, naturally, and in the lonely country places the Pretore exercises a power that is practically irresistible, and that would be a perilous temptation to a Solon.

A crowd had got about the law court this day, for the rumour had run like wildfire that the miller's son at Santa Rosalia had murdered the rural guard. His father and brothers and Gigi Canterelli had come over to see if they could aid, or speak for, him, and they had brought poor old half-frantic Pippo with them; beside these there were the apothecary, and Bindo's friends, and also the Public Minister, as the little lawyer is called who prosecutes for the Municipality, and there were also the Chancellors and the Conciliators of both borough and village.

Messer Nellemane stayed at home; he was never seen in person to appear against any member of the commune, in great cases or small. He always said, with a deprecating smile, that it did not become one who served them in the capacity he filled, to sway the balance of justice either way.

Nevertheless, he was very good friends with the Pretore of Pomodoro and Carciofi; a young advocate, fussy and bustling, and of as shrewd a nose for promotion as ever a dog of the south for truffles; a young advocate who hated Pomodoro and all belonging to it, and its musty court, and its simple population, and the scanty forty pounds a year it gave him, but who, nevertheless, took them all as stepping stones. In the future he, too, meant to be a statesman.

This day the young man, who was a little, sallow, sharp-eyed creature, by no means imposing, even though he donned a black robe and black cap, just such as those that Portia wore, took a violent aversion at first sight to Carmelo as the accused, between the carabiniers, was marched in front of the Pretore's desk.

This day should have been the youth's nuptial day, and his heart was aching, and his blood burning, and his face was very pale; nevertheless he walked erect, and with a firm step trod the steps of the Pretura between the carabiniers with their clanking swords.

Carmelo was the true peasant of his country; with shapely limbs and throat, like a young gladiator's, and a handsome face, with the features regular, and the blue eyes large, and the skin delicate, though of a healthy, sun-tanned hue.

This bold and picturesque-looking lad, who faced him with hardihood and even haughtiness, displeased the young judge, who was himself a city-bred, saturnine, and dissipated weakling. He felt at once assured that this miller's son was a dangerous and violent character, and he listened with willing ear to all the invectives against the accused made by the lawyer, who prosecuted on the behalf of the municipality.

The Pastorini had never known that they ought to bring a lawyer, and old Pippo, in an agony, pulled Gigi Canterelli's coat, and whispered:

'There's a notary against him—there's a man of law against him. O Lord! O Lord! he's no more chance than a lamb when it's hung up by the heels, head downward!'

'Eh!' muttered Gigi with a sigh, 'in our old times one young fellow fought it out with another, when there was any bone to pick, and no one meddled; it was the best man won; now, Lord save us! if but two cats set up their backs and spit, there's law about it.'

'Order there! Silence!' cried the usher; and the case for the prosecution went on glibly till, listening to it, the brains of the Pastorini, father and son, reeled, and almost gave way.

Carmelo began to say to himself in amaze, 'Am I indeed this villain double-dyed?'

For the advocate of the commune, instructed *sub rosâ* by Messer Nellemane, was a very eloquent-tongued man indeed, who, having little to do, and very small means indeed, had always his oratory ready bottled and almost bursting, like ginger-beer upon a summer's day.

When he had done his plea for the prosecution, and had resumed his seat, there was no one to answer or refute him.

Carmelo and his friends knew too late the terrible blunder they had committed in their ignorance of having no other man of law there to reply to him.

The examination of the accused began.

Carmelo, answering as to his age and name, and parentage, added then in a firm voice,

'Bindo Terri poisoned my dog; I beat him; yes, if I had killed him I should have done no wrong; he is a beast; he is a devil; he tortures brutes and men——'

'Silence!' said the Judge. 'You can vilify no one. You are only to answer my questions, one by one, as I put them to you.'

'But he is right! He is right!' shrieked old Pippo, pressing forward to the bar, behind which he and the rest of the public were hemmed in. 'He is right! he is right! By the word of Christ our Saviour! Bindo Terri wanted to stop my brook running; wanted to make me pay for the good God's own clear spring water——'

'Take that fool out of court,' said the Pretore, and the old man was carried out struggling and screaming for justice.

Then the cross-examination of Carmelo began again in such an endless intricacy of questions that the boy's head whirled. Wiser and more worldly trained intelligences than his have been confused, and blurred, and bewildered out of all their own sense of memory and certitude of fact by the brow-beating of such an interrogation.

Did he see Bindo Terri poison his dog? No: he did not see it; but the guard poisoned all dogs he could get at; that any one knew; the guard poisoned Toppa, certainly, certainly. So he kept on saying, again and again, almost stupidly; and the tears welled into his eyes, and began to fall down his cheeks, thinking of the dead dog, and of the maiden sitting weeping at home on the day that should have been her marriage morn.

The Pretore and, after him, the lawyer for the prosecution tormented him over and over again to much the same purport. All Carmelo could say was, 'he poisoned the dog; he poisoned the dog.'

That was all he could say.

He had no proofs.

His father begged to speak for him, but was told it was not to be permitted. Gigi Canterelli, with the moisture in his eyes, begged, too, to testify to his excellent nature and great amiability; and the Vicar of Santa Rosalia entreated to be heard as to the youth's good and kindly character, his docility and his honesty, as one who had known him from his infancy upward.

But this latter witness harmed him rather than benefited him in the eyes of the Pretore, who was a *libero pensiero*; and, being thus liberal in principle, would have garotted all priests, melted down all church bells, and smashed the crucifix in every household.

He said, snappishly, that the preliminary examination was not a time for the testimony of an *amicus curiæ* to be admitted in evidence; such could be heard at the trial itself; and then, after very busily looking over his notes, and conferring with his Chancellor, and muttering, and scribbling, and frowning, and believing that he looked like Jules Favre, whom he had seen in a fortnightly visit to Paris, the young Pretore summed up in a voice shrill and stern, and said that he had never heard of a more unprovoked, brutal, and infamous assault, that there had evidently not been the very slightest excuse or provocation for it, and that as the evidence of the most excellent the apothecary went conclusively to prove that the life of Bindo Terri had been imperilled, and that the said Bindo Terri still lay prostrate in a state that might at any moment bring about a fatal end, and in which it was quite impossible to be able to examine him personally, he deemed it inconsistent with the interests of justice and the safety of the public to leave the accused at liberty, guilty, by his own confession, as he was; therefore he would order Pastorini Carmelo to be kept in durance and surveillance until such time as his trial could be fully heard, and sentence given upon him.

There was a murmur of dissent amongst the crowd.

His father shook like a leaf. His brothers muttered curses deep and fierce.

Carmelo stood like one scared; his eyes wide open, his face flashing crimson, his nostrils breathing hard, as though he were out of breath from running.

'In prison, I!' he cried in a loud voice. 'And why is he let go free, the thief, the spy, the poisoner?'

'Remove him,' said the Pretore sharply, with a frown; and the guards, taking him by each arm, forced him away.

When a little later, when other causes had been heard, the Vicar, a fine-looking and white-haired old man, ventured on a private remonstrance with the young judge, the young man took him sharply up.

'Impossible!' he answered. 'It was a clear assault, a ruffianly assault; and made upon a functionary of the law. The law must be respected. It must make examples.'

So the friends of Carmelo could only drive wearily back in the rickety diligence from Pomodoro to Santa Rosalia with aching hearts and weary bodies; and old Pippo, staggering in, white with lime dust of the road, and hoarse with weeping, could only cry like a child, and sob out in broken whispers the story of this cruel day.

Carmelo himself was detained in the prison of the town, and Viola could only lay aside her bridal gown with the orange petals to keep it sweet, and heads of lavender and dried rose leaves, withered like her hopes and joys.

Bindo Terri was so elated that it was all the apothecary could do to keep him from jumping out of bed and skipping down the stairs into the street.

'But you are in danger of your life,' screamed the Æsculapius, throwing his arms about the victim; and Bindo grinned from ear to ear, showing teeth as white as lilies.

'Let's crack a flask over the good news,' said he, and Æsculapius drank with him.

Meanwhile his master, in the caffè of Nuova Italia, was smoking serenely, and wore a serious and sorrowful cast of countenance.

'A very sad thing to befall an honest family!' said Messer Nellemane. 'But the Law must be respected, and all violence must be repressed.'

The brigadier to whom he spoke assented with his lips, not with his heart; he had been a brave soldier in his day, and did not love his work of torturing the poor, in accordance with the rules of Polizia Igiena e Edilità.

'He was a good youth, this Carmelo,' he said hesitatingly; 'never have I seen him in brawl or trouble of any kind, nor ever the worse for drink, nor ever in bad houses; his momentary passion overcame him.'

'The Law does not recognise passion,' said Messer Nellemane coldly, and the brigadier dared say no more, lest he should be reported to his commanding officer, away in the city, as lax in his discipline and an aider and abettor of offenders.

Thus does a single strong will govern others.

## CHAPTER X.

In the month that Toppa was murdered and his young master imprisoned for avenging him there was an appeal to the country; that is to say, a vast number of attorneys, an equal number of adventurers, several Jews, and a few gentlemen asked the natives of Italy to send them up to Montecitorio.

The Ministry had been defeated on the burning

question of a poll-tax on cows, their husbands, and their children. The Ministry was convinced that all the bovine race should be taxed per head at the place they lived in, as well as taxed at the gates when driven through them for sale, and taxed at the market when changed into meat; all bulls, cows, and calves were to pay a poll-tax of twenty francs a head annually, and as this was considered only to hurt the agricultural interest which a progressive Ministry naturally considered of no account at all, it had been asserted that the tax would be accepted and become law.

There was, however, in the Chambers an ex-notary who cared not at all for bulls, cows, and calves, and as little for the agricultural interest, but cared very much for himself. He had been Home Minister once for six weeks; he had ceased to be it on account of a ridiculous fuss that was made in the papers about his buying a piano with the public money for a lady whose character was light as a syllabub; naturally he always burned to become it once more, and have his own way with pianos and all other articles, including the nation. So he had turned against his old friends, who had not supported him loyally in the matter of the piano, and had set up for himself in business, as it were, and had a separate set of principles and a separate little party, which was to the Chamber in general as is the gadfly to the horse.

With the separate little party he vigorously attacked the cow-tax; bulls, he said, might be called on to support their share in the maintenance of the national expenses, but cows, never! He drew such a touching picture of the cruelty in taxing the milk-giving mothers of the herd, to whom so many human infants, bereft of their natural food, owed life itself, &c., that the ladies in the gallery all wept, and the few gentlemen in the Chamber who owned land took heart of grace, and these being further strengthened by the very large minority, who hated the Ministry for the best and fiercest of all reasons, that they wanted to be in its place, the bill was thrown out amidst hooting and groaning and screaming, and the Ministry desired, or at least offered, to resign.

But the King, who was tired to death of all parties, and of their squabbling, told the House to go to the country, and dissolved Parliament. Thereupon all the attorneys, adventurers, and Jews became hopeful and riotous, and the few gentlemen very anxious, being sadly conscious that every year they grew less and less influential against the noise and the intrigues of the others.

Now Pomodoro had the right to send a deputy for the district in which the commune of Vezzaja and Ghiralda was situated, and Pomodoro had two candidates, one the Marchese Roldano, and the other one Luca Finti, a lawyer. Roldano was a stately, gracious, and very kindly gentleman, who led a life as simple as it was dignified; he had represented Pomodoro many years. Luca Finti was a very clever Neapolitan rogue, who had been in Parliament for other places, could talk a forest-tree into sawdust, as the people said, and was the Liberal, though not the Ministerial, candidate.

The Cavaliere Durellazzo, not a very wise man, had been set by his Prefect in the city, a not easy task. The existing Prefect was of course a Ministerialist; Prefects always are, and in consequence are changed as quickly as signals on a railway. With regard to the elections in the commune of Vezzaja and Ghiralda, the Prefect was in sore trouble. The commune, like the province, was reactionary, and had always returned the Marchese Roldano, whose brother was a cardinal, and whose father had been a Grand Duke's prime minister. Opposed to the Marchese was this Luca Finti, one of the *Dissidenti* who had slipped into the contest before the Ministerialists had put forward their own candidate. If Vezzaja and Ghiralda, and the other two communes which with it made up the Collegio of Pomodoro, divided the little liberal feeling there was by setting up a man all their own, the divided liberal votes would of a certainty let in the reactionary Roldano.

Luca Finti had got a start, and had trumps in his hand, through the good-will of the *strozzino* Zauli, in whose strong boxes mortgages and other engagements of nine-tenths of the country gentlemen of the province were locked up in safety. The Prefect thought he saw nothing for it but to wink at the Finti election and undermine the Finti principles. To get at the Marchese in any such a manner was hopeless. So the Prefect coquetted with the Dissidente, and the Dissidente coquetted with him; Messer Luca Finti being an adept at this kind of political flirtation.

As for his principles, indeed, they were of small compass, and could be put in a handbag and left behind, if need be, by accident. He knew well that he who would travel quickly and scale heights rapidly must carry but little of such baggage.

Although at this moment in the full flower and fury of dissent, he was a very clever man, and had made the Ministry feel that he would no longer rebel and fume if it were worth his while not to do so, and had also made the conservative side believe that with a little persuasion and profit he would not be averse to join his guerilla forces to their veteran phalanx, and march with them against his old comrades.

So the task set before the Cavaliere Durellazzo, as before the other syndics concerned in this election, was to get Messer Luca Finti elected without in any way compromising the Ministry, and in such a manner that at the end of it the Prefect would be able to issue a manifesto describing his own perfect impartiality, and his willingness for every one to act up to conscientious convictions, however opposed to his own those convictions might be.

The Cavaliere Durellazzo ostensibly accepted this onerous enterprise, but it was his secretary who mapped out all the secret campaign.

Moltke, with the ordnance map of France before him, never had graver meditations or finer combinations than had Messer Gaspardo Nellemane now. A little persuasion here, a little pressure there, a hinted threat, a well-timed bribe, a final compression of that punishment-collar which the municipalities put on the throat of the people, and all this to be done under the rose, behind the mask of a strict non-intervention —he never had been happier or of more importance.

As he was a servant of the State, he ought to have had no vote and nothing whatever to do with the elections; but, as Italy does not at present see the force of this great truth, all her prefects and syndics meddle and make in all elections, and all her clerks, guards, and servants of all kinds can vote, and the result is the Montecitorio we all behold and admire.

Messer Nellemane had at once discerned the fitness of Signor Luca Finti, and Signor Luca Finti had at once discerned the talents of Messer Nellemane. To be sure, Messer Nellemane was only the petty clerk of a petty commune, but then Luca Finti had once been only a clerk too, and some said had been things much worse, like Sir Pandarus in 'Troilus and Cressida.'

So there was a fellow-feeling between them, and even had there not been, Messer Nellemane would have supported the candidate that he was ordered to support in his own efficient, adroit, and quiet way, which burrowed unseen like a mole in the ground.

Now Vezzaja and Ghiralda was an agricultural country like nearly all the rest of Italy, and it was very unwilling that any one should represent it who should put that abhorred tax upon the cows, therefore the present election required all the tact and resources that a vigorous and active intelligence could command, and strained the powers of the Government well-wishers to the uttermost.

The Marchese Roldano, moreover, was much respected in the province, and lived like a patriarch in his great old castellated villa, amidst his olive orchards and his chestnut woods, and was not very easy to defeat.

So Messer Nellemane secretly toiled by day and night for the return of Signor Finti, and was so busy that he scarcely remembered Viola, except when he passed the door and saw her sitting spinning or plaiting within, very pale, very wasted, very weary-looking; and at such times his black eyes would gleam as if gas were lighted behind them, and he would feel a thrill of rage, a glow of triumph: but at other times he was too occupied to think of her.

He even thought with a shudder that he might have compromised his public career for a woman! for a poor girl going barefoot in the shallows of the Rosa water!

In the lives of great men love can claim but a second place.

Messer Gaspardo and Messer Luca had many a colloquy together, and found their views of a surprising harmony. When all your politics and policies are summed up in the one intention to do well for yourself, great simplicity is given to your theories, if not to your practice.

Messer Luca Finti was hand-and-glove with the ex-minister who had got into trouble about the piano, and promised if only he should be returned for Pomodoro to do great things for Messer Nellemane, who, for his part, being shrewd enough to know that a man's civility only lasts as long as his need of you, took care to know a great deal about the Finti method of canvassing, which would not have looked well in the light of public opinion; while he also conceived and mainly carried out the grand design by which all the brigade of carabiniers throughout the province was moved about from town to town rapidly and bewilderingly, so that they scored their votes for full six candidates in six different *collegie*, with great success for the Ministerial party and the cow-tax, and placed the Prefect and all his grandeur for ever in the debt of the humble secretary of the village commune.

Not that the cow-tax, though thundered against

by the conservative party, was spoken of either, by any of the ministerials canvassing in the province; they knew better; they made florid and beautiful speeches full of sesquipedalian phrases, in which they spoke about the place of Italy among the great Powers, the dangers of jealousy and invasion from other nations, the magnificence of the future, the blessings of education, the delights of liberty, the wickedness of the Opposition, the sovereign rights of the people; and said it all so magnificently and so bewilderingly that the people never remembered till it was too late that they had said nothing about opposing the cow-tax or indeed any taxes at all, but listened, and gaped, and shouted, and clapped; and being told that they could sit at a European congress to decide on the fate of Epirus, were for the moment oblivious that they had bad bread, dear wine, scant meat, an army of conscripts, and a bureaucracy that devoured them as maggots a cheese. What is political eloquence for, if not to make the people forget all such things as these?

Messer Luca Finti, who had that many-sidedness of mind that he could have found equally brilliant arguments either for or against any given measure that he might have deemed it expedient to support, cared far more to injure the aristocratic party than to damage the Government; the Government, indeed, having been his own party till his leader had been annoyed about the piano. His single object was to get returned; once returned, he, with the other Dissidenti, would trust to their natural talents to worry themselves into office, either by reunion with their whilom friends, or coalition with their eternal foes. Therefore, he had quickly taken the Prefectorial hint not to commit himself on the cow-tax in either way; a discreet neutrality was all that was asked of him, and that was difficult enough in face of the rampant rage of the country proprietors. But Luca Finti, who had once been a little, naked, idle rogue by his native shores of Amalfi, could trust to his mother wit to dazzle out of all remembrance of the main question of the elections, the elective body of the Collegio of Pomodoro. He told them, instead, that it had been only the tact and wisdom of the Dissidenti that had saved them from being involved in the impending war between Russia and China.

Russia and China, he said, were to be left to fight it out, but when the fight was over Italy would allow no treaty to be made that would compromise her rights, and would lay a claim to a portion of Mongolia, as a precaution against the influence of France in Cochin-China.

Here, again, he was loudly applauded. Not a notion had they of where, or what, Mongolia was, but it was something to be got for nothing, and which the French folks would dislike: that was enough. Not to fire a shot, not to draw a sword, but to get an acquisition of territory, and give the victors of Solferino a slap in the face; this seemed to his audience very clever indeed. Only one demurring voice was heard, which screamed, 'Will the Mongolians take the grapes out of the country? The French merchants came buying them all up last year, and it's a shame.' But this speaker, who was a *vinaio*, was hushed down as a rusty and dull conservative.

To sell your grapes to foreigners, and have none at all at home, is a spirited commerce, and fine free trade; that the poor souls around are all poisoned with cheap chemicals in the absence of wine is only an evidence of all that science can do.

Messer Luca Finti said nothing about the grapes, but he wound up with a great deal about Gambetta. One of the dyers nudged another and said, 'That's the King's brother, isn't it?' and the other replied, 'No, no; 'tis the German that took Paris;' and much edified, the assembled voters listened to the sonorous declamation of the new candidate.

When the Marchese Roldano said to them in their own homely phrase: 'Dear friends; bread is dearer in Italy by fifteen centimes a chilo than it is in Paris. I think that fact is more consequnece to you than M. Gambetta,' then the hungry stomachs applauded indeed. But the hungry stomachs were not the voters; and the dyers, and shopkeepers, and small proprietors who had the votes were of opinion that, though no doubt bread was very dear, yet to talk about it did not make pretty speechifying, and said to one another that if Italy got that bit of Mongolia then, no doubt, bread would come down like winking.

Oratorical dust is easily thrown in the eyes of all multitudes, but never so easily as here.

The Marchese called a few of them together in his own room and showed them a map.

'He is laughing at you,' he said to them. 'Look where the Mongolian Empire is, and Russia and China.'

But the map did not convince them. 'If we get it for nothing, without fighting, Mongolia will be a good thing,' they said stubbornly, and the idea grew in Pomodoro that the Marchese was a poor spirit, and unworthy to represent them.

As they were used to be led by the priests, so they were now led by the placemen.

The advantage of the exchange was questionable.

Signore Luca Finti made his oration successfully in the Pretura of Pomodoro, speaking in the same chamber where Carmelo had been brought to judgment, since it was the largest in that town; and the good folks who heard him, understanding about one half that he said, and dazzled by the other half, imbibed only the conviction that they were the glory and wonder of Europe, and said one to another that to be sure the Marchese Roldano had never told them all those fine things.

Then the agents of Signore Finti, sitting there as mere auditors, muttered to their neighbours that it was the interest of the nobility everywhere and at all seasons to keep the people ignorant; and this idea worked its way into the shaven heads of the Pomodorians, and stirred their vanity as yeast stirs the flour, and made them say one to another in the streets in the evening, as they lounged and smoked and chattered, that it was a very fine thing to be a great nation, and to have ships bigger than any that could be boasted of, even by that great *buccatone*[1] and *buscatore*,[2] England.

The Pomodorian mind was not wide, nor was it brilliant; it understood wine, oil, and dyes, but there it closed; it thought England was somewhere down Rome way, as it thought Austria was somewhere over the hills; it still believed in the priest's blessing on the fields, in the poisonous nature of frogs, in the weather prophecies of its *calendario*, in hydrophobia being as common as catarrh, and in

---

[1] Hypocrite.   [2] Brawler, bully.

other things of a like enlightenment; it did not in the least know what a congress meant, nor where Epirus was, and it had a vague notion of Europe as of a disorderly place beyond seas where you sent pictures and wine when you had more than you wanted of either.

Yet so strong is the power of vanity, and so strong is the power of oratory, that Pomodoro voted by a big majority for Messer Luca Finti, because he had told them he would make them a Power, though he had never said he would cheapen bread, extinguish conscription, or lighten any of the burdens with which the land is laden, as a pack-mule is 'chinked' on the march.

Great is the might of words—above all, is it great in Italy.


## CHAPTER XI.

ALL this while that Pomodoro was in a political fever and ferment, Carmelo languished in his prison cell. Every one had quite forgotten him except his father and his brothers and his betrothed. Old Pastorini had to pay heavily for him to have a separate cell and a little better food; at least it seemed a heavy expense for the miller, who was by no means rich, and had a large family dependent on him, and had had his gains much lessened of late years by a great steam-mill that worked at Pomodoro, and took away much of the grain of the neighbourhood. Old Pastorini had gone to an attorney in the town and put his son's cause in his hands, seeing how badly for want of a lawyer things had fared with Carmelo; but the lawyer had said, 'After the elections: after the elections,' and no more could be got out of him, though he accepted his preliminary fees.

'After the elections,' said the miller with a tremulous sigh to his son, in the few times he was allowed to visit the prison.

Carmelo shook his head.

He had known men innocent of any crime kept in prison for months and months, without being allowed a trial; it is probably by way of compensation that assassins and thieves are allowed very often to go scot free for months and months without being had up to justice.

Carmelo had changed greatly; the lithe, active, bright-eyed, sunburned youth, always at work in the air, up when the dusk of dawn veiled the earth, accustomed to spend his blithe strength in healthy labour, was shut up here as a young lion is shut up in a cage, and grew pallid, shrunken, hollow-eyed; a sullen dull anger slumbered in his eyes, and a listless despondency had replaced his calm yet buoyant spirits.

But there was no one to take any heed of that. Even the lawyer retained for him, who visited him once and asked him some rapid questions, said impatiently: 'There are a hundred causes to be heard before yours. I doubt if you will get sentence before All Saints' Day.'

For though the attorney had taken up his cause, being tempted by the sight of the elder Pastorini's well-thumbed national notes, he did not much care for it; he felt that it was not very nice work, to defend a lad unpopular with the municipal powers, and who was guilty of having assaulted a municipal guard. These cases get a lawyer in bad odour.

In the room in the Carcere where he was spending his wretched hours, of no use or profit to himself or to mankind, Carmelo, through the open window, barred close high up in the wall, could hear the roar of the assembled people inside the Pretura, as they were applauding this speech which was Greek to them. The Pretura was opposite to him, and not many metres divided the one building of Law from the other.

He had heard from his gaoler what was going on; why the town was in such tumult night and day; and he knew that one of the Liberals was standing against the old, white-haired, regal-looking Marquis.

'Perhaps if he be elected he would do something for us,' thought Carmelo wistfully. 'Perhaps he would take away all those clerks and guards, and say the poor dogs might use the legs God gave them?'

And Carmelo's heavy heart rose a little, and he felt a little hopeful and glad when his gaoler told him, at twilight, that Luca Finti was elected Deputy for Pomodoro by so large a majority that no ballot was needed.[1]

When the twilight deepened into night bands played, rockets went off, fireworks threw their many-coloured reflections into the prison cell, where Carmelo sat on his wooden bench.

Pomodoro drank too much, and fought a little, and rejoiced greatly, having a vague serious idea

---

[1] Unless one of the candidates has two-thirds of the votes, there is a ballot after the polling.

that it had done something very fine indeed in electing the advocate from Naples.

'Shall we be any the better?' said Carmelo doubtfully to his gaoler, a chatty, good-humoured man, who was sorry for him.

The gaoler shrugged his shoulders.

'He is going to give us gas and a tromböi.'[1]

'Gas! We had never vine disease, nor rose disease, till there was gas in the city,' said Carmelo, and here he did not exaggerate; for in Italy neither were known until gas works were introduced.

The gaoler shrugged his shoulders again.

'Our people want it. He says he will get it.'

'And besides?———'

'Well, nothing much besides, except that we are to be a bigger nation than England or any in Europe.'

'What is England?' said Carmelo.

'It is a place where the poor souls have no wine of their own, I think,' said the gaoler. 'And they make cannons and cheese. You see their people over here now and then. They carry red bibles, and they go about with their mouths open to catch flies,[2] and they run into all the little old dusty places; you must have seen them.'

'And why do we want to have anything to do with them?'

'They will come in ships and fire at us if we are not bigger and stronger than they,' said the gaoler. 'We must build iron houses, that float, and go on the sea, and meet them.'

'What is the sea?' said Carmelo; for how should

---

[1] Tramway.
[2] The *bocca aperta* of the English physiognomy is always a great diversion to all Italians.

he know, he who never had been out of the confines of Santa Rosalia.

But the gaoler was not very sure himself, and so said sharply he 'had no time for talk,' and withdrew the pewter plate that had carried in his prisoner's supper, and fastened the bolts and bars roughly, and then went out to see the fireworks, and talk about England with people who did not ask inconvenient questions.

He found everybody excited and enraptured about the gas that was to come to them through the mediation of the new Deputy. They did not know in the least why they wanted it; they had none of them anything to do after dusk; they had their own pure olive oil to burn, that hurt no eyesight, and gave a sweet pale light that suited the summer nights. But they thought that gas and a tromböi were signs of progress and prosperity. There are many wiser people who make the self-same error.

The railway hissed and roared twenty miles off them, where the city was; they knew that would never come nearer to them; but they saw no reason why they should not rejoice in a tall brick chimney, staring black and foul, and straight and frightful, up against their bright blue skies, and a hideous engine tearing up, and tearing along, their winding country lanes. Other towns, no bigger than theirs, had these blessings; and Signore Luca Finti had promised the same to them.

Meanwhile Messer Luca Finti was sitting supping with the Syndic of Pomodoro and the Giunta, and as the Syndic of Santa Rosalia was indisposed, his excellent *locum tenens* and secretary was invited in his stead, at the new Deputy's request, and tasted the sweets of a just reward.

In the piazza of Santa Rosalia the news was received in another spirit.

Messer Nellemane had worked for Messer Luca Finti, and that one fact was quite enough for the community that enjoyed the many blessings of his reign.

A morning or two after the elections, Viola was sitting at her door with Raggi by her side.

Raggi (an abbreviation of sunbeam), so named because she was of a light yellow colour, was a little dog that the girl had found seven years before, stray and miserable in a vine path, with a little tattered red coat adhering to her body, which showed she must have been a runaway dancing dog.

Raggi was never claimed by any master, and had long made the joy of Viola's life; the tricks and saltatory talent that Raggi, when rested and recovered, voluntarily displayed, proved that her career must have been professional, while her large liquid eyes had a sadness which betokened that she had had her share in those vicissitudes and maltreatments which no artistic career is ever without. Raggi had quickly become the idol of all the children of Santa Rosalia, and was a very happy little dog, though she always remained timid. She was now old, but she would still waltz if any guitar or accordion were sounding, and would walk erect, and beg, and beat an imaginary drum in the prettiest way possible. This morning she was sleeping on her mistress's skirts; and that was what she now liked to do best of all.

As she slept there and Viola plaited, not lifting

her eyes from the tress of straw, there passed by the door Angelo Saghari; the old man who had been rural guard of the place ever since Viola could remember; who had never molested anybody, and had always seemed as harmless as the old grey cat that dozed amongst the twine and sugar of Gigi's general shop. But old Angelo had been threatened with dismissal for supineness, and had been fired to emulation of Bindo's deeds by the fact that half the fines went into the pocket of the guard who was sharp enough to smell out a contravention; from a quiet, good-natured, neighbourly soul he had become as suspicious, spiteful, and cunning an old spy as could be manufactured by the infusion of the spirit of the communal code. The blood of his aged veins was turning sour because Bindo and his colleague were always getting the fines instead of himself, and so angry was he now that woe betided any luckless child who spun a top, or any hapless dog that wagged a tail, within a rood of Angelo.

As he went grumpy and glum, because of these things, his sword hanging at his side, with which he could hack a dog handily, though he never dared draw it on a thief, his eyes spied out little yellow-haired Raggi asleep on her mistress's gown.

The dog was certainly not chained; the dog had not even a collar; the grey hairs of Angelo stood erect with horror.

He had known Raggi seven years, and had stood and laughed a hundred times to see her waltz, and beat the drum, to divert the children in the piazza. But now he only beheld in Raggi an object for contravention. As to Napoleon all men were food for powder, so, to those imbued with the communal code, all living things are food for fines. Can a fine be screwed out of them? that is the only question.

He went up to Viola, therefore, and said roughly: 'Your dog is loose!'

Viola looked up and laughed, despite the sadness of her heart.

'Raggi? Why, it is Raggi! Are they going to tell me to tie Raggi? That would be too cruel; why, Raggi is the darling of everybody. What would the children do without her? Though, to be sure, she is a little rheumatic and stiff now, *poverina*——'

Angelo was frowning heavily, and writing with a pencil in his book.

'I have a right to seize the dog, and I have a mind to do it for your impudent answers,' he said harshly. 'The dog is loose. It is an offence against the laws of the commune, as you are very well aware. Your father will be summoned——'

'But, Angelo!' cried Viola in stupefaction, not believing her own ears. 'Raggi is just as she has been for seven years and more. What has she done? What can you mean? You have patted and petted her yourself all these years, and laughed so to see her dance—you are joking!——'

'You will find it no joke,' said Angelo harshly, feeling a little ashamed of himself. 'Your dog can be no exception to the rest. Your father will have to pay, and if I see the beast loose again, I shall take it to the guard house, and it will be killed unless you pay twenty francs. You are warned.'

Then Angelo shuffled off, feeling that Bindo himself could not have said or done better. Viola took the little yellow dog up in her arms and kissed it convulsively and sobbed over it.

'Oh, Raggi! What has come to the world that we are all treated like galley slaves, and you poor pretty things like wild beasts!' she murmured over the dog; and it seemed to this gentle and pious girl that she could spring at the cruel hearts of all these men, and stab them to death for the sheer sweet sake of justice.

For it is the noblest natures that tyranny drives to frenzy.

'*Dominiddio!*' cried Pippo when he came home. 'I'd throttle Angelo sooner than I'd throttle an adder. Oh, the vile old creature, when he has known me all his life, and saw you baptised with the holy water! Lord, Lord! how are we to live? Was not life hard enough to the likes of us at all times? Is Raggi a wolf or a bear? Can a dog live tied down with a string as you tie a call-bird to a trap? They are mad! They are all gone clean mad, and it is we who have to bear all the brunt of it. The gentlemen can't know of it. The gentlemen can't know!'

The gentlemen did know of it, however, well enough, and when they sat at their weekly meeting, listened to the reports read by Messer Nellemane, and applauded the zeal of the rural guards. None of the gentlemen lived in Santa Rosalia itself, and when they drove through it they liked to have no wooden disc rolling from a child's hand across their road, no dog barking at their gigs' wheels; and cared very little by what means their laws were enforced, or what poor household was sold up under their rules. For thorough, absolute, selfish indifference to the wrongs and the sorrows of the people, there is nothing comparable to the apathy of an Italian of the new *régime*. It is an apathy so obtuse, so self-complacent, and so pachydermatous, that one longs sometimes to see it blasted and shaken into ruins by the roar and leap of an avenging people.

Angelo kept his word, and Pippo was summoned for having Raggi loose, or, according to the amenities of the printed papers, was invited to make amends for a transgression.

Poor old Pippo, being advised by his timid neighbour, Cecco the cooper, to do anything for peace and quietness, went and submitted to be fined two francs, and had to go without wine for a week.

'Two francs because Raggi slept on your gown!' he said to his daughter twenty times a day; it seemed to him an oppression so monstrous that the world had never seen one like it.

Viola, trembling for the safety of Raggi, put an old bit of ribbon about the neck of the dog, and tied a long string to it; but no municipality being able wholly to change the nature of animals, and it being quite impossible to perpetually pin a dog to your side, Raggi walked about the piazza, and went to her playmates the children with the string trailing behind her, and more summonses rained in on Pippo.

Not summonses alone, moreover, for there came with them a taxpaper which claimed, on account of Raggi, seven years' tax at six francs the year, and all the *spese* attending delay added thereto; in all, some seventy odd francs. With this came documents for various contraventions concerning the cutting of the reeds and the running of the brook, condemning Filippo Mazzetti in contumacy for not having attended the various calls for these great and punishable offences; and the sum total of this was so terrible that the old man, when it was read to him by his daughter, dropped down, white as a sheet, and stared with gasping breath and suffocating heart, till the terrified maiden screamed that he was in a fit, and all the neighbours ran in to help.

Pippo was not in a fit: but when one after another these papers rained in upon him with their inexorable demands, the buoyant, brave, ignorant, harmless life of him seemed to collapse under a great terror, as a bird sinks down that is stoned.

He had never complained of his lot, though it had never been a good one; he had never thought it hard to have to labour for his bread all the year round; he had accepted his destiny cheerfully, never quarrelling with God or man about it; but now the docility of his soul turned and writhed, and he called out against his fate, and he rose at every dawn with a great fear, like ice, at his heart. For what does ruin mean to the poor man? It means death; a slow, long death of hard-drawn hunger.

Gentlemen who so lightly make your rules, and pass your fines, do ever you remember that? I think not; I hope not; for your oblivion is your sole excuse, though such oblivion is accursed, and if ever there be justice or judgment, it scarce will hold you guiltless.

Ten days were given wherein to pay these charges: six of these days Pippo spent wandering wearily to and fro, up and down, telling his woes now to this neighbour, now to that, staring on the documents which he could not read, and wondering what on earth he could do. He could see no right at all which could force him to pay these penalties. He had done nothing that he had not been accustomed to do all the years of his life; how could he understand that all these charges had become due, just because a few men gathered together and said they were so? Dogs had been free, the rushes had been free, the water had been free, ever since Pippo could remember; why should they be taxed, and forbidden, and made sins of, just because those communal clerks and guards liked to have it so?

The justice of moral laws even the galley-slave will admit; but the justice of municipal laws no poor man recognises, as indeed there is no reason why he should, since none of these laws serve him.

There was no sense in it all; it was only done to put money in the purses of rogues: Pippo, though a simple docile soul, rebelled.

Life had never been anything wonderful to him; he had always worked hard and eaten little; he had never seen anything beyond the vine-paths about Santa Rosalia and the dusty stones of Pomodoro: wiser people might have wondered that he ever cared to take the trouble to get up of a morning and pull his breeches on, so very little did each day offer to him. But Pippo never wondered; he enjoyed his life very much when he was let alone; he had been very fond of his womenkind; he had once been a bright young fellow with lute and song, and light limbs to dance with, and he had not forgotten all that time; when he could lie in the shade at noontide, and get a little beaker of wine, and chat about nothing cheerily, and smoke his pipe, and hear his village news, Pippo was perfectly happy, and did not want to end his life as Nanni had ended his, with a pinch of charcoal, in a shuttered room, on a bare floor.

It was not much of a life, to be sure; and was wearing away now like a waning light on St. John's Eve; but it was a fresh, simple, pleasant, little life, spent on the edge of the bright Rosa water, and amongst the waving beds of reeds; it seemed to Pippo that he would hear the sough of the rushes and see the glint of the river-reaches even when he should be put away in a deal box against the church wall, or, as the priests said, should be in heaven.

When Dom Lelio would preach about heaven, Pippo, sitting at mass on his wooden chair, would nod and shut his eyes, and dream of paradise, and would never be able to get any other idea of it than that shining water, those waving reeds, and the blue clear sky beyond them.

And he had always said to himself, 'Come what may, God will leave me the river;' and it had always been a great happiness to him to think that this little cot, overlooking the river that he loved, would be dwelt in by him till the saints should bear him across another and a darker stream.

But now,—if he must borrow on it— Pippo felt that nevermore would it really be his own again.

'You borrow twopence on a thing you have, and from that minute those two pennies will eat and eat and eat you till they swell like turkey poults at Ceppo, only it's you who burst for it, not they,' had Pippo's wife always said to him; and the truth of the saying remained in his mind.

Yet what was he to do?

No doubt to you, gentlemen, it is very absurd to want these few francs; you and I give as much for a plant, for a plate, for a chair, for a teacup; to face ruin because you cannot find it seems ridiculous, and yet it was ruin to Pippo.

If he did not pay, the Law would seize his rickety tables, and his earthen pipkins, and his copper pots, and would sell them, and sell his house over his head, and his bed from under him. He had done no harm whatever, and he owed not a farthing; yet he would be treated as if he were the blackest thief, the most shameless debtor, and all the few rags and sticks that he owned in the world would go under the hammer.

Pippo sat on his threshold and leaned his grey head on his hands, and could not understand it. 'If I had done anything,' he said again and again; and, stupid old fellow that he was, could not see his crime.

'They'll fine the butterflies next, I suppose, for flying,' he thought wearily, as those golden, and azure, and tortoise-shell, and white flowers of the air spread their wings against him, or floated through the light above the rushes.

'Could Carmelo's father help us?' asked Viola wistfully; but Pippo shook his finger in denial. He knew that the elder Pastorini had debts of his own from bad trade and the law costs attending his son's trial. For some years the mill had brought in but slender returns, and the Pastorini were generous folks, and never grudged a neighbour a place at their board. This open-handed way of living was well enough in the old times; but nowadays taxation sits like a ghost at every homely table.

No; old Pippo would not borrow of a friend, nor of one whose son would wed his granddaughter. So he sat all alone on the settle in his little stone porch, and totted it all up after his own manner with a bit of chalk. He could not read or write, but he knew the look of figures, and he could sum up correctly. Many men, here, know arithmetic very well who do not know the alphabet. They learn it in self-defence against cheating.

He had all these hateful papers in his hand; papers wordy, and covered all over with writing, which was as Greek to him, but he could understand one thing in them—the sum he was condemned to pay. There was twenty-three, and then there was twenty-five, and then there was thirty-two, and then there was forty, and besides these were five different sums of ten francs each; these last five were for the reed-cutting; and then there was the seventy for Raggi. He told them all up once more, as he had told them all up twenty times before, and he made them in all two hundred and forty-three francs, and the total made his head reel, his eyes swim, his stomach sicken; he could no more get that sum than he could get a gold chariot and six white horses.

'What will happen if I don't pay?' he asked of Cecco for the fiftieth time; and Cecco answered, 'They will sell you up; sell you up as they did Nanni;' and Pippo groaned.

Gentlemen, what would you feel if every week, or every month, some power of the State could call on you for a thousand pounds, and if you failed to pay it could seize on your estates? Gentlemen, you do not remember it, but the five francs, or the five shillings, to the poor is as that thousand pounds would be to you; nay, more, for the seizure of the large sum would be to you at worst a lost superfluity, some luxury, some purchase, some pleasure the less, but to the poor the loss of the little sum may be the loss of bread in health, of medicine in sickness, of the meat that is strength, of the clothing that is decency; the loss of the little sum may be the loss of the one frail plank that stands between poverty and death.

Think of this now and then, gentlemen who make the laws at ease, all the world over, and break the hearts and destroy the homes of the poor with the fines that the English magistracy, the French mayoralties, and the Italian municipalities alike so dearly love to wring from the poor man, standing ignorant, helpless, and utterly unconscious of wrongdoing before these mockers of the majesty of Law!

What with pondering over the summonses about Raggi, and the summonses about the reeds in the river, and the summonses about the brook-water, old Pippo was fairly crazed. He went about the village, shouting like a dazed creature, 'My fathers cut the reeds before me hundreds of years; and hundreds of years the water has run, and God sent it; and the little yellow dog, why, she is known to every man jack of them, and all the babies play with her. What have I got to pay for? what have I got to pay for?——'

And his neighbour always said to him,

'You must always pay if you haven't got a bit of paper. We'll soon have to pay for drawing our breath, or lighting our pipes. I always told you, you should have got a bit of paper.'

'But I can't pay,' said Pippo, shoving his hat on the back of his head, and hitching up the band of his linen trousers with a little puckered, woebegone face, and his tears only not falling because they were dried by his rage.

'If I earn a dozen *soldi* a day, it's the best as

ever I do; and, to be sure, the girl plaits, but plaiting isn't what it was since all those machine-made hats came in, and it's barely enough for her dress that she makes at it; and there's nought besides, nought; and it's a'most as dear to make your bread as buy it now the grist-tax is on; and wine, Lord! wine that I remember twenty years ago you might have almost for the asking of it, there it is now up to a franc, and not seldom up as high as one-thirty—who's to pay, who's to pay, with victuals and drink what they are?'

'If you haven't got a bit of paper you must pay,' said the neighbour, into whose head long years of municipal despotism had hammered this one fact. 'The house is your own, aren't it? You've always said so. Well, you'll have to get something on that.'

'Jesus, help me!' groaned Pippo, to whom the Galilean was not dead.

The house was certainly his; he was not very clear how; but his forefathers had dwelt in it, and he had been born in it; and in an old iron chest with rusty locks there were some old 'bits of paper' that he had been always told established his right to it. But to raise money on it! Pippo did not know much, but he had always heard that attorneys and *strozzini*[1] were the legitimate children of the devil. True, everybody was everywhere raising money in these days; he heard say that all the big lands were writ down in the Mortgage Archives in the city, and half the little estates too; but to Pippo's old-fashioned ideas it seemed quite as shameful to get money on your bit of ground as to carry your pots and pans up to the Monte di Pietà.

[1] Usurers.

He came of that stock of homely, honest, independent peasantry that is still existent in Italy, as in France and England, but which all the new-fangled laws and schools are doing their best to destroy in each of these countries. To borrow, Pippo thought, was quite a thievish thing, and as bad and as mean as to send your girl to her nuptials without her due share of house linen and her decent string of pearls.

Then he had not an idea what his little house was worth: whether twenty pence or twenty million pence. It was a little stone-built place, sound and solid because raised in the old days when work was soundly and solidly done, but it had never a stroke for repair given to it, and it was very small, and had only a narrow kitchen garden behind it, with one aged fig-tree past bearing, a few fruit espaliers, and some vegetables. Pippo did not think any one would give much for it, and the thought of raising a penny on it cut him to the quick. 'For the *strozzini* and the lawyers,' said he in his perplexity, 'if they do but smell at a peach, it is down their throats, stone and all, and never chokes them.'

He had not any dealings with such folks himself, but so he had heard, and so he had seen in his intercourse with his neighbours. Had not Simone Zauli the money-lender, who dwelt at the new white house with the gilded weathercock and the cast-iron gates, on the Pomodoro road, made all his riches thus out of his fellow creatures, beginning as a ragged boy by stealing dogs and selling them alive, or their skins when dead, and then lending other boys trifling sums to lose at lotto or at marra, and so progressing upward in man's and fortune's favours?

Nevertheless little old Pippo said to himself:

'Nanni gave in without a struggle, but I will go and ask them to do right by me. Human hearts are good in the main, and what for should those gentlemen want to hurt a poor soul like myself?'

He thought these things were done because the gentlemen did not know of them; so he resolved to tell the gentlemen; and he brushed himself and put on his Sunday clothes, and betook himself on a round of visits. First, of course, he went to the Syndic's villa, but there he was told that the Count Durellazzo was still away at the Bagni; if it were anything of business, Messer Nellemane down in the village would attend to it.

'Nay! nay! as well send me to Lucifero himself,' muttered Pippo, and turned back to descend the long four miles of stony, shadeless hills that he had painfully climbed.

Bindo Terri, who was up there, flirting and drinking with the Syndic's pretty *massaja*, heard the muttered words and duly reported them.

Bindo had got about his duties once more, and though he had made himself some bruises very cleverly with iodine and indigo, he could not affect to be ailing any longer, and had indeed got sick of lying in bed, despite the fry and the Vin Santo, and so had come up cheerfully to the Syndic's farm to guarantee as 'healthy meat' a bullock just dead of pleuro-pneumonia.

## CHAPTER XII

IT was too late that day to go anywhere else, but the next morning Pippo set forth again. He went to each of the gentlemen of the district who formed the Giunta; there were seven of them. Two of them, as said, were noblemen, two were small gentry; one was a doctor, one was a lawyer, and one was the money-lender Zauli. Pippo tried the nobles first; one was at his estates in another province, and the other, who was at home, said he was very sorry, but he could not interfere; he had no power to alter the law; he was kind, however, and told his *maestro di casa* to send the old man into the kitchen to have a meal; the small gentry said much the same, a little more disagreeably; the lawyer said that they were determined to make their laws respected; and when the old man timidly asked why the law had been made, and suggested that they would be very much better un-made again, grew angry, and told Pippo he was impudent, which was, indeed, the last thing that Pippo ever dreamed of being. The doctor said much the same thing as the lawyer, and as for going to Zauli, Pippo knew that would be of no good; as soon will you get peaches off an ant-eaten tree as mercy out of the heart of a money-lender.

In Pippo's eyes, and in those of most in Santa Rosalia, Simone Zauli was as a great swollen dragon, gorged on the bodies and the souls of other men, and he was the only incarnation that they knew of usury.

Jaded, footsore, very heart-sick, Pippo trotted through the ankle-deep dust, carrying his boots in his hands; he had thought it only respectful to enter the gentlemen's houses with his boots on, but that was no reason why he should wear them out on the common highway. He was very tired when he got home; for one way and another, up and down hill, and to and fro, he had walked five-and-twenty miles, if one. But he ate his bit of supper in silence, and went to bed. In bed another hope dawned on him; a faint one, but still something on which to act.

He said nothing to his daughter, for he held the old-fashioned opinion that women had no head for anything, and had best be told naught, but next morning put on his festa coat and waistcoat, took his straw hat and went through the clouds of dust in the shaky diligence to Pomodoro.

'They do say he is a liberal one and has a heart for the poor,' thought Pippo, and boldly went and asked for Signore Luca Finti, who had taken a lodging in the town, for people were now saying that the new deputy, who was a bachelor, was thinking of nothing less than asking for the hand of Teresina Zauli, an ugly wench, indeed, brown, clumsy, with a bearded lip, and a chignon like a melon, dressed in all the colours of the rainbow, but worth her weight in gold, and owning all the jewels, too, of a dead countess, whose affairs her good father had managed; the countess, being a poor-witted and sad-spirited lady. Teresina Zauli had given her heart to a brave young bailiff who was floridly handsome as a dahlia flower, but that was not the match her father meant for her, and she had soon resigned herself to the idea of being a deputy's wife, and living in Rome, and going to the Quirinal when a state ball was given, as Luca Finti's wife would do unquestionably.

The 'note' of the new deputy being all things to all men, and familiar good-nature to the entire population, the little old dusty figure of Pippo was shown into the chamber where the deputy was taking a light breakfast of stuffed onions and a *risotto* of liver and brains. Signore Finti, thinking the old man came to beg, buttoned up his pockets, but saluted him with a sweet smile and words so bland that Pippo thought at a bound: 'he will get me let off the fines.'

He was benignity and kindness itself, for this Luca Finti was to every one; but when he found what the errand was he grew a little colder, a trifle less affable; for to the mind of the Deputy municipal law was sacred. The bureaucratic mind, all the world over, believes the squeak of the official penny whistle to be as the trump of archangels and the voice from Sinai.

That all the people do not fall down prostrate at the squeak is, to this order of mind, the one unmentionable sin.

With hope Pippo began his tale.

He was a long time telling it, and he told a good deal of it three times over; and he muddled it all together, and at the close of it he damned the State in general, and Messer Gaspardo Nellemane in particular, very finely.

Luca Finti listened patiently; but when Pippo, out of breath, paused in his cursing, he frowned, and drew himself up with the gesture he generally kept for the Tribune.

'I fear you are contumacious.'

'Eh, sir?' said Pippo. 'That's what they say in the summons-papers. Con-tu-ma-cious. It's a mighty long word for poor folks that don't know what it means. What have I done? Nought! Nought! He came prying and poking where he'd no business: he didn't make the reeds in the water; God made them. He didn't set my brook running; God set it. As for the poor little beast, every child

knows her and loves her. I have done nought.
That I'll say if I die for it. I live peaceably, and I
hurt none; and this Jack-in-office comes spying on
me, and worrying me, and beggaring me, and then
he calls it all con-tu-ma-cy! What have I done?'

The Deputy's face clouded and grew grave as he
looked over the papers which Pippo had handed to
him.

'They seem all in order,' he murmured a little
severely: if the penny whistle has shrieked, who
shall dare to find fault with its blast?

'Eh, sir?' said Pippo wistfully.

'I see nothing out of order in these,' said Luca
Finti. 'Really nothing. It may fall hard on you;
but you should have observed the laws.'

'Laws, sir?' said the old man hotly. 'I never
broke the law—never. It never could be put against
me. *They* are not laws, these tomfool's rubbish that
those spies and blackguards lay their heads together
to concoct, that they may wring our money out of
us when they want a breakfast, or a supper, or a
drink, or a trull!'

'Hush—sh—sh!' said the Deputy, putting up
his hand with quite a shiver. 'You must not say
such things. You must never say such things. The
Law is unassailable, and its administrators and representatives must be respected. Those papers are perfectly correct. They are founded on Imperial Law,
and, were they not so, every municipality has a right
to make and to enforce its own laws. The regulations of your commune are admirable ones; wise,
preventive, full of an excellent forethought and
caution. It is your duty, and it ought to be **your**
pleasure, to obey them——'

Messer Luca Finti might have gone on in this strain for an hour, since every Italian is eloquent, or, at any rate, long-winded and master of a million words, but old Pippo, whose slow and patient blood was beginning to boil under the bitterness of his disappointment, interrupted him.

'Listen, your honour; that guard is a rogue that has been a vagabond before all our eyes ever since he could run alone; and the clerk that makes the laws is a rogue too, only a smooth one, in cloth clothes; and wrong, to my knowledge, I never have done; and the brook has been put there by God in heaven, and the reeds any man of us cuts when he pleases, and no one is a penny the worse; and my little old dog is a pet of every baby about in the place, and why shouldn't it sit at the door; and if you only will think on the cruelty of all this, and the shame and the sin against me, an old man, and one who never did harm, and——'

'My dear friend,' said the Deputy wearily, 'your head is a wooden head. You will not understand. You have broken the law. Libel against the officers of the law will not efface that fact, but only increase your criminality. I can do nothing. Nothing whatever.'

'What is the use of you being our Deputy, then, if you cannot see to having us righted?' said Pippo, whose spirit had risen as his heart was breaking.

'You are not wronged,' said Luca Finti with a polite contempt. 'Were you wronged, be sure my protection should be over you. You are not wronged at all, *caro mio*. You have transgressed certain just laws, and you must be made to pay a just penalty for your disobedience. It is no use to groan,' added the Deputy, as Pippo did groan at all the grand words that fell like ice on his ear.

'You should not complain. You should confess yourself to blame. I do not see that the fines are in any way excessive. You must pay them, and you will be a wiser man for the future.'

Pippo stood quite still; the veins swelling on his wrinkled forehead and great angry tears gathering in his eyes.

There is nothing on earth so hard to endure as this tone of easy superiority, of jaunty counsel: to the old man, with whom this matter was ruin itself, every one of the tranquil, insolent, chill words was like the stab of a knife.

He gathered up the papers with a tremulous hand; it was all he could do to keep from bursting out crying like a child.

'There's no right in them, and no justice,' he muttered. 'God forgive you gentlemen who ruin the poor.'

And with that he put his hat on his old white head, and turned his back on Luca Finti, and went out of the door. The Deputy hesitated a moment, then rose and went after him: this was an old fool rightly served, he thought; but then—he wanted to keep up a good name in his newly-won Collegio.

He touched Pippo on the shoulder.

'Here,' he said a little hurriedly. 'You must try and make a collection and pay those amounts so; they are not at all excessive; quite just, quite just; but if you are so poor, take this to begin with; only you must not say I gave it.'

Then he slid into the old man's hand a five-franc note.

Pippo put it back again very quietly.

'Thank you, sir,' he said very quietly too. 'I came for justice not for favour, and I never was a beggar yet.'

Then he went down the stairs, and Messer Luca Finti for the first time in his life felt crest-fallen.

## CHAPTER XIII.

LITTLE Pippo, saying nothing more, went with the bitterness gnawing at his heartstrings, and got leave to visit Carmelo.

It was a sad sight to see that strong healthy, handsome youth, who should have been at work in the mill with the weighty sacks pulling at his arms, shut up in prison, lying on a wooden bench face downwards, doing nothing, grown spiritless, and yet sullen, broken in strength, and yet savage, as the dogs are that these wise laws chain.

Pippo sat down before him; the old man's brown face was pinched and pallid, but he was quite quiet still; he felt like one stunned and paralysed.

'My boy, these devils claim two hundred and forty three francs of me,' he said with a little quiver in his voice. 'If I do not pay they will sell me up; I must get money on the house. You know well a thing borrowed on is as good as lost. I did think to give the girl that house in dower, when she married you. What do you say now? It will come to you mortgaged, and that is no better than a loaf that the mice have gnawed, with all the crumb eat off, but so it must be.'

Carmelo nodded.

Nothing mattered to him much.

'Will not the new deputy do any good for us?' he asked wearily.

'Curse him!' said Pippo. 'He is one of them; a scoundrel climbed up on poor fools' backs, and making more poor fools a ladder to get up higher by, that's all. A scoundrel; a sheer scoundrel, a tongue of oil, a heart of brass! Don't think of him! You won't mind then, Carmelo, if the old house never comes to the girl?—'

Carmelo laughed a little bitterly.

'I am a felon,' said he. 'House or no house, Viola will be too good for me when I come out; I am disgraced.'

'Not you,' said the old man. 'You did right; the prison can do you no shame: all the village says that, and Viola will be as proud to walk before the priest with you, as if you were the king. I thought I would tell you of the house, because you had a right to look for it, and when once there is a loan on it, it is gone for good.'

'Never mind me,' said Carmelo. 'I am so sorry all this loss falls on you. There seems a curse on us. Tell Viola not to fret, to keep a brave heart; I shall be out in three weeks more, for certain I am that when they hear all they will set me free, and then—'

'Then she shall marry you,' said Pippo. 'Not but what if things go on as they are now you will breed but beggars.'

'We must take our chance of that,' said Carmelo. 'If you are sure she will not be ashamed of me—'

'If she were, she would be turned out of my

door, neck and crop,' said Pippo. 'But there is no fear of that. Viola is a good girl and a loyal. I am glad you do not care more for the house.'

'I do not care at all except for you,' said Carmelo, to whom in his durance it seemed that no roof could ever be needed by any one except the broad blue sky.

Then Pippo left him and said to the gaoler at the prison door :

'Can you tell me of a man who lends money?' and the gaoler answered that he knew no one who would lend it without making profit on it, but if there were a profit to be had, then nobody he thought could be fairer than a certain Signore Nicolo Poccianti, who dwelt hard by the west gate, and was a notary and a lender too.

To him went Pippo.

'When you must be hanged, what matters the rope?' he said to himself, and by sunset on the morrow he had three hundred francs in his breeches pocket, and had left his papers that concerned the house with Messer Nicolo, and had put his cross before two witnesses against a long written thing that was read out to him without his understanding any word or any sense of it, and had seen seals and signatures set at the public office to documents a metre in length.

When he took his place in the lumbering diligence to be borne homeward, he felt that the dust of the road and the blue of the sky spun round him. Life was over for him, as much as though the coffin had been nailed down above his body.

His little house had been very dear to him; it had made him feel proud and like a man; there had been always that little place to live and die in, a place all his own, as much as the palace is a monarch's: now that another had a claim on it, all that was over.

'I have borrowed on the house,' he said to his daughter when he reached home, and sank into a chair, pale to the lips, and with all his limbs and frame trembling.

Then he stretched out his hands with a sudden strength of passion.

'God's curse on them!' he cried fiercely; 'God's curse on them!'

## CHAPTER XIV.

NEXT morning timid Cecco the cooper went for Pippo and paid the two hundred and forty three francs claimed by the municipality.

Pippo was in bed with what is called a stroke of heat, and wandered in his speech and seemed stupid. Timid Cecco went and paid it all because the girl asked him to do so, he being very far from sure that he would not be incriminated in some way himself. But when they gave him the receipt for the money, the simple soul was overjoyed, and ran back as fast as ever he could, and tore up Pippo's stairs, and went in triumph to Pippo's bedside.

'Now you have got a bit of paper,' he cried; 'they never can hurt you any more. Keep it close. Never lose it. You've got your bit of paper now!'

The old man lay with his face to the wall, and answered nothing.

Viola, young, and so hopeful, caught Cecco's arm in both her hands.

'Is that true? Is that really true? Will they never be able to torment us any more? Are you quite certain?'

Simple Cecco, in the honesty of his own convictions, patted her hands kindly, and said:

'Of course they can't, my dear, now you have got that bit of paper. You must keep it close, and always have it by to show; this bit of paper. Why, my dear,' continued Cecco, with a touch of patriotic indignation, 'Do you think after taking nigh three hundred francs from your poor grandfather, they wouldn't respect his bit of paper? No, no; they're bad, but not so bad as that.'

'And Raggi may be loose?'

Cecco scratched his head thoughtfully.

'Why, I should say so, my dear: for what else is the tax paid for her, and that bit of paper given?'

The one-idea'd mind of Cecco the cooper could not embrace a state of things in which you should pay heaps of fines and taxes and yet get nothing in return for them.

'Poor grandfather!' said Viola with her onyx-like eyes suffused and tender. 'Pray God send him no more trouble.'

Pippo, as she spoke, sat suddenly up in his bed.

'Nay, nay; Dominiddio has nought to do with sending this sort of trouble,' he said, with a thickened voice and a wild gesture. 'Never lay it on God, my child. This trouble and them who made it are spawned and hatched in hell.'

The girl shuddered.

She had never seen her kindly, placid, pious old grandfather thus.

A lull occurred in the storm of summonses. Some eight or ten days drifted by in peace. Raggi ran about.

At the end of the week Pippo got up and put on his clothes and went out to his daily work.

'Never to cut the reeds! Never to cut the reeds!' he muttered: but he had been cowed and terrified; he did not dare take his reaping-hook and wade in amongst those lithe green blowing rushes. It is the perfection of these laws that they change brave men into soulless machines.

He got his spade and went and dug, in his little bit of ground amongst the potatoes and tomatoes. Seeing him thus labouring the girl took heart, and began to hope all would go well. She did not know enough to realise all the mortgage on the little house implied, and she felt sure that Carmelo would soon be free.

She called Raggi, and ran lightly up to Gigi Canterelli's shop to buy a little maccaroni. She passed Messer Gaspardo Nellemane. She coloured hotly, remembering the gifts of Corpus Domini. He uncovered his head with a bland smile; his eye, glancing from her, fell on little yellow Raggi.

That night he said to Bindo, 'There are still dogs loose despite the law. Enforce our regulations.'

Bindo promised extra zeal, though it was by no means to his views to drill the populace into perfect obedience, but rather to leave a little troop of contraventions straying about like gipsies, on which to pounce down for his fines at leisure, as a hawk picks one out of a brood of young birds for breakfast, and takes another at noonday.

The next day another summons, to 'make accord on a transgression,' was left at Filippo Mazzetti's. Viola received it when her grandfather was in the kitchen garden, and after a moment's hesitation thrust it in her pocket, and waited her opportunity to take counsel with Cecco the cooper.

'It is a mistake,' said Cecco. 'Of course it's a mistake, when you have got the bit of paper! Lend me the bit of paper, and I will go and see to it. I have been once;—I can just as well go again, and not worry your grandfather.'

Cecco was a long, thin man, like a lath, and was very pale, and almost anything in the world set him all of a tremble, as he would say himself, and he shook in his shoes as he went up to the Municipal Palace on his unselfish errand. But he was a good neighbour and friend, and was fond of Viola; and he put a bold front over a quaking spirit as he asked to see Messer Nellemane. It was the hour when the potentate gave gracious audience.

'I have ventured, sir,' he began, with great respect in his tone, for he knew that the Secretary liked and expected much obsequiousness. 'I have ventured, Pippo being ailing himself, as one may say, and not able in any way to come to you, to bring your most illustrious this summons they have sent him by a mistake, sir. Quite a mistake, as you will see, sir, for you will remember only last week giving to me, who came for him then also, a bit of paper that set him free of all these things. This is a mistake, sir——'

'We never make mistakes,' said Messer Nellemane frigidly, and glanced his eye over the summons. 'I cannot suppose for a moment it is a mistake. But it is not in my department. However, as you seem a well-meaning person, I will send for the *usciere*.'

He touched a hand bell.

The *usciere* was out, serving warrants; in his stead fat Maso, who was below cracking walnuts, as he had been eating figs when Carmelo's wedding-party had come, responded to the summons, even tried to look pompous and official, knowing that the master of all their destinies expected it.

'This summons, Signore Tommaso,' said Messer Gaspardo to him, with dignity yet graciousness; 'Will you be as good as to say why it was issued? It is worded so as to call to account Mazzetti Filippo, for a transgression of the law on the 15th *ult.*; that was the day before yesterday. What is his offence?'

'Dog loose, Signore,' said the fat Maso, who knew that his superior liked to do all the eloquence himself, and expected pithy and pregnant replies from his colleagues and inferiors.

'Dog loose? Ah! The witness?' asked Messer Nellemane.

Maso replied promptly, 'The municipal guard, Terri Bindo.'

'All in order—all quite in order,' said Messer Gaspardo complacently, and turned to Cecco. 'You perceive, my friend, there is no mistake. No mistake is ever made here. I should have thought that Mazzetti had had caution and lesson enough; he must be an extremely obstinate and perverse person. His dog was loose the day before yesterday. He must pay two francs, and if he continue his transgression the next penalty must be higher.'

Cecco gasped: he remained standing with his mouth wide open, so amazed and so horror-stricken he was.

'But, your honour,' he said with a trembling and panting voice. 'Please, your honour, here is this bit of paper; you gave it yourself, and the tax-gatherer gave such another; I paid all that mint of money for him only last week; if it don't set him free, what was the use of it? what was the money paid for—?'

This most timid man grew audacious in his grief and amazement. If a bit of paper was no protection, then to Cecco heaven and earth alike were falling.

'What was the money paid for—what was the money paid for?' he stammered in his bewilderment. 'Sixty-five francs of it was every penny for Raggi!'

'Everything is in order,' said Messer Nellemane, coldly eyeing the agitated creature with some scorn and more disgust. 'What this very stubborn friend of yours paid last week were arrears; long due arrears. That payment has nothing to do with this, nor with any future ones that his contumacy may cost him.'

'Lord have mercy on his soul!' groaned Cecco.

Messer Nellemane grew impatient.

'If you are come to pay the fine, pay it. If not, I must remind you that my time is valuable, and so also is that of the other officers of the commune.'

'Lord have mercy on his soul,' ejaculated Cecco, looking all round the room with a scared expression. 'Why, if he were as rich as a wax candle maker he would be ruined at this rate in a month!'

'Are you come to pay the fine?' repeated Messer Nellemane, sharply hitting his desk with his ruler, as Léon Gambetta does when in a rage with Paul de Cassagnac. 'Lord, have mercy!' moaned the cooper for the third time, and fumbled in his breeches pocket and pulled out some very dirty little half-franc notes and halfpence.

'Is it two francs?' he asked faintly.

'Three-fifty with *spese*,'[1] said Maso with great rapidity.

Cecco counted out the sum; he happened to have it in his pocket, for he had just been paid for some wine barrels.

Maso made him out a receipt grudgingly, but Cecco put it back with a feeble gesture.

'What is the use of it if you will come again directly?' said this very stupid man.

'Imbecile!' thundered Messer Nellemane. 'Every charge is separate, and every charge is just. A word more, and I call the guard.'

Poor Cecco went humbly out, fumbling in his pocket at the few pence that were left him, and sorely terrified at his own temerity. He went home, and passing Viola, who stood with anxious face and wistful eyes awaiting his return at her door, he tried to nod quite cheerfully.

'It is all right, my dear. It was a mistake,' he said briskly. 'Only—only—keep Raggi with a string beside you. She will be safest so.'

Then he hurried on to his noonday meal, as he said, fearing she would question him.

'We won't have meat for a few Sundays, Giuditta,' he said to his wife. 'I had a misfortune. I lost the

[1] Costs.

money they paid me for mending the casks. Nay, never tear your hair. It is no such great calamity. How did I lose it?—oh, I don't know; I daresay I pulled it out unawares with my pipe.'

A falsehood that certainly may go heavenward with Uncle Toby's oath.

When his frugal dinner of beans was over Cecco went to his workshop with a heavy heart and a bewildered brain. 'Lord have mercy on us,' he said to himself as he hammered his staves. 'We'll all be ruined men!'

Meanwhile fat Maso was spending the one franc fifty centimes, that he had had for *spese*, on a very comfortable meal of pork chops and fried artichokes in the back room of the shop of Gigi Canterelli, who, as he served him, thought to himself, 'By Bacchus, I should do little harm if I poisoned the whole damned lot of you in your *pasta*!'

For these are the cheerful and loyal feelings in the populace that the present administrators of the Law promote.

## CHAPTER XV.

Pippo was not told of that summons by either his friend or his daughter; but poor little Raggi was always tied to her house door, and could no more dance with the children.

The days were very sad ones to Raggi and her mistress. The girl did all she could to console the little dog; nursed it, caressed it, and robbed herself of soup to make its meals, but nothing could atone to Raggi for that cruel enforced inaction ; and when at night, the doors being closed, it was let loose it had lost the wish to play, being too sad of heart. The children, too, pined for Raggi, and cried at not having the pretty little dancer with them in their sports: but even they were no more allowed to play about the piazza or on the roads, and their young lives were not much brighter than was Raggi's.

Their fathers were poor, and dared not risk incurring the heavy fines which punished all infringement of Messer Nellemane's rules and regulations, and they kept their little sons and daughters in, with harsh threats and harsh measures. For the men themselves grew sullen and irritable. Their hearts were with Carmelo, and their impotent sense of never-ending, ever-increasing wrong wore them down with a leaden weight.

There was another reason, too, for heavy hearts in the village. A new enterprise had brought with it its usual complement of old ways and old interests ruined. It was no less a thing than a projected tramway from the City, sixteen miles away to the north, and Pomodoro, seven miles away on the south ; and this tramway was to pass through Santa Rosalia. Nay, Santa Rosalia was even to pay five thousand francs a year for being thus honoured.

The scheme was due to foreign speculators: foreign speculators are, to free Italy of to-day, what the devouring hordes of the Huns were to the Italy of a thousand and more years ago. The nation is like a young man come into a goodly heritage, with a swarm of money-lenders on him, devouring him at ninety-two per cent. Some of the latter are indigenous to the soil: the majority are English,

Belgian, and American. Unfortunately they are made welcome.

Tory governments have always been twitted with having a job: Italian municipalities, in this respect, are thoroughly Tory.

This tramway was a job gigantic.

The City never needed to go to Pomodoro, and Pomodoro scarcely ever went to the City. But what did that matter? Nothing at all, certainly, to the gentlemen who projected it.

You can take Italians with a trap as you can take birds; for your call-bird put the boast that a thing is American or English, and they will tumble into your trap by thousands. It is a sentiment that one feels ashamed to see in the land of Dante and of Michelangelo: but it is there.

They are smitten with a very disease of imitation.

A country tramway, whether viewed from the point of its cruelty when drawn by horses, or its hideousness when drawn by steam, not to speak of its peril to children, and its disfigurement of nature, may be said to be the vilest abomination hitherto conceived by that procreator of monsters which is called Progress. But the municipal mind is enamoured with them, and likes to see them unrolling their unsightly irons over the birthplace of Virgil, the tomb of Ferruccio, the battle-fields of Scipio and of Hannibal.

There had been much opposition to this one, in the meeting of the Thirty who formed what was called the Provincial Council; but the dissidents had been overruled in the matter: some had houses which the company would buy to demolish; others had angles of hedges that would also be bought at high prices; some sold the fuel that would be burned in the engine. Somehow or other, with such delicate persuasions, everybody was reduced to reason, and the tramway had been decided on; Messer Nellemane being foremost in praise of its project, and his friend the engineer being appointed on its staff. Indeed, it was entirely due to the energy and exertions of Messer Nellemane, working in the name of the Cavaliere Durellazzo, that the abandonment of the tramway was averted.

'The people are never awake to their own benefit,' he said, as he overheard the lamentations of the owners of the diligences and little carts that had hitherto sufficed to carry on the intercourse of Santa Rosalia with the greater world.

He had been fully awake to his, however; and in the arrangement for the payment of the five thousand francs a year by Santa Rosalia had not forgotten his own services, or allowed the Tramway Company to forget them.

Every member of the Provincial Council, too, got, or expected to get, something; and so every one of them decided that tramways were a blessing of Providence; and if the speculators were making a bad speculation, that was their look out; and if the diligence owners and the carters were ruined—why —that was theirs.

The municipalities were all of them pleased, and if the populace raged and groaned, who cared? The municipalities attend no more than a schoolmaster attends to a child's tears over Euclid and syntax. Euclid and syntax are for the child's ultimate good; so are taxes for the public's benefit.

Now the iron rails were, of course, to run in as

straight a line as possible; and that they might do so the little *boschetto* of the mill was amongst things that had to be destroyed.

The engineers of the City end decided that it was not necessary, a little curve could spare the wood; but Pierino Zaffi argued quite the contrary; and, as he was a clever fellow who knew how to put a case, and how to carry it through, he got his way: the *boschetto* of the mill was expropriated, just for all the world as the gardens of the Farnesina were, if we may compare the death of a mouse with the fall of a lion.

Pastorini, poor foolish man, who had been wont to fancy that what was yours was your own, and that neither King nor Pontiff could make away with another man's property, was stunned as by the fall of a mountain on his head when they notified to him, in the municipal peremptory fashion, that his wood was wanted, and would be taken, and levelled to the ground.

When Messer Nellemane, with Messer Pierino Zaffi, with other legislators and engineers, brought the great engineer of the City down into the *boschetto*, without so much as by your leave, or for your leave, as Pastorini said afterwards, and began measuring with tapes and rods, the miller stood at his house door with his mouth wide open and his eyes staring vacantly: then, all of a sudden, he strode across his own land, and seized the first man he came upon by the collar.

'It is my land. It is my land,' he said in a low thick voice. 'No man comes here but by my leave; no, not the King himself, nor the Holy Father.'

'Holy Father!' Messer Nellemane shrugged his

shoulders as he heard. Whatever such a person might have been in the old dark ages, he, too, had had to bow to a municipality now.

'Does the owner object?' said the chief surveyor.

'Of course he objects,' said Messer Nellemane. 'These people always do, to raise the price; there is no cunning so *furbo* as country cunning.'

'That is true,' said the engineer from the City.

'Will you go?' said Demetrio Pastorini fiercely, shaking Pierino Zaffi, who was the man he by chance had seized. 'Will you go? The land is mine, as the church is the Lord's, and his palace the King's. You cannot touch it. You shall not tread on it. Do you hear what I bid you? Depart.'

'Let us humour him, sir,' whispered Messer Nellemane to Cavalier Durellazzo, and their business being already done, they went; Pierino Zaffi white and shaking, for the miller's grasp had not been light, and the aspect of the old man had been terrible.

'I am rid of them,' muttered Pastorini to his eldest daughter, as he strode in from the wood; but his breath oppressed him as he said it, and his brow was crimson, and his tongue seemed to him to cleave to his mouth.

The next week it was certified to him by a public document that his wood would be felled in the ensuing November *pro bono publico*, and that he would receive a certain sum in proportion, valuing the poplars at ten francs each, which was the current price for light timber.

Pastorini, through his dull spectacles, plodded painfully through the decree; then, with his white strong teeth grinding one on another, he tore the sheet in two and put it on the charcoal fire, then burning brightly under the pot of soup.

'We are not to be bought and sold like steers,' he muttered as the paper blazed, 'nillywilly—just at a clerk's will—as though we were dumb stones.'

But there he mistook.

With the excuse of a 'general interest' and a municipal licence, spoliation may be done in the people's name, while the people groan, and starve, and sorrow, and die: unconsenting, but impotent as the ox that is dragged to the slaughter.

Demetrio Pastorini had driven the men off his land, and had burned the paper; he was simple enough, like Pippo, to think he had conquered, that his rights would be respected.

When the diligence drivers and the small carriers gathered about the mill-house in evening time, muttered savage oaths against the coming iron day, and condoled with him for the loss of his wood, he smoked his pipe stolidly and only said: 'No, no! they'll not touch my trees. Mine is mine, come King or Pope against me.'

'But they will fell your wood, they have marked it out; they will be down on you, and cut it, come Ognissanti,' said the neighbours, trying to persuade and to prepare him.

But he only shook his head, and replied to them, 'They'll not touch my trees.'

If this seems to you, gentlemen, exceedingly stupid, you must try and realise what people are like, in a country place, in the green heart of Italy. They are full of intelligence of their own kind, but they do not understand the new ways of freedom;

and they are primitive enough to fancy that a man can do as he will with his own.

Under the Liberal governments of this latter half of the century this is an impression which is rapidly being improved away all over Europe: but it still lingers in old countries and old people as lichens cling about oaks marked for felling.

'They'll not touch my trees,' said the miller, positively, and he passed whole hours at his milldoor, looking up at their columns of autumnal foliage, and listening to the rustling of the leaves as he had never done in any time of his life.

He had always been fond of his *boschetto* and proud of it, and grateful to it; being wise enough to know how it helped to keep the stream deep, and save it from absorption of the sun's rays, save the sun from drinking it up as he was wont to phrase it: and he had deemed this wood of such use and import that he had never followed the common foolish custom of lopping the branches to sell for firing; a custom which is penny wise and pound foolish.

He had always loved his wood, but now it was with an almost savage sense of possession, an almost painful tenderness of affection, that he looked up at the quivering leafy pillars, full in spring of song of birds, and in summer of the laughter of crickets.

'It would be like stealing my daughter,' he said, with his face dark and sullen, as he leaned over the half-door of his house and watched the green river gleam through the still green boughs.

'But they'll not touch them. No, they'll not touch them, that I promise you,' he would say again and again to his children. Sore as his heart was for

Carmelo, he almost chafed more at the thought of the wood felled by strangers.

No one did or said anything else about it to him. The due summons had been served upon him, and of course no more was needed. But he himself made sure that the thing was abandoned and forgotten.

'Did I not tell you they could not do it?' he said to his daughters and sons. 'Nay, nay, the State is not a robber.'

Messer Nellemane going by with his cigar in his mouth for an evening's stroll, used to see him thus gazing up at his poplars, and on such occasions would smile.

'The hot-headed old madman,' he thought. 'Well, there are straight waistcoats for all such.'

Messer Nellemane had a mind at ease. He saw that the face of the maiden who had rejected his honours had grown wasted and pale; he knew that the little Casa della Madonna was mortgaged, which is as good as gone; the lad Carmelo was in prison, and the wood was doomed. What could be better? Borgia had poison and the Tiber for those who thwarted him; the methods of Messer Nellemane were more refined, but I am not sure that they were kinder.

As he stepped along one evening he had to step across the little brook that escaped from Pippo's house and ran across the roadway into the weir. It was now October, and rain had swollen the little stream, and it moistened the boots of this great man, who was a clerk at fifty pounds a year, and yet practically ruled over three thousand people.

He stamped his feet angrily, shaking off the moisture, and seeing old Pippo, who was sitting at his threshold to keep the poor little fettered dog company, and who was staring aimlessly at the river, and doing nothing, as he could not afford to buy osiers to make things that perhaps no one would take, he paused in his walk, and with wet boots approached the basketmaker.

Showing his boot, as you show a dead rabbit to a poacher, as *pièce de conviction* of his crime, Messer Nellemane said sternly:

'Signor Mazzetti, for some months past you have been admonished and fined for allowing this water to run across the road and annoy the public. How much longer do you intend to defer compliance?'

Pippo got up, and took off his hat, from that respect for authority which is strong in the Italian; a good sentiment whose endurance is daily and hourly being strained and whittled away by the *oppressor rusticorum*.

He did not reply at all.

'How long do you intend to defer compliance with the municipal injunction?' said the great man.

'Eh?' said Pippo; he looked sullen and sad, and his head never seemed to him now to be right: 'there's a swarm of bees always buzzing in it,' he said often to his daughter.

'How long will you let this water obstruct the public way?' demanded Messer Nellemane, driven in desperation to use simple language.

Pippo shrugged his shoulders hopelessly.

'How long?' repeated Messer Nellemane with imperious impatience.

'I have nought to do with it,' said Pippo at last, doggedly. 'Dominiddio set it running; He can stop it if He wish.'

'You are impious!' said Messer Nellemane.

'No,' said Pippo, 'no, not I.'

'Such trifling is merely insolence,' cried the other very angrily, and losing something of his dignity, and of his suavity all. 'Yours is a contravention of the most odious kind. You have been warned, mildly chastised, reasoned with in every way; you are obdurate, obstinate, and blasphemous. Do you, or do you not, intend to make the necessary works to remove this nuisance and obstruction?'

Pippo looked at him with sunken, sullen desperate eyes.

'I can do nought,' he said doggedly, and he covered his head as he spoke. 'With one thing and another of your accursed laws you have taken from me all I have. The roof over my head is wholly mine no more. You can torture me as you may; you can't get blood out of a post.'

Then he sat down, and put his pipe in his mouth, and let loose little Raggi.

'You have made slaves of men and beasts,' he said, 'but you have done your worst to me already; you can't get blood out of a post.'

And he took the little dog on his knee and caressed it.

The water rippled and bustled brightly in the sunset light, and toppled over into the river below, as though no presence of a great man were there to trouble it. Messer Nellemane struck his cane into it as though it were an obstinate child that he chastised; he was pale with passion.

'The laws will force you to respect them,' he said furiously. 'That you will find, and to your cost.'

'You can't get blood out of a post,' said Pippo.

'I have bartered my house to pay you, and I'll do no more. Get you gone.'

As he spoke he threw a pebble down the road, and bade the little dog run after it; Raggi ran, nothing loth, and brought it joyfully.

'The dog will ne'er be tied again for you,' said Pippo. 'We pay, and you hurt us just the same. For me, I can pay no more; and were it so that I could, I would not.'

Messer Nellemane said nothing; he opened his note-book and wrote in it, and went away in silence.

Raggi played with the pebbles, and the cooper's children ran out and played too, and shouted and spun tops on the river-side; and Pippo clapped his hands and encouraged them. An old man, a little dog, and five small boys and girls made up this scene of anarchy and revolt, and broke the communal laws in a way that was terrible to behold.

'Laugh, children, laugh while you may,' cried Pippo; 'soon you will starve, and then the Law will laugh at you.'

The children did laugh, and romped on; not understanding.

Excellencies and Ministers—you think Messer Nellemane does not matter; that he is only a clerk and his place is only a village; you think that these people are all poor clods, and know not their right hand from their left; in your high place, whether you were born there, or whether you climbed there, it is so far below you, that poor, little, dusty village, with its stone walls and its narrow rooms, where the people die like flies, and no one cares, and the Sheriff's officers, on the Pale Horse, make their rounds together night and day, and no one hears the death cries, for the voices are too feeble and the roofs are too low; you think it does not matter, and you turn away your eyes, and you manufacture your pretty phrases, and you take your armchair at the Congress table of the Nations, for all that does matter to your thinking is only *la haute politique*. But you mistake; ah, yes, you mistake.

Louis Quatorze made just such a mistake; and the scaffold was built for the children of his blood.

But the Roi Soleil had many an excuse. He was born in the purple; he was reared in oblivion of the people; he honestly believed that God had made him of ivory and them of clay; but you—is it so long since you left your cabin in Sicily, your desk in Piedmont?—are you not sons of the wars of independence?—were you not lulled in your cradle by the shouts of 'Morir per Libertà!' Would you not be nought, unless the people had made you all? unless, with their blood and sweat, they had cemented the mortars of your houses, and with their bodies made the steps by which you have mounted thrones?

Yet once in office you forget!

Once in office, Lethe never gave more utter oblivion than this oblivion of yours. Your portfolios won, what else matters?

Let these people toil, and groan, and die; let the tax-gatherers seize the last rag off their naked and starving bones, wring from them every poor bronze coin that they have gained by the labour of their limbs, and claim impost off the crust of black bread that their hungry babies gnaw; what matter? it is only the people—you, too, were of the people once, but you have forgotten that.

You are in office; you speak with eloquence in the Chamber, and you have your place in the councils of Europe.

Vive la Haute Politique!

We must be a great Power—ay, though in every house lies a corpse, in every river rots another, in every poor man's mouth is a curse, and over all the land there spreads the plague of want, the putrefaction of despair.

Vive la Haute Politique!

What! though you see behind her a spectre, a scaffold, and a tomb?

## CHAPTER XVI.

IF you have only killed your father or mother, or sister or neighbour, that is a trifle, which may well stand over for a year or more; and unless you were caught redhanded in the act, you may go scot free meanwhile. This sort of murder is a merely personal affair, and scarcely concerns anybody. But if you have put your hand upon the sacred person of a guard, ay, though he have been, as often happens, a whilom thief or an ex-forger, then indeed you have committed something very like high treason, and you must be tried and sentenced as speedily as may be, to pacify the outraged majesty of Law.

Italy is like M. Gambetta; with the cap of liberty on their heads they both set up a policeman and say 'worship him.'

It seems hardly worth while to have upset all the

old religions and all the old dynasties only to arrive at this.

The crime of Carmelo having been therefore so heinous, the usual snail's pace of the law was hastened, and by what was almost a miracle of rapidity, he having done this crime in sultry June, was actually brought up to trial at the beginning of October, having spent only four months in prison on suspicion, which is, as things go, really nothing at all.

The Pretore of Pomodoro put on his black cap and robes, and mounted his curule chair, with his mind already made up as to Carmelo, before this state prisoner had ever entered the court-house.

Like the wolves in the 'Animaux Parlants,' lawyers, guards, secretaries, chancellors and syndics make a compact party, sworn never to quarrel, and to grip all that comes in their way. The Pretore, Gino Novi, had never seen either accuser or accused in his life before, but before he had heard two words of the case he had made his mind up against Carmelo; all these officials are little Gambettas, and the Law is their fetish. Offend it, and you are vile as a Jesuit; there is no point in your favour possible.

It was with much impatience that this brisk and smart young man, who had the administration of justice in his power over something like seven thousand people, went through all the forms of trial, as though there were any sort of doubt of the prisoner's criminality.

It was absurd, thought Gino Novi, not to be able to condemn the wretch off-hand; but the law gave him a trial, and he, as I say, like M. Gambetta, revered the Law; indeed, there is hardly anything to which you may not stretch it, and hardly any end it will not answer; when you hold it as a schoolmaster holds the taws you get quite fond of it. It is so unpleasant to others, and so elastic and omnipotent.

Carmelo's advocate was fainthearted; he was equally sure of his fees whether his client were sentenced or set free; and he was afraid that by taking up this case he made himself obnoxious to the Pretore, and to the governing powers generally. It is far more compromising to defend a free citizen who has been wronged by a guard, than it is to defend a brigand who has only murdered travellers and violated women.

His advocate was fainthearted, and his witnesses were not over-wise; they were his own relatives, who got passionate and indignant, and were reproved, and neighbours, such as Gigi Canterelli and Cecco, who were too eager in his defence to be believed. Gigi Canterelli made indeed a bad impression on the court by swearing heartily that Bindo Torri was a '*briccone*' and a '*scelerato*,' but that he was set on by blackguards in black cloth higher than himself, and that everybody knew, for the whole commune was a prey to this set of oppressors and extortioners; for which violent enunciation of the truth the impetuous old grocer was ordered out of court, with a bad mark scored against his name, to be of use the next time that he should have a case at law there, against carriers who had stolen his bags of rice, or against octroi-duties falsely levelled on his cheeses. Never again would Gigi gain any cause that would be heard at the Pretura of Pomodoro.

It is not true that no Italian ever tells the truth, as commentators on the country say, but it is sadly true that when one does he suffers for it.

The trial went on all through the golden October day, wasting the time of many men who should have been at work in the vineyards; and throughout it Carmelo stood between the carabiniers, faint and sick from past confinement and present fatigue, and his old father and his brothers and Pippo listened trembling and indignant, with the sweat rolling off their brows.

When questioned, the prisoner said only, 'I would do the same to-morrow; he poisoned my dog.'

But of this there was, alas for Carmelo! no proof, and if there had been, what would it have served? It was the law of the commune of Vezzaja and Ghiralda that the guardian of the public morals should be the poisoner of dogs.

'I would do the same to-morrow!' said Carmelo with eyes that flashed fire from out of the weary pallor of his face.

Gino Novi looked at him from under his black cinque-cento cap of office, and scowled and shuddered.

'This is the stuff that makes regicides!' he thought.

It is certainly the stuff that made Tell; but the Pretore did not think of it in that sense.

Carmelo's attorney had summoned two or three men whose dogs had been poisoned, and who had traced their death to Bindo; and had also summoned Squillace, the apothecary who had supplied the poison; but when the people came up to the tribunal they were frightened, and hemm'd and haw'd and prevaricated, and scratched their heads and blew their noses, and ended in sheer fright by being sure of nothing, while Signore Squillace perjured himself as handsomely as if he had been a deputy arraigned for bribery, instead of a poor devil paid thirty pounds a year to doctor all the commune.

So the long, dull, sad, terrible day wore away, with the sun beating at the thick panes of the casements, and the dirty, garlic-scented crowd of Pomodoro pressed together behind the bar, thick as bees in swarming-time. The advocate's heart was not in his work; it put him in bad odour, and every now and then the eye of the Pretore menaced him, and then he lost the thread of his subject, and began to think that a few months in prison would not hurt a young fellow, and to remember that he himself was a very poor man with a *jolie ribambelle* of hungry children.

He examined his witnesses badly, he helped to hush-hush Gigi Canterelli, he pleaded loosely, spoke at random, showed he thought ill of his client, and had not courage to bring into evidence any one of the many rascalities of Bindo Terri's past, or the many villanies of his present.

It was one of those trials common enough in Italy, where the verdict is a foregone conclusion. No one except the Pastorini boys and old Pippo was astonished when Gino Novi, with his sharp black eyes glittering like lancets, sentenced Carmelo to seven months' imprisonment for his assault upon an officer of the law. He would have been better pleased to give seven years, but he was a wise young man, who never let his passions get the mastery of him, and kept himself close within precedents and statutes.

Seven months!

All the bitter winter, and part of the lovely spring, were to pass over the young head of Carmelo in the narrow den of the prison.

When he heard, he opened his great blue eyes, with a frantic terror in them, his lips grew blue, he shivered all over and dropped down in a dead faint. He had eaten nothing all day, and he had been standing many hours.

The elder Pastorini, a strong man, shook like a woman; his veins swelled on his forehead; his eyes grew dull; the men around him forced him out into the open air; they thought he would fall in apoplexy.

When he was in the air he staggered, and gave a great gasp for breath.

'This is for what we toil!' he shouted, 'this is for what we give our last coin to the tax-gatherer, and our last child to the barracks, and our last breath to the hospital! God above us! We are meeker, duller, stupider fools than any sheep that crouches to the shearing! Men, you have known me all my life. I have been peaceable, neighbourly, respectful to law and State, heedful to pay debt and impost; you have known me all my life. I have reared my sons in honesty and simple worth. I have done no harm, I never wronged man, woman, child, or beast. Have I deserved this that they do to me? Men, as God lives, this night would I bear steel and torch through the kingdom to kill these wretches that ruin us, these worms that crawl to their masters, but sting the poor as the viper stings. As God lives, I pray—I pray—for revolution, for red blood, for bitter battle, for human justice; I pray——'

Then his voice choked, and he lifted his arms in the air, and the men caught him to save his fall.

Meanwhile, in the court old Pippo had risen on trembling limbs, and with his hat doffed, and his white hair shining in the sunshine, called aloud to the judge, 'Dear sir, most illustrious, you cannot mean it; you cannot have the heart to mean it.

The lad is good as gold. You cannot brand him felon and bracket him with thieves? Dear sir—honoured judge—do hear me. He is to marry my daughter. His marriage lines are all drawn out, and the girl sits at home weeping, and the bridal gown lies in a drawer, and the orange flowers are all yellow and shrivelled, and they lie on it to keep it from moth. Good sir! Most high and honourable sir, do hear me! The dear lad already has suffered four mortal months in the town gaol. It is enough. It is too much! He did no harm. If you only but knew the rogue, the thief, the impostor, the villain, that they make a guard——'

'Take that old madman out of court,' hissed the Pretore; and Pippo was hustled and pulled down by the officials from where he stood, and thrown, as if he were a stone, through the doors.

'Defamation of an officer of the law,' muttered Gino Novi, as he closed his great case of papers and hurried from his throne, as twilight dimmed the court, to go and eat a supper of robins and tripe, fried ham and lentils, in his own room behind the chamber of justice, where he had invited Messer Gaspardo Nellemane and Messer Luca Finti to pass a jovial hour with him, and lose a friendly coin or two over draughts and dice.

'Very insubordinate and revolutionary people in this commune, I fear; no veneration for authority,' said he; and his two guests, who quite forgot that but for revolution they would at this hour have been respectively selling their father's battered iron and rotting fish, shook their heads and said there was a bad spirit abroad—the people certainly had no respect for authority.

For these good gentlemen were like all their class, the very oddest mixture of Prussian despotism and Parisian radicalism. They hated all those who were above them, and despised all those who were below them; there was only one strata of humanity that they thought worth consideration or preservation, i.e. their own.

When Italy shall purge herself of these, the opportunists of public benches and public desks—the licensed and registered brigands of the public purse—then, and then only may she lift off the burden of her taxes, and breathe freely, and have title to be a voice in Europe. Will this day ever come? By the educated will of the people, perhaps. Perhaps—never.

Nepotism and Impiegatism are as thorns in her flesh; fixed there in festered wounds, and maybe, past all surgery. They are as thorns that pierce, as leeches that suck; when the flesh is bloodless, then it rots and the body falls.

## CHAPTER XVII.

ALL the winter would roll away ere he would behold the eyes of his betrothed; he who should have wedded her in the mid-summer months, when the crickets were chaunting in the trees, and the magnolias and the rose-laurels were all ablaze with bloom. During the four months since his arrest he had striven to keep his reason and his patience, saying always to himself that he would be set free at once when his cause should be clearly heard. Hope had sustained him all that while, but now he had no hope.

The sentence had been passed; the doors had closed, the bolts been fastened on him.

He was in prison for seven months.

Ah! judges and gentlemen of the council, who put youths in your prison cells for bathing in a river in the heat, for rescuing a dog from the slaughterer, from begging for a coin when their old mothers or their young babes starve and perish, how much I should like you to taste that prison yourselves! The Bastille was the royal dungeon of the noblesse, and scarcely deserved the rage of the people; but these petty bastilles all over the land, where by petty laws the honest, the poor, the helpless, the courageous, for every trifling act of life are thrown to break their hearts as they may, and from which they can only issue with blackened names and ruined characters—when will these accursed places, that mingle the righteous with the unrighteous, the godly and the innocent with the thief and the assassin, surrender to the summons of the nation, and be dismantled and destroyed?

Never so long as Messer Nellemane and his kind shall reign; and make of every brave impulse of pity, of every despairing cry of want, a crime.

Carmelo, lying on the hard narrow bed of the prison cell, recovered from his swoon, stared with dull aching eyes up at the ceiling; the prison had been an old palace once, and on the ceiling, which was a section of what had been once a grand and vaulted roofing of a banqueting hall, there was still in unfaded frescoes a little group of angels bearing palms and flying up against the stars.

Those angels seemed a mockery to Carmelo; the innocent lad to whom the saints and the sons of God had been no whit less real than the poplars on the river shore, hated them now, and thought them cruel deceptions, beautiful fair lies.

'If they were really up there beyond the sun, they would not let these things be,' he said between his teeth, lying on his back, and knowing that for seven long months he would be a prisoner, treated like a felon, because a vile wrong had been done to him, and he had justly chastised it.

Carmelo had always been in the open air, up whilst the skies were still dark, on the road with the mule, at work under the trees, fishing in the Rosa water, dashing the ruddy grain down into the black mouth of the shaft; on feast days and holy days strolling through the lanes and fields with a flower behind his ear, or thrumming his mandoline in the moonlight under the porch; a free life and a happy one, doing no harm and thinking none, enjoying vaguely but intensely, as the bull enjoys the pastures when the springtide grass is sweet in the dew of dawn; a natural life and a wholesome life, with free movement of the limbs and unpolluted air in the lungs, dumb in outward expression, but keen to inward pleasure from scent, and sight, and sound.

To him every moment in this close den, without a breath of air, with scarce a gleam of sunlight, was despair. A day in a prison to a free-born son of the soil, used to work with the broad bright sky alone above his head, is more agony than a year of it is to a cramped city-worker used only to the twilight of a machine-room or a workshop, only to an air full of smuts and smoke, and the stench of acids, and the dust of filed steel or sifted coal. The suffering of the two cannot be compared, and one among many of the injustices the law, all over the world, commits is that it never takes into consideration what a man's past has been. There are those to whom a prison is a hell; there are those to whom it is something better than the life they led.

Carmelo lay on his rough sacking, and stared at the painted angels that the last glow of the sunset had illumined, and he thought that on the morrow he would be a madman and know nothing. That was his fear. His brain boiled and burned in his skull, and his heart seemed to pant and leap like a wounded hare springing before the hounds.

When the gaoler looked in at morning, the lad was in high fever: they called the parish doctor of Pomodoro, he pronounced it to be congestion of the brain. They took him in a litter to the infirmary, a dark, foul smelling, ill-kept place, where the doctor tried experiments on the patients as he pleased, and cut up dogs and cats alive in a back room, and flattered himself that this was science.

When will the truth be written of hospitals anywhere? If ever it were written, the faculty would swear it all a lie.

No one hardly ever recovered in this infirmary, certainly none were ever the better for it. All Carmelo's auburn locks were shaved off, and many ounces of blood were taken from him, and little else was done; he was a prisoner, and really it did not matter. His father, who was not allowed to see him, drew his last franc out of the Cassa di Risparmio[1] to bespeak the doctor's care for him, and the doctor took

[1] Savings-bank.

the fees; secretly, as he was forbidden by the rules to touch a centime.

'The dear lad, he has ruined me!' thought the old man, who was feeble and broken in health since the fit before the Pretura, and who had spent nearly his all over the long account of the notary; 'dear lad, he has ruined me! Yet he is as innocent as a babe unborn!'

The miller was not a weak man, nor given to such weaknesses, but the hot tears rose in his eyes and fell down his furrowed cheeks as he left the hospital bed. He was not allowed to stay there, nor to send any sister or brother of Carmelo's to him, and he felt as though his tough heart would break, as he got up behind his good grey horse and jolted over the ruts of the road in the twilight of the November afternoon.

Why had all this ever come upon him? Who put these thieves and tyrants there on those stools of office?

The Government had done, he supposed. To him, the Government meant the King. He cursed the King. How could he tell that the King had no more to do with these things than with the melons and pumpkins that had ripened with the summer sun under his garden wall?

It is the White Cross of Savoy which the ink-splashes of Messer Nellemane's documents stain in the people's eyes.

How can you expect them to comprehend the contradictions of constitutionalism?

The King caused it all, and set Messer Nellemane on that office throne; so thought Demetrio Pastorini, and so think tens of thousands; but the thought failed to console the old miller as he went along the dusky road that he knew so well; indeed it made his pain the more bitter to him, because he had lost a dearly beloved and only brother in days when they were young, in those wars against the 'stranieri' which they were told had given them freedom.

So weary were his thoughts and so preoccupied, and so dim were his eyes with tears, that if the good grey horse had not been acquainted with the way for fifteen years, he might have missed it for aught that his master did to guide him.

'*Hè—o! Ouf!*' cried the old man to the horse in surprise, as his own mill-house loomed through the grey shadows, and the horse checked his trot without the command.

In the mist of the autumn night that was closing in, he could see the figure of his eldest daughter as she ran out to him; she was sobbing, and the sound of her sobs was borne to him through the cold, quiet, misty air.

'Oh father,' she stammered, 'Oh father!' and then she came to the side of the cart, and lifted herself up on the side of the wheel and caught his hand: 'Oh father!' she cried again.

The old man trembled.

'What is it new of sorrow?' he said: he spoke almost roughly from very fear.

The girl standing up on the shaft caught his hand:

'Oh father, do not mind too much—the trees!'

'The trees!'

He said no more; he got down off the cart and threw the reins of rope to the youngest boy.

'Lead the horse to the stable,' he said unsteadily 'The trees? what of the trees?'

He strode off in the darkness towards the river, and the girl followed him.

'Oh father!' she said again with a great sob.

There was very little light but the gleam of the moon as the clouds swept by; it was enough to show him what had been done in his absence.

Three of the poplars had been felled.

'Oh father!' said the girl catching at his hands once more. 'We did all we could to stop them, but they would not wait. There were six of them with hatchets, and an overseer. They said they had the right by law. Oh father!——'

## CHAPTER XVIII.

Before the week was out the trees were all down, and the wood by the mill was a thing of memory alone. Demetrio Pastorini was powerless. He had misunderstood his own rights and the ways of the laws.

When the wood-cutters and the overseer came on the morrow, he was like one beside himself. He got down his old gun from the shelf, and would have shot the first man that dared approach the *boschetto*, but his young sons and daughters weeping about him made his nerve and his purpose fail; they got the weapon from him, and besought him for their sakes to be patient.

'Patient!' he cried to them. 'Shall we be patient while we are stripped alive as the live lamb is stripped of her skin, she bleeding at every pore? Patient? you are poltroons! You eat the dust! You are no children of my blood. Let me be!'

But they clung about him notwithstanding, and pleaded that better was it to suffer wrong than to do it, and sweeter in heaven's sight; and so besought him, in the name of Christ and of their own, that he, being a religious man, and one most affectionate, gave way at last, and dropped into his wooden chair and wept, and bore as best he could the sound of crashing axe, of falling trunk, of wrenching wood, of shivering leaf.

'Must the King, who has dominion from sea to sea, over all the land and the greatness of it, must he grudge me my little all?' he cried in his agony, as he heard the blows of the hatchet on the trees.

## CHAPTER XIX.

BEFORE the week was out the poplars were all down, as I have said, and the birds that had made their homes in them had flown, shrilly piping in their woe, across the Rosa water.

Messer Nellemane visited the spot often.

The municipal soul loves destruction. Whether it beholds a noble and fair monument of ancient times being changed to dust and rubble by the hammers of masons, or whether it sees a gracious sylvan haunt alter to a desolation of sand and stones beneath the hatchets of wood-cutters, the municipal soul is equally full of an exceeding joy, of an unspeakable contentment.

Messer Nellemane, who possessed the municipal

soul in its entire perfection, was thus happy now; and his happiness was further pointed by the acid pungency of a grudge paid off, a vengeance accomplished.

It was a sad sight to other eyes than his: the mossy bank where Toppa had used to roam stamped down into mud, the brave trees felled, their yellow leaves churned into a paste of earth and water, the branches piled in squares to be sold for firewood, the tall trunks trimmed and set in rows to be disposed of as timber; all the place unsightly, naked, miserable, where all had been so lately freshness, and peace, and forest loveliness.

The white wall of the mill-house stood bare and ugly, no friendly shadows cast on it from waving boughs. The heart of the miller seemed broken in his breast; he could scarce bear to pass his door; he could not bear to look across the stream.

He never spoke of it to any one since the trees had gone.

Once his third son, little Dante, said timidly:

'Is it well, father, that they should sell the wood like that? They have not paid you.'

Then Demetrio Pastorini said to him:

'If they sold your sister to the brothel would you squabble to share the price? Pay? no, they will never pay. They are thieves. Thieves do not pay for what they take.'

Then the young man was afraid, and did not dare to speak of the wood again.

After a while the timber was carried away, and the boughs also; no one knew where they went; it was understood to go to the City. No one ventured to inquire, since the stern lips of Pastorini were dumb.

If he had spoken he would have learned little, he would have heard that the engineers had valued his possession, and the municipality had contracted to pay for it: that was all he would have been told. He did not know that he was highly honoured, and that they were treating him exactly as the princely owner of Farnesina was treated before him.

This destruction of the boschetto, which had been a favourite haunt for feast days with the neighbours, and the dread of the iron way that was to follow it, harassed and saddened all the people in Santa Rosalia, and added to the gloom of a wet and stormy November, which was in turn followed by an unusual and severe winter.

The harvest had been good, and so had been the vintage, and so also proved the olive-gathering, rain notwithstanding, and as foreign papers innocently wrote, nothing was wanting to the happiness of the country.

But the foreign papers only read the statistics of corn, wine, and oil, and did not try to see any further; indeed, having started with this fixed idea of Italian happiness, would not have believed any explanations proving the contrary. Foreign papers did not understand that, as the local taxes always go up in proportion to the excellence of harvest and vintage, that excellence is not the unmixed gain which it is supposed to be, and, indeed, is scant profit to any one.

The more you have, the more I take, say the municipalities to the communities; there can be no more admirable recipe for keeping a populace poor.

## CHAPTER XX.

In Santa Rosalia the winter was hard and, for this country, long. Snow came; not the snow of cold countries, with all the glories of an ice-clad, frost-hung world; not snow pure, serene, beautiful, with holly-berries red against it, and firtrees dark, not the snow of lands where snow means Noël, Santa Claus, or Father Christmas; but snow that fell in the night and melted in the day, and left a muddy, slushy, watery, slippery slough of despond in its place: snow that killed the olive, broke the arbutus boughs, withered into death the passion-flower, and changed to putrefaction the aloe and the cactus; snow that blurred out all the sunny pastoral loveliness, and made the landscape grey and sear.

In this sort of winter-time the poor are the first to pine and perish everywhere, but soonest of all in this land of sunshine and south wind.

The impetuous Rosa was as over full of water as it had been low and shallow in the midsummer; it ran out over its banks and flooded the fields, where Science brought in with Liberty had felled the trees and hedges that had used to serve as dykes.

There was no work in the flooded or in the frozen fields; the contadini wanted no labourers; there was nothing to be done anywhere; there was a score of empty hands ready if ever such a little job needed the doing.

The houses, all built for warm weather, with their open loggie and their ill-fitting windows, were swept through by the north wind as though they had been canvas tents. There was scant fuel; the old times were gone when they could glean it on all the hillsides, for the best reason, that nearly all the woods were felled. Wine was so dear no poor man could drink it, and bread was frightfully dear, too. The people cowered over their little brown pots of lighted *brace*, and did not complain. When any one gave them a coin they were passionately grateful.

Most winters they suffered like this; but this winter the suffering was greater than usual. A few said something about getting work in the Maremma, where all work is done in winter; but they might as well have spoken of getting work in the moon; they could as well get to the one as the other. They had no idea how to travel there, and nothing to travel with; besides, nine-tenths of them were women and children, for whom the Maremma had no need and no room.

Of course these people were very thankless and unreasonable. There was a railway twelve miles off, there was going to be gas in Pomodoro, and there was Messer Nellemane in their midst, all three monuments of progress.

But these silly people persisted in feeling that they would prefer cheap wine, cheap bread, and stomachs full of both, even to a railway, gas, or Messer Nellemane.

The winter is never very long in Italy, yet this seemed very long indeed. The mill wheels, after having been immovable from drought, were now useless from ice, and the miller, from a plump, jovial, strong man, had become thin, haggard, and silent, feeling the weight of bitter sorrow and the aching of money-cares.

In Pippo's little house the blue Madonna heard no laughter and saw no fire-gleam.

The old man had grown taciturn and irritable. Misfortune is no sweetener of temper or of bread. He would sit long together, crouched in a corner immovable, and his lips were at such times always moving inaudibly; he was counting up the sums of which they had robbed him; counting them again and again; a hundred times a day, a hundred times a night.

They had but little to live on: no one bought straw plaiting in winter, and, as he could not cut the osiers in the river, the rush-working of Pippo bought but small profit.

When they could have a dish of oil and beans they were very thankful; when they could not they boiled a little bread in water with a bit of garlic, and tried to believe it was soup.

Now and then they had a drop of bad coffee without milk: that was all: as wine they had *mezzo-vino*, that is, the last juices of the already-squeezed grape-skins diluted with water, a drink to which vinegar were sweetness.

The Italian poor know as little of the bacon, and potatoes, and tea of the English labourer, as they do of the champagne and mutton of the English mechanic.

In summer time they can do well enough: there is the gracious sun shining on them, and there is always work to be had; but in winter there is terrible suffering, the more terrible, I think, because so quiet: the people die, that is all.

'Patience,' they say, to the last; but their patience brings them nothing.

In Santa Rosalia there was great want, and there was nobody to succour it: the nobles of the province were away in the City keeping carnival, and no *fattore* ever cares for the poor: he gets labour cheap if he requires it, that is his view of the universal misery.

Vezzaja and Ghiralda possessed a charitable society; it was named after that purest of all saints, the Confraternità di San Francisco di Asissi, and it dated back to the thirteenth century.

Originally it had been a very noble society, and had owned broad lands, of which many estates still remained to it. It had been self-denying, generous, religious, in the highest sense of that word, and gentle and simple had been proud to be its ministers; but of this character there did not now remain to it so much as there did remain of its revenues. The rich were very willing to be on its staff; but the poor were not very willing to apply to it; it had a way of considering a case for three months, and then ordering as relief a few pounds of bread, which, when a whole family was waiting, and starving, and dying, was a little too dilatory to be very efficient.

But the fraternity of St. Francis still had its old palace in Pomodoro; still had its historical archives and its pious repute; still had nobles and gentlemen on its committee; and if it only gave a little bread now and then—well—pauperism, they say, should not be encouraged; and if its funds were never very clearly accounted for, we know these mediæval institutions cannot be worked in the mediæval way nowadays: St. Francis saluted Lady Poverty; but we keep her well outside the door while we ask for her certificate.

Now old 'Nunziatina had an attack of bronchitis at this time, and though she recovered, which was little short of a miracle, she was by no means so strong again as she had been; and her draughty room under the tiles, scorching in summer, and frozen in winter, shared with three other old women, and without any stove, or any glass in the window, was not an abode to favour convalescence. The *vicario* of Santa Maria seeing this, bethought him of the Fraternity of St. Francis, and gave her a letter to its committee, urging her age, and honesty, and recent sickness, as fit reasons why she should benefit by this noble charity.

There was a quantity of money locked up in the revenues of this Fraternity, and it had been intended for the poor; but then the present age, the age of Messer Nellemane, knows better than to spend it on the poor.

Those old times were so different to ours: different methods of administration become a necessity in modern days. The Fraternity made a great flourish, and printed long reports, and still charmed the province into subscriptions and donations; but if St. Francis could have been present when the accounts were made up, his benignant eyes would have blazed with the fury of his offended God.

Annunziata blessed Dom Lelio, and took the letter and the sixty centimes he gave her for the diligence, and betook herself, and her staff, and her broad hat, and her short petticoat into the rickety vehicle with much joy and hopefulness of spirit. If she could get a certain little pension, if it were only a franc a week, she felt that she could praise heaven with a full heart. Her trotting round to all the outlying farmhouses and villages with her basket was getting very toilsome to her.

Now, the President of the Fraternity was a certain most noble Count Saverio, who had a high repute as a philanthropist, and whose villa was close by to Pomodoro.

The Count gave his services, which were highly appreciated, nominally for nothing, saying, with much eloquence, that all his life was dedicated to service of God and the poor; and if he did do a good deal at the Bourse, and buy a great many *terni* at Lotto, that was his own affair, and in no way concerned St. Francis. Besides he did it through agents; and his own name never was heard except in connection with philanthropy.

This very noble and pious gentleman received old 'Nunziatina, who made him a nice curtsey, and wished him every blessing in her cheery cordial way, which was as pleasant to hear as a bird's chirping; he was sitting surrounded with ledgers and folios, in the muniment room of the castellated house of this ancient brotherhood; and he spoke so prettily and amiably to her that she felt quite sure of ten francs a month.

He was a long time looking over her papers and reading the priest's recommendation; and then he smiled, and fussed about, and rang for his clerk, and whispered with him, and scribbled something and slipped it in a drawer, and then, finally looking across his writing-table at Annunziata, said very pleasantly:

'Money-charities we never give; but come again on this day month, and we will see if any exception can be made in your favour. I will put your case before the board: my compliments and reverence to the good Dom Lelio.'

The old woman made him another deep curtsey, and went away with a cruel disappointment nipping her old heart.

She did not protest. Italians rarely do.

That day the Count Saverio met Messer Nellemane in the streets of Pomodoro.

'Oh! by the way,' said the Count, 'one of the people of your village was sent to me to-day by the *vicario*. Perhaps you can tell me something of her, for Dom Lelio's heart is apt to run away with his head. He wants us to grant her permanent weekly relief; an old woman, an odd-looking old trot, by name Taormina Annunziata, a widow.'

Messer Nellemane looked shocked.

'Dom Lelio is very unwise,' he said gravely. 'The person you speak of is one of the worst people in the *borgo*. A professional beggar. A confirmed beggar. She is very well off, they tell me; but she has that passion and preference for mendicancy which is like a disease.'

'Dear, dear!' said the President. 'That is terrible. We must never encourage mendicancy. Dom Lelio should not put the society in such a position.'

'What would you, Signore Conte?—He is a priest!' said Messer Gaspardo with that scoff which is always on the lips of the Liberal; but seldom finds an echo in the hearts of the people.

The President smiled a little deprecatory smile, for of course he was a Liberal too, but as he was head of a semi-religious corporation he could not quite laugh at the priesthood.

The month passed over Annunziata's grey head

painfully; it was very cold, and she could make but little way about to those outlying farms where they had given her the most food. But her niece spared her all she could, and she said to herself every day, 'The gentleman promised he would think it over; he will be sure to do something for me when I go;' and being of a very sanguine temperament, she managed to live on hope.

Her most dazzling idea was that they might allow her half a franc a day, but that she felt was too brilliant to be realised; if she got ten francs a month she felt she could ask nothing better of the saints in heaven or the gentlemen on earth.

It was with a glad spirit that she set out to Pomodoro on a chilly morning on the day appointed; she had smartened herself up as well as she knew how; she liked to look respectable. She had her black hat tied under her chin, with a yellow handkerchief and a blue woollen skirt that a *fattoressa* up in the hills had given her at Ceppo, and a little rough red jacket that belonged to Viola.

She was very smart, indeed, for Annunziata was far above the idea of the professed beggar, that rags and dirt were more likely to provoke charity than cleanliness and order. She was no beggar at all; she never stretched her hand out for a farthing; she was old and people were kind to her: that was all.

With a smile of happy expectancy she stood once more before the Signore Conte Saverio in the muniment room.

But the President had no smile in return for her. He looked up with a stern glance from his books and papers, and he frowned as he saw who was the petitioner.

'You were so good as to tell me to come this day, sir,' said the little old woman, as he remained silent. 'You were so very kind as to say you would give me something, and all the month I have been living on your word, sir, for the winter is hard.'

Count Saverio, who had such a milk-and-honey-reputation to lose that an act of severity was disagreeable to him, coughed and cleared his throat, and then said with the air of a father reproving a child: '*Cara mia*, it pains me very greatly to have pained you, but I can only say that the good Dom Lelio has been very much to blame. This honourable and charitable fraternity is established on the scope and to the end of the relief—the judicious relief—of the deserving poor, of the honest poor, of the laborious poor. It was never intended to support a beggar.'

'No, sir?' said Annunziata, puzzled and not following his drift, for she never thought of herself as a beggar.

'It was never intended to encourage mendicancy,' pursued the President, gathering a heavier frown as he warmed with his theme. 'Mendicancy is the curse of the country. It is the heaviest sin to foster it. All our efforts are directed to its suppression. The first qualification to be fit to claim the aid of our society is *never to have begged*. Now you—you are an habitual mendicant; you habitually subsist on public alms. No doubt some frightful improvidence in your youth has brought you to this pass in your old age? With that we have nothing to do; all that concerns us is to obey the laws of the Fraternity. You are not eligible for election; you are not even eligible for momentary relief from our funds. You are a beggar.'

Annunziata stared hard at him, her little bright bird-like eyes wide open with amazement.

'A beggar, sir? I?' she stammered. 'No, that I never was. People are good to me and I bless them. As for spending when I was young, sir, that I never did, for I was left a widow when I was forty-two, sir—my man fell off a house-top, and I had to bring up four children, and I did bring them up well, sir, all beautiful grown men and maidens, though every one of them are in Paradise now— and I always was very poor, sir, though it is true that when I was young the land was happy and the people too, not starved, and pinched, and squeezed like lemons in a presser as they are now-a-days. But spend I never could, sir, because I never had but just enough to keep life in my children and me, and now that I am old, sir, seventy-six come the blessed day of St. Peter, the people that have known me all my life are good to me, and may the saints remember them for it, for what can a woman of my age earn, though I do say I can see to plait still?'

'Enough!' said the Count sternly. 'You may gloss it over as you please, you are a beggar; you have no other means of subsistence than by the charity of others.'

'No, sir; and that is why I come here,' said Annunziata, who was not without a spirit.

'Beggars are ineligible,' said the President impatiently as well as severely this time. 'You are a beggar. Dom Lelio committed an offence against the law in recommending you for the charity of this community. We have nothing to do with you. Our rules would forbid us if we were inclined. You had no business whatever to come here; I am occupied. I must request you to withdraw.'

'I beg your pardon, sir; pray do not hurt Dom Lelio for me. He meant what he did in all goodness,' said Annunziata with a quivering lip; and then she dropped her little curtsey and went out, and going across the street, at the cold dark shelter of the opposite church sank on her knees on the pavement before the nearest altar and sobbed bitterly.

We who eat and drink as we wish every day, and on the score of our appetites suffer nought save perhaps something from the Nemesis of dyspepsia, we can ill realise what the disappointment is of a denial that refuses daily bread, and leaves an old and painful life alone to the menace of a death by hunger; we cannot understand, try how we will, what they mean—the empty cupboard, the cold hearth, the bed of sacking, the gnawing pangs, the famine faintness, the slow, long, cruel hours that creep on from dawn to dark, from dark to dawn again, and bring no friend, no food, no hope, no rescue.

These all faced Annunziata in her future: that poor little sorrowful future that stood between her and her grave; so short in years as it must be, so long in misery as it would be.

Rheumatism racked her bones, and she knew that soon she would be bedridden, and then—well—the people gave to her when they saw her cheery face and her empty basket, but when she lay in her bed, and they saw her no more, they would forget.

They would none of them come to her, any more than they would go to her tomb, when it should be made, a mere nameless hole under the rank grass of the common burying-ground.

The world does not take into account people who have nothing. They should be provident in their youth, and save money even if they have not enough to hold body and soul together, and never enough to satisfy hunger!

They should save money.

Stentorello is the type of the Italian on the stage, and the people in truth are perhaps too miserly and fond of gain; but is there much wonder at that in this country? There is no poor rate, and no workhouse, and nothing for the honest poor except a metre or so of ground in the cemeteries.

That is not a prospect to strengthen bare arms in the battle of life, or moisten parched lips dry with toil. The dead wasp is thought of by its kind, but the dead poor have no such remembrance from theirs.

Viola was watching for her as the diligence rolled heavily into the piazza at Santa Rosalia. The girl sprang to her and looked in her face, and her own face fell at what she read there.

'They have refused you!' she cried.

'Yes, dear,' said Annunziata with a quiver in her voice. 'They think I am a beggar, and that I never am and never was, as you know, for I never ask aught; never, never! they give me what they like to give me, and I am thankful.'

'When you have nothing, how can you help that?' said the girl, with a sob of indignation.

Annunziata bore up somehow or other against her lot and endured her hard pallet, her damp chamber, her dry atom of bread, because she still believed, against all witness to the contrary, that her God cared for her; that somehow or other when her soul should leave her little shrivelled, brown body, she would see the light of a gladder day than ever shone on earth.

She was an old woman, and had been bred up in the old faiths; faiths that were not clear indeed to her, nor ever reasoned on, but yet gave her consolation, and a great, if a vague, hope. Now that we tell the poor there is no such hope, that when they have worked and starved long enough, then they will perish altogether, like bits of candle that have burnt themselves out, that they are mere machines made of carbon and hydrogen, which, when they have had due friction, will then crumble back into the dust; now that we tell them all this, and call this the spread of education, will they be as patient?

Will not they, too, since this short life is all, insist at any price of blood that it shall be made sweet and made strong for them?

Will they not seize by violence on violent drugs, and drink themselves drunk on the alcohol of communism?

Why should they not? Since there is nothing beyond this life, why should they toil that you and I may be at ease?

Take hope from the heart of man, and you make him a beast of prey.

The philosopher stands at his desk in the lecture hall, and demonstrates away the soul of man, and with exact thought measures out his atoms and resolves him back to gas and air. But the revolutionary, below in the crowd, hears, and only translates what he hears thus to his brethren: 'Let us drink while we may; property is robbery; this life is all; let us kill and eat; there is no God.'

The philosopher may cry to the winds, 'Love virtue for its own sake.'

The communist is more logical than he.

## CHAPTER XXI.

MEANWHILE in the prison of Pomodoro, Carmelo, thanks rather to his youth than to his leech, recovered despite the bleeding, the camomel, the stench of foul drains, the diet, and the obscurity; in six weeks' time he was almost ready to go back to his prison cell; he looked but a shadow of himself; he was thin and pale, his eyes were moody, and cast downward; his ruddy, sun-tanned skin had grown pallid and yellow.

He had recovered, but he had a worse poison in him than even the poison of fever, for in the bed next to his there was lying a German with anemia and other ills, and this man talked to him in his own tongue by hours together in the long watches of the night, when they had no other companions than the newts and the rats and the beetles that ran over their couches. The German, a travelling mechanic, was a socialist and an internationalist; and into this ignorant virgin mind of Carmelo, all seething and fermenting now under an unendurable sense of wrong, he poured the black stream of his own beliefs and desires.

Carmelo did not understand a tithe part, but he

understood enough, after many a night's colloquy, to breathe in eagerly this vengeance on society which looked like justice, this insanity for equality which looked like reason. Until wrong had been done to him he had been a perfectly contented lad, troubling himself about nothing outside his own duties and occupation, for, scarcely knowing how to read, he knew nothing of any other world beyond that of the mill-house. He had been bred up to be respectful to the gentry and the clergy; to be decent and honest in life, and to be quite happy so long as his father was pleased with him. This had been always Carmelo, until that hapless hour when poor Toppa had been treacherously done to death.

But injustice and despotism change the pure blood of youth into a dark and sullen current. Carmelo, who had only rightly punished a poisoner, was treated like a criminal and thrown amongst thieves and assassins.

One of the cruellest sins of any State, in giving petty and tyrannous authority into petty and tyrannous hands, is that it thus brings into hatred and disgust the true and high authority of moral law.

'Where is God? He cannot hear, He cannot care; nor can the saints, since He and they let me lie here and make a king of Bindo Terri,' thought Carmelo, lying on his bed, with all the bright and vigorous force of his young limbs gone out of them.

If they were indeed throned in heaven, as the priests always said, would they let the poor suffer, and the scoundrels thrive, and the fines be wrung out of starving bodies, and the parasite of the public torture and arraign and sentence honest winners of their daily bread?

Carmelo still shrank from the bold blasphemies of the socialistic doctrines; but the German was wary and skilful, he softened for this foolish young Christian the atheism of the texts he quoted upon all religions, and only recited again and again their condemnations of all existing laws, and their invitation to a perfect future, when there would be on all the earth 'only free men in a free fraternity.'

Carmelo listened, and his sick soul was seduced by the dangerous stimulant of these doctrines, whose greatest danger lies in the fact that there is in all their exaggeration an essential, an undeniable, truth.

He was at war with all the world, with all these unknown, unseen, forces which had been stronger than he; his ear and his heart were open to words that told him of the tyranny of property, of the favouritism of law, of the sins of society by which millions groaned in want, and died unpitied.

The German, exiled from his own country for his opinions, was a keen and restless student and an ardent propagandist; he was a disciple of the most extreme creeds, and deemed, as most of those men now do, all remedy useless save 'pan-destruction.'

Well aware that he was dying, and a prey at times to great agony, he beheld in the young Italian his last proselyte, and threw all the last energies of his waning life into the rescue, as he deemed it, of this dumb soul, into the effort to give light to the blind eyes of Carmelo, for he found that Carmelo was ignorance itself; thought heaven had placed the king upon the throne; thought heaven had made one set of men to toil, and another set to do nothing and enjoy; had a vague idea of the Government as of a sort of god hedged round with cannon; fancied the good weather and the bad came from divine pleasure or wrath, and was certain that grain would not come up unless the priest made the round of the fields and blessed them.

The autumn nights were long and cold; in the infirmary they were allowed no charcoal and no light, but the fiery utterances of the Internationalist lit up and warmed the darkness. Carmelo who knew naught that occurred outside the hedges of Santa Rosalia, listened as in his childish days he had listened to the priest's wonder-stories of S. Ursula or SS. Cosmo and Damian, to the recital of the movement going secretly onward in Italy; of the insurrections of San Lupo, of Gallo, of Calatabiano; of the 'Circoli Barsanti,' and the section of the 'Figli di Lavoro'; of the memorable words of Garibaldi in 1873, that were there a society of devils to combat despotism, he would join it; of the Internationalist federation of Rimini which decrees 'the earth to who cultivates it, the machine to who uses it, the house to who builds it;' of the programme of Piacenza, 'every one has right to what is necessary, no one has right to what is superfluous;' of the declaration of the fraternity of Montenero, Antignani, Ardenza, and San-Jacopo that 'the State is the negation of liberty; authority creates nothing and corrupts everything; change of government is useless; if a man have a thorn in his foot, it is of no use for him to change his boots, he must pluck out the thorn;' and, with these, of many a burning and bitter paragraph from the *Plebe* of Milan, from the *Petroleo* of Ferrara, from the *Proletario* of Turin, and the unhesitating dictate of the *Campana*, that 'all authority, human and divine, shall perish and disappear, from God downward to the last agent of police.'

The innocent soul of Carmelo revolted from these arguments which tore down his Christ from his crucifix, and dashed his stoup of holy water to the ground; yet the wrong that festered in him made his mind open to all these dreams of freedom and of justice, all these promises of a millennium upon earth.

If such minds as Rousseau's, Fourier's, Proudhon's, Bakounine's, do not see the falsehood that is mingled with this truth, how shall Carmelo see it, or the like of Carmelo?

The Italian is, as I say, not by nature a revolutionary, but when he is one he goes beyond all others, because, perhaps, he has more than all others to suffer in the contrast between his dead hopes and his present misery. No one seems to remember that the Italian Socialists have rejected Marx and decreed Mazzini a reactionist, whilst they subscribe blindly and without change to all the terrible creed of Bakounine.

No one seems to remember this, or heed it; yet Bakounine's is a creed of nothing less than universal destruction. The disciples of it grow every day in numbers throughout Italy, but since the arrests of 1874, they call themselves by a harmless name [1] and so no one is afraid.

No one is afraid; and the State continues to give them justification by leaving in every commune the breed of Messer Nellemane and of Bindo Terri.

'It is a question of hunger,' the Marquis Pepoli said once of the revolts of Budria and Molinella.

---

[1] Circoli per i studi sociali.

Perhaps partly : not altogether. But who makes the hunger? who keeps the stomachs empty, the hearths cold, the box of the commune full by fines?

The Municipalities.

Here is the thorn that must be pulled from the foot of Italy if the canker and fester of it are not to spread through the whole body.

Carmelo, of course, could not understand a hundredth part of what the German unfolded to him, but the vague meaning that he gleaned dazzled and awed him, and the poison of injustice already given him to drink had left him thirsty for this other poison of revenge.

Carmelo was a brave lad, a lad honest, clean-living, and harmless in thought and deed; he was dealt with as if he were a criminal, and the bitter sense of his wrongs made it precious to him to hear of sovereign rights that he shared with all mankind.

He had been dimly conscious of a right to live in his own way so long as he did no harm to his fellows; he had been by nature independent and of fearless spirit; but of late the petty tyrannies enfolding the lives of the poor had been to him like a choking chain, and he had begun to tremble. He saw men impoverished, and hunted down to beggary, or death, by this thing which they called Law, and which he knew only to be extortion; and he had lost hope and manliness; and in the stead of these there had come on him a moody and morbid resentment, chilled with dread.

He was as ready for the tempting of his teacher, as clay is made moist for the hand and the wheel of the potter.

One night, when the moon was shining in through

the grated hole that served as casement, the German mechanic died.

Carmelo was too feeble to rise; he sat up in his bed and saw the ghastly agony, and heard the death-rattle, of this man, who seemed to him his only friend. He strove to call for help, but his tongue clave to his mouth, and when at length he could find his trembling voice he shouted in vain; no one heard.

The horror of that hour aged him by many years.

He dragged his weak limbs out of bed and strove to hold the man in his convulsions, but death was stronger than he, and flung him backward rudely on his own mattress.

With the moonlight on his ghastly face the German struggled with his doom, choking and vomiting blood. Once only, with consciousness in his eyes, he stared upward in the eyes of Carmelo.

'The people—the people—suffer,' he muttered through his clenching teeth.

Then he gave a bitter cry and died.

Carmelo was alone through all the long chill night with the body of the dead man beside him.

## CHAPTER XXII.

AFTER her fruitless journey to Pomodoro, Annunziata could not get about at all, on account of snow that fell, and of a thaw that left the roads mere torrents of slush.

She had but little blood in her veins, and but little bread in her cupboard; she and the three other old souls huddled themselves together over a single *scaldino* of charcoal that they clubbed their pence to get, and spent most of their time in bed, in hope of of so keeping their slow circulation from absolute stagnation. They were four miserable little pallet-beds, one in each corner, and the spiders and beetles and mice ran over them, and the old women were too feeble to chase them away.

Dom Lelio did all he could; and Viola went daily, and denied herself that she might keep her great-aunt from starving, but when all was done that could be by these two, Annunziata had but little of all that old age needs. Dom Lelio had but a franc a-day, and in Pippo's house want was a ghost that had no rest and gave none.

'They cannot call her a beggar now,' said Viola bitterly, as she stood beside the hard bed in which the old woman was stretched, with her legs useless from rheumatism.

The heart of the girl was sick with hope deferred, and that vague fear of something yet worse to come which a long succession of undeserved misfortunes will leave on the brightest nature.

It was now the end of February and the weather, as it often does here, grew colder by far than it had been when the days were short. The village was a sorry scene, the ill-made roads were little better than bogs, and the angry river went swirling and rushing, yellow and muddy with all the clay that it washed down from its treeless banks.

'One would say the Rosa were mad to think the *boschetto* is gone,' thought the eldest girl Dina Pastorini, as the north wind, without that screen of trees, beat with all its might against the millhouse.

Her father had changed as greatly as Pippo.

He was never irritable, because he was a sweet-tempered and just man, who could not bear to farther afflict his children.

But all the honest mirth and cheery content were gone out of him; he who had been so loquacious and mirthful now never smiled and seldom spoke; his brow was always dark and his eyes were always dull. Missing that glad and pleasant shade, so green through three of the seasons, that had been before his eyes ever since he had opened them at birth, seemed to him to have made him half-blind.

Besides, he was always saying in his thoughts: 'How shall we tell Carmelo? how will he bear it when he sees?' Carmelo, who beyond them all had loved the bright *boschetto*, and had passed so many a holiday hour sitting on the mossy edge of it with his square net floating on the stream below, and white Toppa sleeping by his side or hunting lizards in the flower-filled grass.

The father dared not think of it. He had suffered greatly himself, but he feared that his son would suffer yet more.

As for such solace as might have come to a man struggling with many burdens from the help of money, none was given to him. The municipality had offered a certain sum of money indeed for the riverside wood, but they had not paid it. In Rome they were five years paying for the Farnesina gardens, destroying them, as it were, on credit; in Santa Rosalia they would probably be twice as long paying the miller.

If he wanted to make them pay he would have to go to law with them, and that no one of the class that the Pastorini belonged to would ever dare to do, knowing the remedy to be worse than the disease. The Giunta was supposed to deal with these matters, but in reality it only met to give adhesion to what Cavaliere Durellazzo said, and what he said was what he had been prompted to say by his right hand and chief counsellor, Messer Nellemane.

Now, as every one will understand without saying, they could scarcely be expected to find money for Demetrio Pastorini, since they were obliged to pay beforehand all those gentlemen who had opposed the tramway.

So the miller's empty pockets were not the heavier by a coin at the present for the expropriation of his wood, and he suffered in a time of peace and, as the foreign newspapers had it, of prosperity, precisely what he would have suffered had an invading army encamped in Vezzaja and Ghiralda and burned it right and left on leaving it.

'Ah, my girl,' he said once to Viola, of whom he had grown fond in their mutual trials, 'I almost would sooner our dear lad stayed on in prison than that he should come to see what he will see.'

Viola sighed heavily, and did not say that she felt otherwise, only in her young heart there was that hope which is in youth like the golden gorse, always in bloom, even in bad weather and on barren soil.

She thought always: 'When Carmelo comes home things will change; all will be well.'

It was now the close of February; she was counting the weeks, the days, the hours till Carmelo's release.

She could not read much, but she had one of those little calendars which are the oracles of the poor, and she could make out their signs and the days of the months, and in this she had marked each cruel week as it crawled by and left her lover shut in prison walls.

There were only two months more now to divide them, and though Carmelo truly would return to trouble and pain, she could not, like his father, wish him absent.

Yet so many sorrows fell upon them, that the bit of charcoal with which she marked evil days in her calendar had made almost every page a smudge of black.

Early in the year her grandfather had received a long and formal printed paper, calling on him to remove the nuisance of the water before his door. Pippo had crammed the thing on to the top of the live cinders in the *brascie* bowl, and there had let it smoulder into ashes.

A few days later Pierino Zaffi had been seen about the place, examining the little spring and measuring it, and in the name of the commune had entered the house and traced the offending water to its source amongst the frozen orto ground. He had said nothing and had gone.

In a week's time there had come another document, and that Viola took to Cecco to read, her grandfather being absent at the time.

This one ordered Filippo Mazzetti forthwith to execute works that would direct his spring underground; to cover it was forbidden, because no means by which it could be covered would fail to obstruct the public path.

He was ordered to commence this work within thirty days; if delayed, the offender would be fined for every day's delay.

The spectacles rose on Cecco's nose, and the hair upon his head as he read, and his face grew aghast with horror.

'After all that money that I paid for Pippo,' he gasped; 'after that bit of paper which set him free of all!'

He who was disposed to revere and obey the law was paralysed with terror.

Was this its justice? this the way it kept its troth with men?

Cecco gave up faith in humanity, and almost abandoned faith in heaven.

Viola was crying bitterly.

'What does it mean?' gasped Cecco wildly. 'What does it mean? Can your grandfather pay masons and plumbers for six months like a duke?'

'It means ruin!' sobbed the girl. 'He has nothing in the world; how can he put the water under the earth? And Carmelo coming home in a month!'

Of this new calamity they were compelled to tell Pippo. He heard quite quietly, but there was a savage wild light in his eye.

He stretched his hand out and took the paper and folded it up once, twice, thrice; then he held it in the palm of his hand and spat on it; then he lighted a lucifer match and set fire to it.

It blazed a moment, then curled up, and became a little heap of black ash on the stones of the floor.

He stayed Viola and Cecco with a gesture, as they would have spoken.

'Never a word,' he said, 'never a word. If they send me a hundred such, so will I treat them all. They cannot get blood out of a post. Let them do their worst—'

'But'—his friend began.

'Not a word,' said Pippo, and he spat on the ashes. Then he went on with his work.

Half an hour later he looked up from his weaving, and his eyes were shining savagely from under his white hair.

'Girl,' he said to his granddaughter, 'I call to mind a night before you were born. There came news of a great battle; they called it San Martino.[1] They told us to light up; so did we all. In your little window I set the oil flaming. They said we were free—God have mercy on us for being fools!'

Then he went on plaiting his osiers.

The girl wept.


## CHAPTER XXIII.

A LITTLE while after that, there came a hue and cry of mad dogs in Santa Rosalia. These cries are very common. They bring in plenty of dog skins for the guards to sell.

If any dog be hunted by boys, be thirsty for water he cannot find, or be gaunt or faint from hunger and ill-treatment, straightway is he declared *arrabiato*, and up on the walls there appear placards that every dog seen about will be killed. Then Bindo, with his poisoned polpetti and his pistol, is busy and happy all over the land.

A woman was bitten the other day by one of these mad dogs, and was recovered by the bone of a saint being laid by her pillow, but present munici-

[1] Solferino is so called by the Italians.

palities are not desirous to bring out the virtues of saints, and they do like to sell the skins of dogs; so they scream at every possible wag of a tail or sign of a growl, and fly to poison and to pistols.

Such a panic seized the municipality of Vezzaja and Ghiralda in this month of February, when Pippo was being summoned again and again for little Raggi and putting the summons in the fire.

If you tunnel a mountain and stifle a score of men you are a public benefactor; if you keep a factory, in which no one lives over thirty years of age from the noxious dust or noxious gas inhaled in the work, no one finds human life at all too precious for you to use up as you like in your own interests; but if ever a dog snap at somebody—ah! then of what sanctity is human life! what horror is anything that menaces it!

Messer Nellemane, in the absence of Cavaliere Durellazzo, who was at his candle-warehouses, took fright now, nothing loth to do so, and had placards stuck up, announcing that the guards were authorised to destroy every dog they saw loose.

The dullest imagination can conjecture the 'lovely time' that Bindo and Angelo had in the commune, and no one dared to check their slaughtering hand, remembering the fate that had befallen Carmelo.

Viola, terrified, kept little Raggi in the house, and shut her up in the orto, and kept her out of danger all she could, and at night would start up and feel for the little floss silk curls of the dog as it lay at the foot of her bed, waking from a dream that Raggi had been seized and killed.

'I said the dog should never be kept in for those

devils,' growled her grandfather: but the girl pleaded to him that her trouble was for Raggi's own sake.

The old man let her do as she would; he was growing apathetic, yet desperate; though he had burned the Giunta's order about his brook, the memory of it and the dread of what they might do to him haunted him night and day. And he was so very poor; he did not so much mind depriving himself of wine and tobacco, but it hurt him terribly to see Viola's clothes mended till they were but patchwork, and her feet going bare.

Viola had always been the neatest and cleanest as well as the comeliest maiden in the province. Clean she was still, but neat you cannot be when you are so very poor that even to buy a few pins, a little thread, a bit of tape, is quite beyond your means.

This is the poverty that the world does not understand, and, not apprehending, does not pity; famine it understands, the famine that desolates Cashmere and Bombay, but not the poverty which can just put enough in the body to keep life alive uncomplainingly, but has not a coin beyond for any need or pleasure of life.

It was a great sorrow, too, to Viola not to be able to be decently dressed for mass as she had used to be; but she did not think so much of that as she did of her inability to give her grandfather a scrap or two of meat in his broth and her equal powerlessness to defend Raggi.

At Christmas she had sold her little string of seed pearls to a richer maiden, the big butcher's daughter, and the money they had fetched had long since gone in charcoal and bread for themselves and soup for

Annunziata. Money runs away so fast when it has no companions in your drawer.

One morning whilst the placards concerning dogs were still upon the walls, and the reign of terror still dominated all Vezzaja and Ghiralda, Viola had her week's washing to do. She needed not to go for this, as most had to do, to the edge of the river, or to the springs on the hillsides, because the brook that offended the Giunta filled a tank in their own little garden.

There she washed the sheets and shirts and other linen that she and Pippo used, and washed her great-aunt's linen, too, if such poor little rags can be dignified by the name; and she was at this work all the chilly forenoon with the bitter north wind whistling round her head and nipping the red flowers of the almond trees near her.

She had shut the house door, and Raggi was with her running loose about the little place; Pippo was out trying to get an order for skips or baskets or the osier-covers of wine-flasks.

Viola looked often for the little dog and saw it lying out of the wind under the wall, but about eleven o'clock, having wrung out her linen, she was so busied hanging it up on the clothes' line, tied to the delicate almond trees, that she never heard the wind blow open the entrance door, and when her work was done at noon she missed Raggi.

The little dog never left her side usually, but Raggi had a little friend in Cecco's youngest boy, a gentle mite of four years old, a cripple with a cherub's face and curling golden hair.

Whenever Raggi heard the tic-tac of the poor little man's crutch, she always trotted out to it, for

Lillo, as they called the child, would share his bread and milk with her, and throw his little wooden ball to please her, and loved her dearly. Raggi—perhaps with that divine pity which dogs have—divined the sad destiny of crippled Lillo, and so gave him her preference.

This forenoon she heard the sound of the crutch on the stones of the threshold, and got up and went to it, not knowing she was doing any harm.

Lillo, delighted to see his playmate, covered her with kisses and hobbled along to his father's house, and there got a bit of bread; and hobbled farther with the dog by his side out to the few willows that there fringed the river bank, and sat down in the sun and shared his bread with her.

Lillo and Raggi were very merry, indeed, about nothing; seeking stones in the grass, making a feast of the crust, and playing with the dry twigs that the wind scattered so plentifully. Raggi's yellow curls blew, and Lillo's blew, too, and the one barked, and the other sang and laughed, and both were as happy as two little mortals could be, with that sweetest of all happiness which is born out of nothing beyond the mere glad sense of living.

But along the road by the river there came a grim shadow; the shadow of a man in grey clothes, with a feather in his hat and a sword by his side.

His eyes flashed over the little child and the little dog sitting together under the willows, and his ear caught the sound of that quick little bark, that gay little laugh.

He drew his pistol and shot the dog.

As the dog dropped on its side the child fell backward, screaming violently.

People ran out from their houses, and Bindo Terri walked away as one who has done his duty and earned his wage.

Viola had run out with the rest; she fell on her knees by Raggi.

Blood was pouring from its mouth, but it moved its little curly tail feebly in welcome and farewell. Then the little bright eyes glazed and seemed to sink into its head, its heart beat convulsively through a few seconds more, it stretched its limbs out feebly, and then was still for ever.

It lay dead in a pool of its own blood.

Never more would Lillo laugh under the willows, and break his bread with Raggi. Never more would Raggi dance to the children's piping. And little Lillo, never very wise, was imbecile from that hour; a frightened, cowering, mindless thing.

But what mattered that? The law had asserted its majesty and vindicated its rights.

When the old man Pippo dug a small grave under the blossoming almond-trees, and laid the blood-stained body of the little dog in it, covered with moss and grass, he groaned as he turned each sod.

'Assassins and thieves are set above us, and work their wicked will, and no one cares. How long, O Lord? how long?'

## CHAPTER XXIV.

As by a very irony and wantonness of cruelty, that very night there was left at his house by the usciere a mandate from the court of Pomodoro to pay the sum of fifty-seven francs on account of the little dog.

As he had neglected to answer the summons for contravention, the charges against him for contumacy had been taken as usual to the senior court, and had been proved and assessed against him with costs.

Two francs for every time that poor little Raggi had been seen loose soon told up to a high sum total, and the public accuser who officiates for the commune on such occasions had stated that, but for the mercifulness of that administration, the number of summonses would have been much greater. They regretted, they said, to be severe on a poor man, but the law must be respected. The law must be respected, said all the officials in a chorus.

That document, like the others, found the fire.

'They may kill me as they killed the little dog,' said Pippo; ''twould be less trouble, and done once for all.'

Viola was weeping as though her tears would, to use Dante's words, destroy her very heart; and in the cooper's house a sad mother sat by a little bed where a golden-headed child, with vacant, terrified eyes, was pointing for ever in the air, and stammering uncouth, shapeless sounds, and then shivering as though with ague, and cowering down under the clothes.

Bright-haired Lillo's body lived, but his mind was as dead as Raggi's, buried in her grave underneath the almonds.

'Carmelo must not know,' said Viola over and over again in the darkness of the night, sobbing and missing her little furry friend, who for seven years had slept upon her bed; and when the morning dawned she begged of Lillo's mother and father, and of all about the house, that never would they let Carmelo know that Raggi had been killed by Bindo Terri, and the child thus lost his wits from terror.

All promised her, but she could not be sure that the promise would be kept, for she knew how every little story leaks from the dry cask of empty heads, and she was afraid, terribly afraid. Sometimes she thought that she would lose her brain, like little timid Lillo.

Her father, too, was for ever saying, 'Let them kill me as they have killed the dog. They have made me a beggar.'

The cold was passing away. The damp was drying up, the corn lands were green with young wheat, and soon amidst the grass the violets were giving place to the daffodils, and on the hill-sides the peach-trees and pear-trees were throwing out their sprays of blossom, making the steep slopes beautiful.

But spring brought no joy to the small house of the Madonna; and by the mill upon the river, in lieu of lovely pillars of lightest green, thickening and deepening with every day, in lieu of that leafy screen, full of the nests of doves and merles and nightingales, there was a waste land of mud and shingle, a barren spot, of no use or good to man or beast or bird.

Nothing had been done with it. The holes yawned where the trees had been uprooted, and the water-beetles crawled undisturbed over the heaps of mud. The tramway was not made; the foreign speculators and the home municipalities were quarrelling, and until their quarrels were ended the work could not be begun. The speculators said the municipalities had cheated, and the municipalities gave the speculators a tu-quoque. It was a quarrel like a croupier's and a gamester's.

Of all these things the population of the commune understood nothing; they were like a horse who has his mane docked and his chin singed; he feels uncomfortable, but he does not know what is done to him.

Italy is always being docked and singed; being amiable, she does not kick her groom, but she is always smarting, and the flies are always raising gall upon her loins.

The sweet spring came; and so sweet is it, here, that it is joy enough to live only to go out into the fields all laden with blossom, and feel your heart dance with the daffodils in the full sense of Wordsworth's words.

But the poor have not leisure for this, nor have they insight for it, and the spring brought no solace to Santa Rosalia.

Another trouble, and a yet greater anxiety, fell on Demetrio Pastorini at this time.

There was another miller on the other side of the village, who had never done very much work, because the water was so much shallower there, and who indeed did not care about it, being a very well-to-do man, owning an oil-shop and warehouse in Pomodoro. His name was Remigio Rossi; he had never been looked on at all as a rival by Carmelo's family, and did not seek to be one.

But one fine day four oxen appeared on the river-edge, dragging a huge, black, shapeless, uncouth-looking object behind them; and a few days later, Pippo and Viola, looking out of their house door, saw a long black chimney, and a cone of black smoke, coming out of the roof of Remigio's mill, which was within ten yards of them.

Pippo ran and shouted with all his might that the place was a-fire, but people standing on the bank, looking on, said to him,

'Be still, you, for an old fool; that is the new machine a-grinding.'

Demetrio Pastorini, who was a home-biding man, and never went to public-houses of any kind for gossip, and so never heard anything that was going on until a dozen days after all Santa Rosalia knew it, saw this black thing spitting smoke, and heard all at a blow, as it were, that the miller Remigio Rossi had obtained a steam-engine from the city, by means of which he could grind grain in fair weather or foul, and snap his finger and thumb at all shallow waters.

The steam-mill was a hideous blot on the landscape, and its ugly iron chimney vomited filthy odours and darkening vapours over all the green country and glancing waters, and made a mass of ash and cinders and general blackness and sootiness all about the pretty grass bank on which the building stood.

The engines were set going with plenty of last year's grain, by favour of the Cavaliere Durellazzo; and hearing their whirring and booming, and seeing the heavy veil of its smoke, the elder Pastorini turned away, 'death in his heart,' for hope was for ever gone out of him.

How could he wrestle against this thing? he with his mill wheels high and dry, for five months out of the year, since the woods had been cut on the banks?

'So you bring devils of fire and iron to ruin your old neighbour, Remigio?' he said reproachfully when he met him at mass on the Sunday.

Remigio, who was a good-natured man, though, like most of them, he loved money too well, looked sheepishly.

'I do not wish to injure anybody,' he said, with some embarrassment. 'But one was sorely wanted now the Rosa is such a captious thing; and as the Giunta find half the cost, it being for the good of the place——'

'Oh, the Giunta find half the money, do they?' said Pastorini, with his heart sinking heavier and heavier. 'And I suppose they will take half the profits too?'

Remigio winked, then shuffled into church.

The next day Pastorini, who was by no means behind the scenes in these matters, went and asked innocently for an audience with the Cavaliere Durellazzo: it was the syndic's day for audiences.

As usual, the Cavaliere Durellazzo was absent; but his secretary would see any one. After a little delay the miller found himself in the presence of Messer Nellemane, who smiled affably, and, without rising from his writing chair, said, 'Can I be of any use to you, my friend?'

Then Demetrio Pastorini, not being glib of tongue, except under pressure of excitement, with some hesitation, and with great repetition and amplification, related the object of his coming, and set forth the fact that his people had been millers on the Rosa water over three hundred years, well counted and proved, and very likely many more; and then he proceeded to urge that having thus a kind of inherited fief and ancestral right as it were in the stream, it was beyond all justice, not to say all law, to have a steam mill set up in face of him.

Messer Nellemane listened very patiently; and when at last the miller paused for want of breath, said gently:

'You are under an entire misapprehension, my friend. Did not Remigio Rossi occupy the mill by the piazza for very many years?'

Pastorini admitted the fact.

'And you never, that I heard of, objected to that water mill being there?'

'It did no business,' said the miller.

'Excuse me,' said Messer Nellemane, 'that is quite beside the question. If it had done, you could not have thought of compelling its removal?'

'I never should have asked it,' said Pastorini. 'Live and let live is my motto. That mill was an honest thing. It worked by water; and it was in worse water than I was——'

Messer Nellemane grew a trifle impatient; the obtuseness of the public always irritated him; but he kept his serene smile.

'All that is beyond the question. You contest the legality of Rossi's mill. Now, whether it be a water mill or a steam mill, it has, or it has not, the same rights to the ground it stands upon: you do not seem to me to see that; yet, if you reflect a moment, dear sir, you will be persuaded that the manner of working the mill has nothing at all to do with the matter.'

'Merciful heaven!' cried Pastorini, goaded into torture by this mild and logical reasoning. 'It has everything to do with it. The mill had the same rights as mine—no less; no more. When Rossi was content with the seasons God sent, and the whim of the Rosa, I had nothing to say: the river is free.'

'A moment ago you claimed it as the property of your family,' said his listener very gently: the miller did not heed.

'Fair contest I would never be a foe to, nor would any son of mine,' he said, a little hotly. 'Come rich, come poor, the river is free; a prince and a beggar may strip and sport in it——'

'More pity,' said Messer Nellemane, whose propriety was often offended by little, live, dancing *amorini* bent on a bath in the heat of midsummer.

'The river's a free thing; but use it fair,' said the miller, growing heated. 'Don't put a hissing boiler on it, and grind, when it's God's will that the water's out; why do you come on the river to do that? it's like the men I've heard of that blow fish out of the waters with gunpowder, and rob all honest anglers with their nets and rods.'

'Dynamite,' corrected Messer Nellemane. 'It is not allowed by our rules.'

'Then why do you allow the steam mill?' pursued Pastorini. 'It's to me what the blasting is to the fishers. One man will gorge, and all the others starve. I never said I had a right to the Rosa; but I do say I have a right to grind grain for Santa Rosalia and all the farms around. This thing isn't fair; it isn't honest; it will eat me up, and make my children hunger; for, of course, all the folks will go where the work is done quickest.'

'You have precisely expressed the reason of its invention,' said Messer Nellemane blandly, and toying with a pen. 'In these times work, to please the public, must be done quickly, and done at any moment. It is most painful to me that this innovation should be displeasing to you; but we are compelled to think of the general interest, not of individual aims. It is absurd that, in these times of great inventions, a whole commune should have to wait with its harvests unground because a little river has run dry; so many complaints have been made on this subject to us that we have deemed ourselves bound to find some remedy for them, and as Remigio Rossi was a public-spirited man with some capital, the most excellent the Cavaliere Durellazzo and the Giunta decided on giving him some help to the better carrying out of this project.'

Pastorini stood confounded and dumb. He had intended to cast the loan for the steam mill in the face of this representative of the municipality; but lo! it was boasted of to him as an act of public utility and benignity!

His slow gentle wits were not quick enough or keen enough to combat those of Messer Nellemane.

He stood turning his straw hat in his hands, and stammering stupidly: 'But the thing's not honest. It's not fair. It is to be beat by devils———' till his auditor amiably reminded him that time was precious, and that there were many persons awaiting audience below.

'Can I do nothing then?' said the miller, staring blindly about him.

'Nothing in this matter. When the Giunta has once given its approbation———'

'Damn the Giunta, and damn you!' said Demetrio Pastorini bitterly. 'You have thrown my poor lad in prison, and you will now take the bread out of our mouths.'

Messer Nellemane rang a little bell, and Bindo Terri appeared, and showed the miller the door.

'All that family is a little amiss here,' said Messer Nellemane, touching his own forehead with a commiserating smile.

## CHAPTER XXV.

The miller went to a lawyer in Pomodoro; and the lawyer told him he could do nothing; he could perhaps petition the Prefect.

So Pastorini bade him, in mercy's name, draw up the petition, which was done, and cost forty francs.

The Prefect's secretary read it, and referred it to the Consiglio Provinciale; the Consiglio Provinciale referred it to their engineer, who was the engineer of the commune, one Pierino Zaffi. He informed the Consiglio Provinciale that the mill was necessary, not insalubrious, and very advantageous to the commune; the Consiglio Provinciale said so in turn to the Prefect, and he certified that he could not go against the decision of the provincial council.

In such a circle does the poor mill horse of the public turn.

Nothing was to be done.

Pastorini knew very well that Ruin would soon look over his white garden gate.

The steam-mill would take all his custom away, and now that the trees were felled, the water would most likely be shallower, and sooner shallow, every summer. Besides the Pastorini felt themselves growing friendless: for the first time for many years the big butcher had been asked to direct the procession of Corpus Domini instead of the miller; people were cool where they had been cordial. Without more selfishness than is common to human nature, Santa Rosalia felt that it was perilous to be good friends with a family so marked out for punishment by Providence and Messer Nellemane.

'A tin-kettle threshing the corn, and an iron pot grinding of it! Oh Lord, what times!' said old Pippo, as the mill smoke came in through his window and smothered him in his bed.

Messer Nellemane was in good and affable spirits; all things were going well with him. The new deputy, not unmindful of the tampering that had gone on with the election lists, and the plurality of voting achieved by the gendarmerie, and other signal services to the State, in which the secretary of Santa Rosalia had been of no small use, both in invention and execution, was more than cordial to his humble ally, and predicted all manner of great things for the future of so intelligent a public servant.

'In a free country like this,' said Signore Luca Finti, 'industry and talent can never long fail to obtain recognition. When these miscreants are out of office, and our turn of power comes, you will not be forgotten, my dear friend.'

And Messer Nellemane was so clever that the Prefect of the province, who had been put in his place by the miscreants, also commended him for his discretion and zeal in certain things that had been convenient to the Prefecture in those elections, and the sub-Prefect said to him :

'So long as we are in power, you, I promise, shall not be forgotten. Such servants of the State as yourself are quite invaluable in these times when we have so much to fear from the Reactionary and Clerical element, and yet on the other hand must avoid being swamped by the deluge of Communism.'

Messer Nellemane said earnestly that he had no feeling except of horror either for Clericalism or Communism.

He thought the good of the State required the strictest moderation and impartiality, and, as he said it very truthfully, he felt quite safe whether the Ministry went out or in, and especially as the new deputy and the sub-prefect would never compare notes because they abhorred each other as only Ministerialists and Dissidenti can.

Messer Nellemane's Utopia was like that of most Liberals of the present era ; it was a neat cut-and-dried despotism, which should call itself a democracy, and in which the people should have as little voice as the nobles, and the church be only permitted to exist if it became a school-house for the semination of State doctrines.

This Liberalism keeps one eye on Gambetta and the other on Bismarck, and is so absorbed in these two, and in trying to combine an imitation of both, that it never sees coming after it with seven-leagued strides the avenger—Bakounine.

## CHAPTER XXVI.

It was the day for Carmelo to come out of prison; it was a lovely May morning, as May is lovely in this land alone.

Plentiful rains had fallen in the night; the tall, green-waving wheat, the mulberry and walnut trees, the willows along the river, the moss-grown grass between the poplars, all were green and sparkling with moisture; here and there an acacia rose up in blossom like the white column of a fountain, here and there glowed a Judas (*circis siliquastrum*), with the roseate blush of its abundant flowers; over all was blowing a sweet sea wind from the west.

Demetrio Pastorini said to the maiden:

'Alas! that he should come home to see what he will see!—'

'He will see us all well,' said Viola, with a true woman's belief that this must compensate for all.

'The lad is sorely changed,' said the father with a sigh; 'remember that, Viola. When wrong is done to a man it changes the honey of the human heart to gall. He is no more the bright, soft, innocent youth that you and we have loved. He will need much wisdom from you, and much consolation.'

'I will try my best,' said the girl, 'I will try to win him back to his old self, and teach him to forget.'

'That is not easy,' said Pastorini; 'when the mildew is on the grain, who shall make it fair wheat again? And he comes to two sore troubled households. But he is young and you are good.'

I love him dearly,' said Viola, with tears in her large eyes.

'That I know,' said his father

Then he kissed her, and got ready the grey mare, and Dina walked back with her to her own little house while the men went on their way.

'That young Pastorini will be out of prison to-day,' Messer Nellemane was saying at that moment to the brigadier; 'you will keep him under your eye, for I think he is a dangerous character.'

'Of course,' said the gendarme.

Once in prison, you are for ever down in the books of the police, and subject to examination and interrogation at any word or act that seems to them to be suspicious. You never wholly escape. You are as a bird let loose, and flying with a recall-thread tied to its foot. Human justice is a sadly deficient thing.

Pippo and the Pastorini, father and sons, went to Pomodoro to meet him; Viola stayed in her house; there is enough of the old sentiment amongst the people, still, to make them think women should not parade their persons, or their affections, or meddle with public things.

When they greeted Carmelo, and the formalities were fulfilled that set him free, he grasped his father's hand and Pippo's, but said never a word. He walked out into the open air, into the broad sunlight, with an uncertain step as if he were purblind; his face had a stupid look, and his mouth, that had been so fresh and smiling, was pale and sullenly compressed. All his youth seemed to have gone out of him; he was wasted and thin, and his clothes hung on him loosely, twice too large. Only twelve months before he had borne the Maggio so merrily with carol and chant!

'You have had a long time of it,' said the Usciere jocosely to him. 'You will take good care how you touch a guard again, *birricchino mio.*'

Carmelo looked on the ground; there was a fierce fire in his eyes; he kept a sullen silence.

'My son has been cruelly wronged,' said the elder Pastorini with tears in his voice. 'If there were any justice in the land, not an hour would he have spent in your accursed place.'

'The law never wrongs any one,' said the Usciere, who lived by the law.

'The real good honest law perhaps does not,' said Pastorini, 'but these rogues who make laws out of their own heads that they may fill their pockets—'

'Hush! or they will lock you up,' whispered Pippo, who ever since he had mortgaged his house had been timid and yet sullen. 'Let us be going; there is Viola at home.'

At the maiden's name a momentary light passed over Carmelo's face and into his heavy eyes; but it soon faded and left again unillumined the sullen gloom that months of imprisonment had brought there.

'Let us go,' he said, and glanced back over his shoulder with a shudder at the prison.

They had brought the mill-horse and cart to meet him, and he felt a sob rise in his throat as he saw the familiar old grey beast, and heard the whinny of pleasure with which the poor thing recognised him.

Their hearts were rather heavy than joyful as they drove behind the grey along the dusty road, with the vineyards on either side of them, and the long low azure forms of the mountains beyond those.

The father felt a bitter pang that one of his sons should go back thus to his birth-place; his name had always been stainless, and though he knew that Carmelo had done no wrong, still in all prisons there is a taint of shame that clings.

The young man never spoke; his brother had the reins; he sat behind with old Pippo, his face turned backward, so that he saw the red roofs and dusky towers of Pomodoro grow less and less, until the rise of the road hid them.

'Accursed place! accursed place!' he muttered once; then his head dropped on his breast, and his lips never unclosed till the cart had jolted over a bridge that crossed the winding Rosa and entered his village. Then he put his hand on his brother's arm, and motioned him to check the horse.

'Let me get down; let me see her alone.'

They let him get down.

He stood an instant, and looked at the white, square, bald building that was the Palazzo Communale. He looked and lifted his hand in the air.

'I would do the same again were the time to come again!' he said solemnly. 'My poor dead dog! do they think the prison has made me forget you—or forgive them?'

His face was very pale and very stern; his eyes had a great darkness and yet a great fire in them, as the skies have when behind the purple rain-clouds flash the lightnings.

The men in the cart were afraid.

'He is not in his right mind,' said Pippo in a frightened voice to his father.

Pastorini shook his head.

'Let him go to the girl. She will be his best cure. We should but do him harm. You will bring them both up to us a little later, when he is calm. He is sorely changed, my lad, my poor lad!'

It was early morning; no one saw Carmelo return. He went across the threshold of the house of the Madonna, and fell at the feet of Viola, who watched and prayed for him.

His father followed him wistfully with his eyes, shading his own with his hand.

'What will he say of the trees?' he cried in a sort of despair. 'I have not broken it to him. What will he say? what will he say?'

Pippo answered nothing: he thought the trees but a trivial woe beside his own dead weight of ruin; but he would not say so; he had a kind heart, which was awake, though his head was failing.

The miller drove on slowly through the village; and Pippo slipped down and glided away by himself, and sat down by the river-side under the willows by the reeds.

It was early, and no one scarcely had seen the miller's cart come through the village, and those who had seen, had kept behind their door-posts and their casements, saying to themselves, 'Will it be prudent to be friends with the lad?'

For whosoever would be friends with the liberated criminal, the whole borgo knew well, would be marked and cashiered in the black books of the *oppressor rusticorum*. Their hearts were altogether with Carmelo; he had done thoroughly right, so they all thought, but who would dare to say so, or dare to act as if he thought so?

In these modern times of cowardice, when great Ministers dare not say the thing they think, and high magistrates stoop to execute decrees that they abhor, it is scarcely to be hoped for that moral courage will be a plant of very sturdy growth in the souls of carpenters and coopers, and bakers and plumbers and day-labourers, who toil for scarce a shilling a day. A bad name with the guards, a series of fines and taxes, the loss of municipal work or gentlemen's patronage—these soon ruin a poor tradesman or workman.

So we will not be too harsh against the little folk of Santa Rosalia that they hung back somewhat, and were not quick to look out of their doors as usual when the miller's well-known grey horse trotted slowly through the street.

Only Gigi Canterelli ran out of his shop and waved his hat, and shouted, '*Bravo! benone!*' and fearful Cecco, who was standing at the entrance of his workshop, having no work to do, seeing Pippo sitting disconsolate amidst the rushes, ran to him and cried, 'Dear friend! Is he home? Oh the joy of it! Never mind the gaol now; never mind it a bit; everybody knows the rights of the tale!'

And when Pippo, who did not think it right to leave the youth and the maiden together more than ten minutes, got up to go into his house, Cecco would go with him, and shook the hands of Carmelo, and kissed him on both cheeks, and said, 'Now you are home all will go well,' and then kissed Viola and went on his knees before the crucifix and blessed Christ, and got up again, and laughed and cried, and sang and danced, and behaved altogether so foolishly for a staid old cooper of sixty years, that Pippo could not help laughing too, and the young man and maiden were glad of this cover to their own too great emotion.

'Let us go,' said Pippo, 'your father will be wondering——'

Carmelo, with Viola's hand in his, looked more as he had used to look; his eyes had a soft and tearful light, and his lips had something of their old smile on them. He spoke but little: even for her he had few words.

But when Pippo said to him that it was time they should be going to the mill, and thereon the three went out from the house into the piazza, the harder, darker look came once more upon his face, and his eyes grew fierce as he strode through the dust with his head erect as if in challenge.

'I could kill them all!' he muttered, and his hand clenched hard on the hand of Viola.

As they went across the threshold, Carmelo looked over his shoulder:

'Where is little Raggi? She always jumped about me so.'

And he began to call and whistle for her as of yore.

Viola burst out crying and caught hold of his arm.

'Oh Carmelo! oh, dear one, don't do that! Raggi is dead.'

'Dead! what did she die of? Poor pretty merry Raggi!'

'She died of—of—old age,' said Viola between her sobs; 'don't talk of her, please don't.'

'Of old age?' said Carmelo doubtingly. 'She was not a pup, to be sure, but she was so full of pranks and play. Poor little Raggi! Are you sure it was not poison?'

His face grew overcast again, and the gloom of it did not lighten as he moved into the street and saw the neighbours hurry inside their doorways.

'One would say I brought the plague,' he said savagely.

'Come on, never mind them. They are afraid the guards are looking, that is all. It will all be again just as it used to be when you shall have been home a week,' said the cooper hurriedly, and they passed across the square.

It was now the hour when all Santa Rosalia was up and doing; when every door was open, and every window unshuttered, when the children were trotting to school, and the mothers gossiping as they made their small purchases for dinner at noon. But now the women hustled away into holes and corners, and the men became suddenly very busy with casks or barrels, with brushes or pails, with meat or flour, with a mule in a cart, or an ox at a butcher's door, with anything and everything so that no one saw Carmelo.

He raised his head higher, and his eyes grew sterner and fiercer: he knew very well why these lazy laughter-loving people were all so suddenly busy and engrossed.

There was only Gigi Canterelli who ran once more out of his shop door and welcomed him with both hands.

'The beasts of the Municipality will never sup or dine in my back room any more,' thought he, 'but what matter—they must ruin me if they wish; I cannot let the good lad go by without a greeting.'

But his was the only greeting that welcomed Carmelo in all the length of the village street, though women and men both looked wistfully after him and said one to another : 'Poor lad, he was in the right; will it do to be friends with him, think you? God knows he is good as gold.'

He understood what they were thinking, and so did his companions.

'Oh, the shame of them! the cruelty of them!' thought Viola, trying not to let her tears fall. 'Instead of giving him welcome and sympathy!'

'Men and women are just like sheep,' thought her father. 'A crack of the whip and they scatter: they never stay by one that falls on the road.'

'It is not to be expected that they will get into trouble for the lad,' thought Cecco; 'and yet one would have fancied they would just have given him good day.'

Now on the steps of the Palazzo Communale there was lounging Bindo, in his guard's uniform, with his short sword swinging at his side, and his big memorandum book bulging out of his pocket; his hat was cocked on one side, and his moustaches were curled up to his eyes, and he looked very much as if he had stepped off the stage from taking part in an opera bouffe.

He saw the four persons coming past the building on their way from Pippo's house to the mill on the Rosa. He said to a carabinier who was also at the doorway, 'Come along with me, there is that blackguard out of prison.'

He swaggered down the steps and stood in the middle of the road so that they were obliged to pass him.

The face of Carmelo grew crimson and then livid as he saw the poisoner of Toppa.

'Here is this gaol bird,' called Bindo Terri out loud to the carabinier, as they went by. 'He will think twice before he assaults us again; but I will be bound he will end in the galleys. Keep your eye on him, brigadier, for he is dangerous.'

But for the pressure on his hand of Viola's entreating gesture, and the low supplication of old Pippo's quavering voice, the municipal guard would once more have measured his length on the dust under the weight of Carmelo's avenging arm.

For their sakes he mastered the passion that convulsed him. They passed on in silence, submissive to insult and to injury, as the people have always to be before the petty tyrannies that are called Law.

'Heed him not, my beloved,' said the maiden near him. 'Be calm and strong. That will be your best vengeance.'

They were words of wisdom, but life cannot always be guided by wisdom.

Old Annunziata met him now also. She had begun to hobble about again with the warm weather; she cried as she welcomed him: 'Oh, my dear lad,' she said, 'I shall always think it was myself with that basket of eggs that was the beginning of all your troubles.'

'Not you,' said Carmelo, kindly. 'Eggs or no eggs, these beasts would have done for me somehow.'

'But they brought it against you—'

'Yes, with lies tacked to it as you tack paper to a kite's tail to carry it higher,' said Cecco the cooper.

Then they all went on again, together.

They were all silent.

They were all thinking, What will he say when he sees the trees are down?

Carmelo, full of bitter thoughts and tender memories, did, indeed, strain his eyes eagerly along the road for the first sight of his father's house.

'There it is!' he cried eagerly as a turn in the river-road brought the white building with its red-tiled roof into view; then he stopped and drew a deep breath.

'But there are no trees!' he cried. Every one was silent.

'Has father cut them down?' he cried, staring all the while straight before him.

Then Viola took courage and answered him.

'They were taken by the municipality, dear; it seems there is some public thing to be done; they want the ground——'

She was dumb, as one of the terrible oaths of Italy that burn and harrow like vitriol rolled out of Carmelo's lips and made the listeners shudder.

He uttered nothing more, but walked on towards the mill-house where his father and his brothers and sisters were waiting for him at the little low gate.

They hung about him, and they kissed him, and wept over him, but he made them no caress in answer; he did not respond to them by any word or sign; even his youngest sister, little Isola, clinging about his knees, got no kiss from him; he looked only at his father, and from his father to the heaps of rubbish where the wood had been.

'You let that be done?'

'Son of mine,' said the miller, humbly and wearily, 'could you fight against the pricks? I could not.'

Carmelo dropped on the wooden bench by the

door above the stones where Toppa was buried, and buried his face in his hands. It was a sad home-coming.

The day was beautiful; the fields were in all their first summer greenness; the waters were green, too, with the reflection of them; the air was full of the scent of new-mown hay and of the vine-blossoms. His sister had made ready a plenteous meal; blackbirds and chaffinches sang in the hedge of arbutus and bay; the old place looked bright and kindly, but nothing changed the cloud on Carmelo's face, nothing made him smile.

He had been wronged, and a great wrong is to the nature as a cancer is to the body; there is no health.

Carmelo leaned his head on his arm and noticed none of them. It seemed to him that twenty years had rolled over him since the morning when, thinking no evil and fearing none, he had gone out on the grass to call the dog for his bread. It seemed to him that his very soul had been changed, and that in the stead of his heart there had been put into him a burning stone.

He loved Viola; the old happy, innocent, simple affection was still very sweet to him, but even that was dulled and dwarfed by his own immense anguish and wrath. A just chastisement may benefit a man, though it seldom does, but an unjust one changes all his blood to gall.

All pleasure in his future was gone out of him; all joy was dead. Some animal passions had awakened in him during his long isolation, but all peaceful serene happiness had perished. He did not reason on this, because he was but a simple unlearned youth, but he felt it, and he hated the world of men and doubted God.

The cooper Cecco, and the elder Pastorini, and the youngest of the sons tried to make a little mirth and gossipry; but in vain old wine was poured out, in vain the men strove to laugh and chatter; a great heaviness of sorrow and of dread was over all. Viola's face was as white as the narcissus poeticus hanging their fragrant bells in the strip of mill garden, and Carmelo scarcely tasted bit or drop. In the midst of the meal his youngest sister Isola, only seven years old, burst out crying.

'Carmelino has not kissed me once!' she said, amidst her sobs.

Carmelo looked up and his mouth and eyelids quivered. He rose, caught the child in his arms, and hurried out by the open door, and there, on the old oak seat above the stone that covered the body of the dog, he bent his face over the golden head of his little sister and wept bitterly.

Within doors Demetrio Pastorini struck the wooden table heavily with his clenched fist.

He had all his life been a most peaceful man, and a more harmless, jovial, kindly, easy in temper, and patient from sense of duty and love of quiet; but now all his blood stirred darkly within him.

'We are mules and bats, blind and dumb, and knowing not when we are smitten,' he said, with a deep rage in his thickened voice. 'We are more foolish than the beasts that perish, since we live and submit to our tormentors.'

They were all silent.

It was a sad home-coming.

## CHAPTER XXVII.

The Italians are patient to a great degree. There is here as much hunger as there is in Ireland, and there are proprietors as indifferent as the absentees, but here there is no agrarian crime, no revolt against masters or landlords, no effort to shirk just payments or even unjust ones.

'Our people do not understand their rights,' said a prefect to me. I thought: 'When they do—— well,—there will not be many prefects.'

This is the fact: they do not understand; they let their sons go to the conscription, their bread money to the municipal extortioners, their last tool in fine to the tax-gatherer, their last shirt in pawn to the Monte di Pietà, and then they shut themselves up and die of hunger secretly, or throw themselves in the river without a word of complaint to any one. They do not understand their rights, and they are not at all envious of the pretty happy people driving by with prancing horses. The cursing envy of the Irish or French poor is not in the Italian; if he can sit in the sun and cut a slice of melon in summer, a slice of sausage in winter, he is content, and ready to laugh and be merry with you.

Foreigners judge the Italians by Menotti's restless emigrants and Mazzini's mystic disciples, but in real truth these make up but a small portion of the nation; to the great bulk of it revolt is alien, and a good-humoured and docile obedience most natural.

Now, no doubt it would have been far better had Carmelo gone elsewhere to seek a living. But to the higher sort of Italian poor it never occurs to leave their home. The same love that bound Dante to the *cerchio antico* binds the Italian cotter or workman to his native village. When they are taken perforce away as by conscription they hunger ceaselessly till they see their hill-side farm or cottage in the plains. Emigration does not attract them; even a change to a near city or a neighbouring province appals them as a kind of expatriation.

'I want to go to my native country' (*paese nativo*), said one of the men in my employ. 'It is such a long time since I was there.'

By his native country he meant an olive-clad hill that rose in sight about two miles off; he had not been there since Pasqua, and he spoke on S. Giovanni's day!

The *paese nativo* is what they love, and to this sentiment their rulers owe their incredible and illimitable patience which forbears from revolution. Leave them in their *paese nativo*, and you may do almost any oppression or extortion to them that you will.

Therefore neither to him or his did it ever occur that Carmelo would do well to leave Santa Rosalia. Besides he was the elder son, and had always been promised that the mill should pass to him, after an old rule of the family that ignored all the primogeniture-abolition of '48.

The eldest Pastorini had always had the mill, and the others had always lived there if they liked, and worked at other trades; and Demetrio Pastorini was strongly conservative, as indeed every rural Italian is in mind and blood, abhorring change, and never understanding it, or being willing to allow for it in any way.

Therefore, as I say, there was no thought that Carmelo would do well to put some breadth of strange land between himself and his foes; but although things were going so ill at the mill-house, his marriage was never doubted or spoken of as a matter that would brook delay.

'They have suffered enough,' said Pastorini, 'and nothing will chase away the gloom that has gathered upon him like the face of the woman he loves always by him by day or by night.'

'My son,' he said therefore to Carmelo that night. 'You are come home to us in evil times. The trees are down, and never a soldo will I see for them. That is certain. The steam mill of Rossi's is taking all our custom away; some go because it gets done quick, and more go because they think to please the Syndic, and the gentlemen, that set it up there. I am not at all sure, my lad, that the place will bring us bread a year more. And I owe money, that I will not deny to you. I owe money, but I have not heart to stand in the way of the only joy you can grasp. You shall wed the girl to-morrow.'

So the very morning after his return, all formalities having been gone through well-nigh twelve months before, they went quietly and with no mirth up to the church of San Giuseppe, and were wedded before the altar by Dom Lelio.

There were few dry eyes there amongst their friends: she had thought of little Raggi, and had put an almond sprig in her bosom off the tree that grew by the little grave, and the two old men stood beside her, careworn, and with a vague and ghastly dread weighing on their souls.

Would these two, whose lives were made one, find anything in the future except toil and pain? Would their children be begotten for anything beyond hunger and care? Would they be allowed to see their years go by in such peace as sweetens labour? Would not their hearts be harrowed and their cupboards bare?

There would be enough if they were let alone, but not enough for tax and fine, for torment and extortion.

Carmelo said very little. He felt scarce any joy. The dull, sullen shame of his captivity was still on him. The bitter rage of his wrongs suffocated almost all gentler thoughts, all tenderer emotions. He loved the maiden who had been so true to him; but the days of dalliance seemed gone for ever from him: he said to himself, 'Have I a right to procreate innocent creatures to be as wretched as I have been, and to bear the burdens that our people bear?'

For he had learned to think, in the long watches of those nights, in hospital and prison; and all that the communist had taught him was for ever fermenting in his mind.

The marriage service was said and over very early in the morning, for they wished to make no fuss, and draw no eyes upon them, save the kindly ones of a few old neighbours who had known them both from their birth. The child Isola had gathered a great bunch of the wild narcissus, which filled the church with its fragrance; that was their only emblem of rejoicing. Viola wore the grey gown she had laid aside in the past summer; and the good vicar blessed them with a quiver in his voice, and they went as quietly and sadly home again; the stick of old

Pippo keeping tune and time on the stones with Annunziata's crutch.

Then every one went to his work again, and there was no attempt at any kind of festivity: it would have been unfitting, and Carmelo would have had no heart for such a thing.

He and Viola went home with the old man to the little square house to break bread with him ere she departed for ever. They had offered to live with him there a few months before taking up their abode at the mill; but Pippo had refused the offer, sweet as it was to him, for he said to himself: 'They will distrain all I have: the girl will be best away from that.'

He had a little meal for them, and they sat at it silently: no one had appetite to eat. It was like a funeral rather than a bridal feast. None of the broad jokes common at such times were heard, and no levity could lift its head under such sorrow.

It wrung the heart of Viola to leave the old man all alone to do his chores, and make his bread and bed; but Pippo, harshly at the last, said that he would have it so, and so best liked it: and she submitted.

The mill was but half-a-mile off down the river: she promised herself that she would run in to him a dozen times a day to do all that was needed. With the miller's three girls there would be little for her to do in her father-in-law's house, and Carmelo was fond of Pippo.

Pippo filled a glass with wine and lifted it solemnly upward.

'My girl,' he said gravely, 'be as good a wife as you have been a good child to me, and you will be as a vein of gold to those you go to dwell with. You have had sore trouble here. May it never find you where you go now. Demetrio, drink with me: health and long life to your son and your son's sons when you and I be underneath the sod.'

Then, with twilight, the young people went away to the mill-house, where there were now no nightingales safe in leafy trees to sing through the hours of their nuptial night; and old Pippo was left alone in his little, dull, and quiet place, where there was no sound but of the Rosa water breaking on the sand beneath the willows.

He looked through his back door at little Raggi's grave.

'My wee dog,' he said to it. 'I shall soon be like you now. Let the thieves come and seize; they cannot get blood out of a post; and it does not matter for me, since you and the girl are gone.'

Then he sat him down by the cold hearth, with his hands on his knees, and his head on his breast, and never stirred till midnight came.

## CHAPTER XXVIII.

WITH the return of mild weather Annunziata had lost her rheumatic pains, and had been able to get off her bed and put on her huge leather boots, that had once belonged to a cattle-dealer, and begin to go about again, up and down the near hills, and to and fro the roads.

The poor old soul had always been certain in

her own mind that her basket of eggs had been at the bottom of Carmelo's troubles, and she never could forgive herself for having complained about them, especially as when the case was brought on at Pomodoro, where it had been sent by Messer Nellemane, she had been forced to attend as an accuser, and had cried so much that the Pretore had abused her, and had felt a great deal more remorse than Pompéo of Sestriano did when they ordered him six weeks' imprisonment.

'And know another time, you, that it is a breach of the law to conceal a theft, and that such concealment on the part of the person robbed makes such person liable to heavy penalties,' had thundered the young judge at Annunziata, who had cried again as if her heart would break, but, being an obstinate old woman, would insist on answering that she could not for the life of her see why anybody should mind her being robbed if she did not.

'That shows how lamentably, how culpably, ignorant you are of the first rudiments of morality and public duty,' said the Pretore, who was as like Messer Nellemane in his ideas and his expressions of them, as a green bunch of grapes is like a ripened one. He was exactly like him, without his mellowed suavity, and exquisite patience with foolish people, which were gifts of time and nature that Messer Nellemane had carefully cultivated with a view to the future, when he should be a Minister, and hold the heart of the State in his hands.

Annunziata had still gone on crying, having seen the smith of Sestriano led off by carabiniers.

'And he will murder me when he comes out,' she had cried, 'and small blame will it be to him, the poor thing, for he was drunk as drunk could be, or never would he have touched the eggs!'

'If he murder you, he will go to the galleys,' had said the guards as they took her away.

'And what good will that be to me when I am dead?' had said 'Nunziatina. 'And he is a good man enough when the drink is not in him; that I have always told you.'

On the whole, the ungovernable resolution to have her own way, and the answers that she had thus made to those in authority over her, had produced an impression against her in the minds of all the officials, who had agreed that she was an insolent and cantankerous old woman.

'If there were but a Vagrant Act, I would consign her to the lock-up at once,' had said the Pretore to Messer Nellemane, who said in his turn:

'I think the Cavaliere Durellazzo will bring in something of the kind; we are overrun with beggars; but, of course, unless this larger commune do the same, it will scarcely be effective.'

'I will speak to our Syndic,' had answered the Pretore.

The Syndic of Pomodoro was the elder brother of that excellent Count Saverio who was the president of the charitable Confraternità di San Francesco di Asissi.

'Are there many mendicants about?' the Syndic had asked his brother, after having been spoken to by the Pretore.

Count Saverio had thrown up his hands, implying that they were many as the sands of the sea.

'They are a great anxiety to us,' he had added, 'for they are always applying to us, and you know our rules do not permit us to relieve beggars. It there were any law by which one could deal with them——'

'There ought to be one,' had said the Syndic of Pomodoro. I will speak to Durellazzo.'

So in the council chamber of the Giunta in the Palazzo Communale, Messer Nellemane had known very well that it was the marriage day of Viola, but was at the same time enjoying such a victory of reason over prejudice that he had no time to indulge in any of the sentiments of a passion disappointed and outrivalled.

By his representations to the Cav. Durellazzo, and the Cav. Durellazzo's representations to the Giunta, he had succeeded in having adopted for Vezzaja and Ghiralda, as he and the Pretore had desired, the laws of the cities against vagrancy and mendicancy.

There had been a strong prejudice against this course in the Giunta; for Italians, until their humanity is effaced by Impiegatism, do not incline to severity; climate and custom alike making them lenient.

But Cav. Durellazzo read a report prepared by his secretary, and endorsed by himself, that presented quite appalling evidence of the persons who lived by beggary or alms of some sort. The order of which Messer Nellemane is the type, is never greater or happier than when preparing a report of this kind, which, dealing with the exact science of statistics, deals a death-blow to those unproductive and erratic classes which every bureaucracy abhors.

The report concluded with a short moral essay on the beauties of providence and industry, and the patriotism and public spirit that were required in all members of the public to enable them to extinguish their individual sentiments and private pity, and look on the question from the higher standing-point of general interest and the good of all humanity.

It was a very warm day in March; the council chamber was small, and, as children say, stuffy; the Giunta was half asleep, and all that was awake of it was longing for a flask of wine; the voice of the Cavaliere Durellazzo was sonorous, but provocative of somnolence; the Giunta assented to the new law with the pliancy of men whose bodies are moist, and whose throats are dry; it was embodied in an appendix of thirty-five new regulations and sent to the Prefect to be approved.

This is a mere form, like sending a death warrant to a sovereign.

The Prefect approved of course, naturally; first of all, it was not his interest to quarrel with the commune; secondly, he assented to these new rules without even thinking what the long documents forwarded to him meant. He was in a hurry to get to the city races, and he also was warm.

The prefect's secretary sent them to the Home Minister, but he was in all the fiery heat of conflict on Montecitorio, and had much to do to keep his own place, and had no time to give to the affairs of a remote municipality hidden away under corn and vines. He assented too: it is always the strongest possible point with ministers and prefects that the country communes are autonomous. When somebody remarked to him that they were ill governed, he said it was their own fault: if they chose to elect asses, they must; it was no business of anybody's. So the law against vagrants was incorporated into the code of Vezzaja and Ghiralda, and was pasted up upon the walls in large letters, which, as nine-tenths of the population could not read, was not to any great purpose.

There, alas! were a great many old folks too old to do anything, who lived with their families, and who, to avoid being a burden to them, went about to all the villas and got pence here, bread there, a cup of *mezzovino*, or an old bundle of scraps, as it might chance. If you had called these people beggars, they would have been amazed. They were all well known, never asked for what was not offered to them, and had been hard-working men and women until their sight or their limbs had failed them.

These old folks the new rules stunned and slew like a pole-axe.

They did no harm; not a mite of harm; and as the State provided no poor-house for them, they could not see that there was any such very great guilt in taking from their richer neighbours a little aid that the richer were never harmed by, and gave willingly.

But, in these days, Christian Europe decides that not only the poor man lying by the wayside, but also the Samaritan who helps him, are sinners against political economy, and its law forbids what its religion orders: people must settle the contradiction as they deem best; they generally are content to settle it by buttoning up their pockets and passing by on the other side. This was the consequence of the new rules for the suppression of mendicancy in Vezzaja and Ghiralda.

Now the suppression of mendicancy is a very good thing; but, as you never can suppress poverty, it would be better to provide a substitute for him before you shelve the Samaritan.

I know a very good man last winter who gave away soup-tickets to all who asked him; and he could not understand how anybody wanted anything more. Now a bowl of soup is a very good thing; but I never knew anybody who could live on it, and I have known a good many who felt ashamed to present the ticket and take the soup there in public. Why are you expected to have no sensitive nerves and no pride because you are starving? I cannot see why you should be myself; but it is a fact that such things are not permitted to you.

Messer Nellemane went a step farther than my good man: he thought people should not have soup at all unless they bought it.

His rules were framed on this principle, which he considered to be a sound and healthy one; and as they were also adopted for the larger commune of Pomodoro-Carciofi, he thought they would sweep the land as clean as a steam reaper-and-binder sweeps a corn field, leaving gleaners empty-handed.

As none of the old men and women involved, understood anything at all of these fresh laws, printed up in big type on the walls of the Communal Palace, they were swept into the net as easily as quails are at Naples.

If a regiment of the blind, the infirm, and the very aged would have been any use to the Minister of War, he could have had a large one from these nettings of Messer Nellemane.

But, alas! they were of no use for anything; and, being nigh their end, so took it to heart when they were locked up that most of them died incontinently; and though nobody really would believe it, for it sounds too absurd, many a humble little home under the pines of the hill-side, or down amongst the maize and vines of the level ground was the sadder, because an old granddam or grandsire sat no more on the wooden settle cheerily telling the tale of his day's wanderings.

These laws came into effect on the first day of June, just twenty days after Carmelo and Viola were married, and one fine afternoon, as Annunziata was trotting about with her stick, feeling happy because her rheumatism was gone for the moment, and because her girl was happily wedded, she was touched on the shoulder by Bindo Terri, the municipal guard, and arrested.

In vain she wept, and prayed, and sobbed, and moaned that she had always been an honest woman. She was a mendicant under the Act; she had no private means of subsistence, nor did she work for her living; she was clearly a mendicant.

She was taken off to the guard-house with her basket, full of scraps and pence and odds and ends, as proof of her guilt, found upon her, and without any more words or any hearing at all, was carried away to Pomodoro and there consigned to prison.

'It is the new law,' said Bindo, and that was all he would say to her: he was very stern and very arrogant, and very much puffed up with this addition to the joys and the powers of his office.

'Do not tell Carmelo; for the of love God, do not tell, or he will come burning the town down to get me out!' cried the simple soul to Bindo.

And so distraught and wretched was this poor old trot at the thought of the disgrace and sorrow she should bring on those she loved, that she fretted herself in half an hour into such a state of body and mind, that the gaoler forthwith pronounced her in his own mind to be mad, and sent her to the same hospital where young Carmelo had languished through the winter nights and spring-tide days.

It was precisely for such cases as hers that the Confraternità di S. Francesco had been instituted, but, as the modern moralities of that society forbade them to encourage beggars, the Count Saverio, though he heard of her case, could not on principle bestir himself on her behalf.

He was, indeed, at the moment he heard of it, occupied with his stock-broker, who interested him much more, and he said quickly to the clerk who told him of it:

'A vagrant; a confirmed mendicant. No, we could not interfere; it would be an injurious example. We are bound to take broad views: to consider the public.'

Meantime, Bindo hied quickly homeward and said to his young brother, who resembled him as one pea resembles another:

'I took up the old 'Nunziatina this morning. Let some lad go say so at the millhouse; best not go yourself.'

The lad winked and ran off; half an hour later, as the family at the mill were sitting down to their frugal noonday meal, Viola and Carmelo at the places that would be theirs all their lives, a grinning youngster looked in at the house door and cried to them:

'Your old woman is in prison—the new law's out to day!—they have taken her to the town——'

Then he ran away swiftly to escape from the chastisement he merited.

They all rose to their feet; Viola was trembling very much:

'It cannot be true. It cannot be true. They never would touch 'Nunziatina. All the world knows her!'

'I will go and see,' said Carmelo, and his face was very dark.

'No!' said Demetrio Pastorini. 'Get not yourself into more trouble. Most like it is but an idle word. Stay you with your wife; and Dante, do you harness me Bigio.'

'Nay, father, that cannot be,' said Carmelo. 'It is Viola's aunt that is in peril and misery. Come with me if you will, but let me go.'

'Be it so,' said Pastorini. 'But remember, for the love of the saints, no violence. You are not alone in life now.'

Carmelo looked out of the door at the bank of mud, where once had been his bright *boschetto*.

'We are slaves,' he said bitterly. 'Slaves can but submit.'

'What did my brother die for in the wars?' said his father.

Viola entreated to go with them, and, being not a month after her marriage, neither man could find heart to refuse her.

The way to Pomodoro, as the way to all things southward, lay along that river road which was to be disfigured by the tramway at such time as speculators and municipalities should have finished their squabbles. There was a short cut that passed by her grandfather's cottage, too narrow for waggons and carriages, but broad enough for a little *baroccio* like the miller's.

They passed that way to save time, and say a word to Pippo.

But as they drew nigh the cottage, close enough to discern the blue Madonna, Viola, whose eyes were quickest to see their beloved little, humble home, cried out:

'*Nonno* is moving away!—moving away and never telling us!'

Carmelo checked the horse and sprang to the ground: his cheeks grew very white; his teeth clenched; he had caught sight of other figures than Pippo's amidst the chairs and tables, the mattresses and saucepans, the bowls and jugs that were put out in a heap beyond the door.

The figures he had seen were the Usciere and his assistants, two straggling do-nothings of the place, who lent themselves to this despised office for sake of the two francs a day they got by it, and the pleasure of seeing the pain of better people than themselves, which is a joy to scoundrels, always.

'Your grandsire is only cleaning, Viola,' he said hurriedly. 'Only cleaning his things. I think I will go and help him if you will go on with father to Pomodoro.'

But Viola also had seen what he had seen.

'They are *selling* his things!' she said, with a piercing scream, and ere either man could stay her she had sprung off the cart on to the shaft, and from the shaft on to the ground, and had run onward across the path into the house.

The elder Pastorini threw the reins on his grey

steed's back, and got down likewise. Carmelo was already on the grass.

'Oh, *nonno, nonno*, what is it?' cried Viola, as she ran into the entrance room, and saw her grandfather sitting there in his basket chair by the cold hearth, just as he had done through all the long, lonely evening of her nuptial day.

Pippo lifted his head; his face was set and stern, but calm.

'They are selling the old things,' he said. 'I thought they could not get blood out of a post, but it seems they can.'

Then he put his pipe in his mouth again.

Viola threw herself on her knees by the old man, and hid her face on his arm.

'Oh, *nonno, nonno!*' she moaned, 'why did you not let me stay with you? I would never have left you if I had known.'

'No,' said the old man, with his mouth quivering a little on the pipe stem that it clenched. 'I knew well you wouldn't, my lass. You were aye thoughtful of me. But you could have done not a mite of good, and you would only have lost your own joy.'

On the threshold Carmelo had seized by the shoulders one of the men who was carrying out the bed that had been Viola's, and was shouting in his ear:

'Thief, and the servant of thieves, let go! Carry off one of these things from this house and I will brain you all——'

Then old Pippo rose, and struck on the floor with his stick.

'Carmelo, son of Demetrio,' he cried in a stern

loud voice. 'You are wedded-mate to my girl, but you are no master of mine, and in my house have no voice. What I bid you do, do; but nought else. Come quiet to my side, and let them work their will.'

Obedience and respect to elders are fine old primitive virtues that are still strong, like the olive and the chestnut on their hills, in the heart of the Italian. Carmelo heard, and hesitated a moment, then took his hand off the man's shoulders, and looked wistfully at Pippo.

'You will not resist?' he muttered.

'Where is the good of resisting? When you cannot make resistance good, it is but a silliness and a paltriness. They are stronger than we. They take the goods. Let them, and go your ways. Make not your wife mourn for you in the Murata; that would be harder to bear than loss of cup and platter, bed and board.'

Carmelo stood still, like a chidden child.

Outside the elder Pastorini was speaking with the Usciere, begging for delay, and praying of him to put back the goods into the house.

'If you pay me this sum down now, I will, though it is late,' said the Usciere.

Demetrio Pastorini felt a mist in his eyes, and a ball in his throat.

The figures that he saw were a total of nigh two hundred francs, nigh 8*l*. if you put it in English sovereigns, and Demetrio had no money at home, nay, was in debt to more than one, now that the steam mill took from him the wheat of more than half the peasantry; for folks will run to what is new, and what is popular, and what brings them credit.

He stood irresolute, meditating whether he could

raise money by any means, and the men went on with their work, hauling out into the open air the poor sticks that made the furniture of Pippo. Rich and rare things look sorry when thus treated and thrown together in the sun and dust; these poor little things of Pippo's looked little more than fit for firewood or the dust-heap.

'They give us all this trouble,' said the Usciere, like an ill-used man. 'They give us all this trouble with their obstinacy, and we take all they have, and then when it is all put together it is not worth a kick from a dog.'

He gave a shove as he spoke to the mound of things, and a copper vessel or two rolled down in a clatter.

They were all silent; the assistants were making a great noise bringing down the steep stone stair an old chest of drawers, older than Pippo himself. It was the chest in which Viola had kept her mother's wedding gown until the day of her own marriage, with the orange leaves and the lavender to drive away the moths.

Viola, on her knees by the old man's side, was rocking herself violently to and fro, weeping.

'And Annunziata, Annunziata!' she murmured in her sobs.

Carmelo stood aloof; his arms folded, his face very dark.

'What of her?' asked Pippo.

'They have taken her up; she is in prison; they call her a beggar.'

Pippo gave a short hard laugh, as his teeth still held the pipe stem.

'Why don't they get out the guns, and set us all

in a row, and fire us down? 'twould be quicker done, and easier.'

'It is the new law,' said the voice of the Usciere, who was lending a hand to get out the walnut drawers.

'Law, law, law!' muttered Pippo, with his eyes savage like a wild cat's, under his white eyebrows. 'There's law for this and that and t'other, till the land is sick; but there's no law against the poor starving to death: there's no law against their dying naked on the naked floor. Will you tax the mother's breasts next, or the babe's swaddling clothes? You're ripe to do it. But the mothers should cheat you, and dash out the brains of their sucklings on the house wall, ere they be old enough to sweat and pine and drag the cannon for the State that curses them.'

Then the old man dashed his pipe upon the ground and rose.

'Get you all gone to Annunziata,' he said, as he forced Viola roughly from the ground. 'Get you gone to her, and leave me alone with the thieves. I have the roof above me yet, and I am not a maiden to mourn for a lost looking-glass. I can lie on the floor well enow, and a bit of dry bread needs no platter. Get you gone.'

They had no choice but to obey him. Carmelo's downcast lowering eyes, and compressed and pallid lips told his father with how violent an effort did he keep down his arm and his words; his father knew, too, that this effort was strung, nearly to breaking point, and he was thankful that Pippo's will set him free to carry away the lad ere he should do to these enemies what no man could absolve or efface.

They got up into the cart again, and drove on by the edge of the river; Viola was still weeping convulsively.

'Grandfather, who has led such an honest, hardworking life, and never owed one penny!' she said amidst her tears. 'And what is it all for? It is not a debt. It is no debt, and who has any right to make these claims?—'

Carmelo's hand grasped hers.

He could not speak.

All the words of the dead German were echoing in his ears, and he was saying to himself, as Pippo had done,

'How long, O Lord? O Lord?'

Viola thought to herself with shrinking and sorrow:

'If I had let Messer Gaspardo make a bad woman of me, all these my dear ones would not have suffered thus.'

And no doubt Messer Nellemane was the cause of all their woes.

But what shall we say of the State and the Law that make Messer Nellemane possible?

## CHAPTER XXIX.

THE cart drove on, and the old man Pippo sat himself down in the chimney corner, though it was a warm day, and fine of course, and saying never a word, and making no sign, he let the plunderers carry on their work of pillage. The spirit had gone out of him; something of vacancy had come over his face and into his eyes; his hands were joined on his knees, and he kept muttering:

'Two and three make five, and four is nine, and six is fifteen——'

And so on through all the numerals; he was adding up all the sums that the municipality had claimed from him; those that had been paid by him, and those for which the law was now seizing his goods.

It was a long sum, and it bothered his head; he had never been good at figures.

He sat there till it was quite dark; long after the distrainers had ransacked every hole and corner, and carried off every pot and pan, and gone away leaving him nought but his four bare walls and the roof above him.

When it was quite dark, and the stars were beginning to tremble in the summer skies, the cart came by his door again and stopped, and Viola came to him.

She was shivering very much and sobbing. Pippo did not either hear or see her at first; the figures were in his ears, in his heart, in his brain, before his sight. She had to shake him by the shoulder to rouse him; and even then he looked stupid.

'What did you find?' he said then, and he thought his mouth moved with difficulty, and his tongue seemed fastened.

'We found her locked up,' sobbed his granddaughter. 'And we could do nothing, nothing. They will not let her out, and she is so wretched, and I feared all the while that Carmelo would break into some violence; it was all his father and I could do to keep him still——'

'They have locked her up, have they?'

'Yes! And she is always crying to them to let her see the sun!' and Viola's tears choked her voice as she spoke.

'They have locked her up, have they?' said Pippo stupidly. 'And they have taken all my things. Well, I do not know, my lass, why folk should try to be decent and honest; we are fools for our pains.'

Then he turned round to the cold fireplace once more and began counting.

'Two and three make five, and four is nine, and six is fifteen——'

Viola went to the door and spoke.

'Let me stay with him this night; I cannot leave him alone; indeed, indeed, I cannot!'

'I will stay too,' said Carmelo; and he came down from the cart, and bade his father drive home.

Pippo did not notice him; he was always counting.

There was no light but from the moon, for the men of the law had taken away both lamp and oil. There was nothing to use; nothing to serve; no table to spread.

Viola, checking her bitter sobs, sought in the old wall-cupboards she knew so well for a broken plate or a bent spoon, but all was gone. There was only a little rusty tin can and a half-loaf of bread; nothing else anywhere was to be found in all the house.

Carmelo stooped down and made a little fire with some charcoal-dust that lay in the stove, and she pumped some fresh water, and put it, with some of the bread, and an onion, from the garden in the little pot to boil. There was not a stoup of wine nor a pinch of rice in all the place.

All this while Pippo was busy counting. The young people crouched together on the ground, and the old man sat on the wooden settle; the white moon shone in through the square window; the room was full of smoke and bad smells from the steam-mill; in other years at this season every chamber had been sweet with the scent of the lilacs by the river.

Suddenly a mouse ran across the feet of Pippo; the mouse roused him; he lifted his head from his breast and saw the figures of his children crouching together on the stones in the moonlight.

Then he looked round the empty, naked room, and laughed a little harshly.

'They have got blood out of a post; they have got blood out of a post, have my gentlemen. They think I'll kill myself like Nanni. It's four hundred and sixty-five francs in all, and I am to drive my brook underground, and spend all my mint of money on masons and engineering folk. What would the king say? what would the king say? And the old woman locked up like a purse-lifter or a trull. This is what we lit up our oil for the day after San Martino! There's the moon, but where's the lilacs? I don't smell them. What's that smoke coming in my house? What smoke is that? Get out, you foul thing, get out! They have sold me up, but I am master here yet!'

He got on his feet and struck at the smoke wildly, beating the air with his hands; then, finding nothing resist him, he looked round angrily, and slowly recognised Carmelo and Viola.

'Why wait you here?' he said thickly. 'Go you home, my dears. You are lovers still, and the night is sweet to you; get you home. Nay, I would be alone. I have my house over my head; I am not out in the street yet.'

And he would take no denial, but thrust them away almost roughly, and shut to the door; then he sat himself down again, and again began counting, 'Two and three make five, and four are nine, and six make fifteen,' and so on through all the figures they had brought against him, repeating them over and over again, all through the dreary hours of the night.

'He will lose his mind, saying over those figures!' sobbed Viola, as they stood in the night air, no more, as of old, clear, silvery and sweet, but full of noxious steam and stench.

Carmelo wound his arm about her; he dared not trust himself to speak.

## CHAPTER XXX.

THE law has been compared by some writers to Fate. It may, perhaps, be more accurately compared to the Juggernaut, which rolls on regardless whether it crushes straw or diamonds, youth or age, beauty or deformity.

The Juggernaut having been set in motion by Messer Nellemane, it rolled over Pippo quite regardless of his circumstances; and a few mornings after the Usciere had taken away everything except the little rusty pot, the law, which is never conscious of being ridiculous, served a summons to this old destitute man to pay sixty francs for a month's delay in executing the work above the running water commanded by the commune.

Pippo could not read, but he knew the look of the summons paper with the arms of the province a-top of its long pages. He laughed a shrill, hard little laugh, and twisted the paper up and lit his pipe with it.

He had a stupid and vacant look on his face, and he was very taciturn; and when alone at work could always be heard muttering over and adding up those figures; but he had set his back up straight against his lot; he would not die like Nanni.

He went on with his basket-work and vegetable garden; one neighbour brought in an old chair, and another a kettle, and another some cracked plates, and Dom Lelio lent him a mattress; and so Pippo began life again at nigh seventy years of age; an age when hope is only a remembered thing, like a fair bird flown away long ago down the golden mists of the valley of youth.

They had been allowed to see 'Nunziatina once more, but the interview was but added pain to her and to themselves. She was almost distraught; her dim eyes were streaming with tears, and her voice was hoarse with screaming. She could be made to understand nothing; she could not fancy anything except that they thought her guilty of some crime.

'Let me get out; let me go free!' she was crying with all her force. 'I want the air; I want to see the sky. This is the day I am always to go to Varammista for my bread, and the pretty foreign child comes and gives me something more herself, and smiles with her blue eyes; let me get out; I have got a rose at home on purpose for the little miss; let me go to my own home. I shall die away from my own house.'

The little musty place where she had cooked and worked, and eaten and slept for forty years, ever since her husband's death, was dearer to her than her palace to a queen.

'Dear lad, don't you get into trouble for me,' she said to Carmelo. 'But let me out they must. I have done no harm at all. I only want to go home. Tell them to let me go home; I don't want a cart or anything; I can walk every step of the way.'

But no one would let her out; and there they had to leave her. But for the entreating pressure of Viola's hand upon his arm, Carmelo would have done that day what would have lodged him anew in the Carcere of Pomodoro. Sadly they had left her, and sadly they had returned.

Carmelo had only one thing of any value in the world; it was a watch that his grandfather had given him, leaving it to him by will as to his favourite. It was an old silver watch, two hundred years old, with fine *repoussé* work of cherubs and foliage around it: it went well still, and was as big as a peach. Carmelo loved and honoured it so that he never wore it except on feast-days and Sundays. He wound it up only on those rarer occasions; at other times it lay in his drawer, wrapped in a silk handkerchief.

The day after he had seen Annunziata for the second time, in the prison of Pomodoro, he waited carefully till Viola was busy washing linen and his father was out of sight; then he stepped upstairs, took the watch out of its drawer and slipped it in his pocket. Then he went and harnessed the mule.

'I am going to take that flour back to Varammista,' he called in at the kitchen window.

The flour had been ground for the fattore of that place. His brothers helped him up with the sacks, and he drove away, no one thinking that he was on any uncommon errand.

He drove to Varammista (where unhappily he found the owners who liked Annunziata were absent), and left his sacks with their fattore, then on into the town that he hated. His face was flushed, and he carried his head high as he went through the streets. He fancied everyone was pointing at him.

There was a shop in the place that was a jeweller's and an antiquity seller's, both in one, kept by a man of whom in the happy weeks before his marriage Carmelo had bought some little coral and silver earrings for Viola.

Carmelo walked into the shop now, and held out the watch. 'How much?' he asked.

The jeweller stared, and took the watch in one hand; he had often seen and often coveted it.

'Twenty francs?' he said, hesitatingly. 'You know it will only sell for old silver. No one will buy a watch that is not new.'

'That is a lie,' said Carmelo, 'for you told me yourself that all that work round it made it of value; yourself, you said so two years ago, at the wine fair, when I showed it you.'

'I only said that to please you,' said the jeweller, who, however, longed for the watch.

After chaffing and disputing a quarter of an hour, Carmelo was sick of heart, and said passionately:

'Give me fifty francs, and you shall have it. You know well enough I would not let it go but for some dire necessity.'

'You are always in trouble,' said the jeweller testily; but he paid the money and locked the old watch up in a desk: he knew a collector of such things who would give him ten napoleons any day for it.

Carmelo went out of the shop; his face was a dusky red; he felt ashamed. But he kept to his purpose. He took the fifty francs and went to the prison. If anyone would pay so much caution money as guarantee that the offence would not be repeated, those guilty of begging were let go out again.

'My father has sent me to pay the money for 'Nunziatina,' he said unsteadily to the gaoler. 'May she come out with me now?'

'Ugh! We do not do things as fast as all that,' they said to him.

Nevertheless, they were obliged to abide by their own rules, and the next night Annunziata, weeping and laughing, was at home in her own room.

Viola missed the watch.

'Oh, my love, how good you are!' she cried.

Carmelo blushed and shook his head.

'Do not praise me, sweetheart. Your people are mine.'

After that action something of the gloom and bitterness that had been on him, lifted, and once or twice he smiled his old merry smile, and little Isola threw her arms about him, and cried:

'Oh, Carmelino mio! Forget all the wicked men, and let us be happy.'

'I will forget them if they will let me, dear,' said Carmelo.

And so he would, and, thus forgetting, would have been a blameless, useful, and contented man.

But the State, which creates Messer Nellemane, does not care to have useful, harmless, and contented men in its cities and communes. It thinks it of far greater importance that no dog should be seen in the streets, no poverty be exempt from a tax, and no man be able to call his soul his own; it likes to have its *gros bataillons* of unwilling conscripts, and it thinks it more profitable to have its galleys and its hospitals full than to remit a tax, or cease to keep ten clerks to do the work of one.

## CHAPTER XXXI.

PASTORINI grew very anxious; his many boys and girls had always been as much as he could find food and clothes for in the best of times, and now they were very heavy on him. Dina indeed was to marry in a year or so, but her betrothed was poor. The other girls were all young and, though handy and helpful, could not bring in anything; and though, when plenty of grist came to the mill, he could make ends meet, now that Rossi's iron servant took two-thirds of the grain away he grew very harassed, and afraid, especially as he foresaw, as I have said, that with the summer the water would be shallower than ever now that the trees were gone; and in effect it had become so as early as June, a thing never known before, and the big black wheels stood high and dry with the weeds on them dying in the sun, whilst farther below on the Rosa the black devil, as the people called it, vomited smoke and worked all day and all night.

It was a hideous blot on the landscape; it spread dirt and dust and poisonous vapours all around it; and the little children near it grew pallid and sickly little things instead of the Correggio-like loves, all rosy and brown, that they had been. But Messer Nellemane, sitting before the Nuova Italia (though, if he had confessed the truth, he was choked by the smoke as well as lesser people) said to everyone:

'What a pleasure it is to see that pillar of progress arisen in our midst;' and all Santa Rosalia understood, by his look and his smile, that whosoever would wish to please the municipality must carry his grain to Remigio Rossi.

The place had been, of yore, sweet with the scent of the flowers on the river-bank according to each season, of the meadow-thyme and the fragrant yellow tulip, of the vine-blossom and the sturdy rosemary, of the acacias and the catalpas, of the magnolias and the Chinese olives; now there was only a stench of oil and hot iron, and the smoke of burning lignite; but the present generation has been taught to think this is a change for the better, and Messer Nellemane was essentially a man of modern mind.

An engine smelt sweeter to him than a lilac-bush; and he thought hurry, strife, noise, and money-making much finer things than 'fair quiet, and sweet rest.'

Dear Old Leisure, with his smile of peace and hands of blessing, was but an old-fashioned obstructionist to him.

The last day of the past month of March had been the day on which the first half-yearly payment of the interest of his mortgage was due from Pippo; an interest of fifty per cent., which, on a loan of three hundred francs with all the costs thereof—as he phrased it, a hundred scudi—was a hundred and fifty every twelve months.

Pippo had by no means understood what mortgages were; the law of hypothec was Greek to him; when the day came round, of course he had not the money, and truly had never in any way realised the arrangement to which he had put his cross before witnesses. The time went by without any great disquietude, except that uneasy sense of debt and burden which was so new and horrible to him. His head had got muddled, and as he could not read he could not clear himself by any study of papers.

When the Usciere had seized his things he had said to himself: 'I shall have to tell that advocate down in Pomodoro, for I never will be able to pay him aught yearly.'

But his head never seemed right now; he forgot things, and could not recollect words very often when he wanted them, and so the matter kept slipping his mind, and when he remembered it he thought to himself: 'Well, he will get the house at my death, so he will be no loser.'

That was his unlearned view of hypothec.

The lawyer neither sent nor wrote to him, so naturally he was confirmed in his delusion. It was now August, and in his empty home he was making a good fight against fortune. His work brought him in, on an average, not eighty centimes a day, but that was enough for his few and frugal wants.

'If my health only will serve,' he said to himself, weaving the osiers that he had now to buy, 'I should like to see Viola's boy on my knees.'

That fancy kept up his spirit, though his head would always buzz. The child would be best unborn, he knew, but still he wished to live to see it.

Now to Messer Nellemane there were a perverseness and almost an insolence in this old man, so very small, poor, and helpless, presuming to live on, and lift his head up again after such a series of deserved chastisements as he had received.

To see Pippo sitting at work in the doorway was irritating to him, and not atoned for by the fact that Pippo was surrounded as he sat by all the foul fumes and vapours of the steam mill across the river. And there was the running water, too, always bubbling across the roadway, and the months slipping away one after another, with the old man still at liberty to sit in the air and mock the municipal majesty by disobedience.

What was to be done?

Messer Nellemane was for ever turning over the problem in his mind, and even stooped to the humility of asking the advice of the deputy of Pomodoro, who was in the neighbourhood, being on the point of marriage with the Zauli heiress.

'I should have the work executed if really necessary for the public good,' said Signore Luca Finti gravely, 'and then I should debit the offending proprietor with the cost of the works. That is the usual course taken in Rome.'

Messer Nellemane thanked his distinguished adviser cordially, and proceeded to get out several blank forms, signed by the Cavaliere Durellazzo, which it was needful to fill in before acting.

The whole of Santa Rosalia was in a mess with public works; those for the steam mill had left heaps of black rubbish about, those for the tramway had left many mounds of as yet unlaid iron rails; the old bridge, which was as firm as a rock, and quite wide enough for the bullocks and mules that alone passed over it, was being pulled about and widened by the Giunta; altogether the pretty little green village had that dusty, unkempt, stony, desolate look which so many 'improved' places have in Rome and Venice, and which is an aspect always as sweet to the municipalic mind, as a wasted province is to a conqueror.

The conqueror sees his victories in the smoking fields; the Municipality sees its commissions and concessions in the rubbish heaps.

So one day Pippo had several workpeople whom he knew, masons and plumbers and the like, come about his premises; and they made as though they would pass through the house into the kitchen garden behind where Raggi was buried under the willows. But Pippo slammed the door in their faces.

'No, no,' said he, 'they have taken all I had out of it, but the four walls are mine still. Into it not a man comes without my leave and license.'

The men beat on the door, and told him through the door that they came to work for the municipality.

'You don't come to work for me; and into my house you come not,' said Pippo. 'A hundred scudi your municipality has robbed me of, and I do not open my door to the thieves of a thief. Get you gone.'

Most of the workmen were old neighbours of his, and were for going away in silence, but amongst them were two masons from another part of the world, employed, and brought there by Pierino Zaffi.

These called to him to let them in, in the name of the law, and, as he made them no reply, they went and asked of Messer Nellemane permission to open the door by force.

To them Messer Nellemane replied:

'I do not love force; it is the weapon of the barbarian. I think we will wait a few days. Mazzetti may hear reason.'

So he postponed the execution of the work, and counted up the days that had elapsed since Pippo had been ordered to begin the work; and the many times he had been summoned to appear and answer for his transgressions; all those various summonses which the old rebel had put in the fire.

Then he took the diligence over to Pomodoro, and had a little talk with the advocate Niccolo Poccianti, who lived by the Pretura.

'I am afraid for your grandfather, *carina*,' said the cooper to Viola. 'Always alone like that, and the house so miserable, and over the wall I hear him always muttering, muttering, muttering those accursed figures over and over again; I am afraid for him, my lass.'

'And I too,' said Viola, with a sob in her throat. 'But what can we do? Carmelo and I would go and stay with him, but he will not have us; he thinks we are happier here.'

I am afraid for him,' said Cecco. 'He is made

of stouter stuff than Nanni was, but the best pipkin breaks with much knocking and much fire.'

'What can I do?' said Viola, in despair.

She would have gone through flame and water to help her grandfather, and would have borne any trouble to save it for him, but she could not tell what to do.

Sickness, sorrow, trial, burdens of poverty and pain, these the poor can understand well enough; they are familiar companions that have rocked their cradles and will go with them to their graves; but these oppressions, these exactions, these harassing debts that they are sold up for, yet which they know they never owed and never ought to pay, these bewilder them, break their nerve, and dull their brain.

Viola would have gone and besought the mercy of the Syndic, but she knew that she would only see his secretary.

She took a pilgrimage barefoot to a famous Madonna ten miles away on the hills, and there knelt and prayed humbly, and set up a candle in the shrine, all glittering with ex-votos, and the gems and metals of similar devotees, and she asked nothing for herself; she only asked for the old man.

'For Carmelo and I are young,' she said to herself, 'and we love each other, and we are together: that is so much; we ought not to want any more.'

Whilst she was still on her knees in the chapel on the side of the mountain, with the plain below like a sea, so grey was it with olive woods, the inspiration came into her to go and find the Prefect of the province at his own palace in the city.

It was to her as strange, as daring, and as distant, a travel as it would be to us to go through the terrible cañons of the Colorado, or scale the height of Chimborazo's summit. She had never been even so far as Pomodoro, and the mere thought of the great glittering city whose domes she could just see on the farthest edge of the plains, was one quite awful and terrible to her.

Nevertheless, when she came down in the twilight from the holy place, and met her husband at the foot of the hill, her mind was made up, and she said to him : ' Our Lady has told me to go to the city and see the Prefect, and that there I shall find help for *Nonno*.'

Carmelo would not say her nay, but he smiled a little bitterly.

'You may walk barefoot, my love, from here to Rome ; nothing will avail, until the people write their rights in blood upon the soil that should belong to them.'

Viola shuddered.

'Hush! That would be doing evil that good might come.'

'It is what we must do,' he answered gloomily ; and they spoke but little more, as they trod the long tedious ways between the stone walls and the cropped trees.

A day or two later she had her way, and her father-in-law drove her to the city. Carmelo stayed within the mill.

She had put on her grey gown that she was married in, and had an amber-coloured handkerchief tied over her raven locks. She looked very pale, but she was a beautiful woman in all the charm of youth, though careworn, and too grave for her few years.

They started very early—at dawn, indeed—for the sake of Bigio, and the way seemed very long; Viola's heart beat hurriedly, and with fear and hope alternately, as she saw the great marble dome of the basilica of Santa Maria, famous in history and in art, rise with its golden cross higher and higher, as Mont Blanc looms white across the foliage of the Val d'Aosta.

'And I will say a word for myself, too, if we get audience,' said the miller, as they drove under the massive brown gateway through the crowd of chattering people, and the market-carts waiting for the weighing and taxing of their goods.

Before the city can eat anything, drink any wine, burn any fuel, the country-folk who bring in what it wants are treated as contraband traders, and made to wait through vexatious hours of heat, or rain, or snow, as it may be, till they are taxed and fined. In this year of grace 1880, the machinery of the State is still so clumsy that it can devise no wiser means to maintain itself than to employ the antiquated dragon of the Octroi, which often obliges the people, and their horses, and mules, and cattle, and fowls, to wait all the long wet night in the high road, so as to be ready against the opening of the gates. They have pulled down all the fine old towers and walls; but they keep up the barriers of the Gabella.

Viola was awed by the noise, the width, the height, the crowds around her, but she was scarcely sensible of any of the grandeur of the frowning palaces, the foaming fountains, the spacious bridges, the marble statues; all her soul and mind were absorbed in her errand. A great purpose gives a sense of invisibility.

Pastorini stabled the grey horse near the market place, and then they sought the Prefecture. There it was in the centre of a square, a grand, solemn, mighty place, that in olden times had been the abode of mighty men; half fortress, half palace, built in the thirteenth century and faced with variegated marbles, and with once gorgeous frescoes on its frieze.

The miller and Viola entered the vast courtyard where water was rushing from the open jaws of stone lions: the Italian peasant has nothing in him of the vulgarity of trepidation before greatness and its emblems; the instincts of liberty and art are in him, all stifled though they be, and he stands graceful and unabashed before a monarch.

They asked to see the Prefect: they were told his Excellency was out; what did they want? They were sent here, sent there, a servant saw them, a clerk saw them; they were indolently told to wait.

They sat down in the court; a janissary, splendidly clothed, and with a gilt stick, told them they could not sit there.

Pastorini knew that the Prefect had in his day been a soldier of liberty, that he was very liberal, even 'red' in his opinions; that he had all the medals and ribbons of the wars of independence on his breast; that he was a trusted friend and ally of that advanced Ministry which the party of Messer Luca Finti was always trying to dislodge: Pastorini had heard this, and he hoped much from this soldier in power. His own brother had died at San Martino; the miller was simple enough to think this must be a link to all the Liberali.

They went outside and sat on the stone ledge that ran round the pediment of the palace. They sat there one hour, two hours, three hours; then they grew faint; they went into a little by-street, and took a bit of bread, and a little wine; then they turned back to the Prefecture and sat there again. Troops went by; cartloads of flowers, carriages with fine liveries, a band passed playing, the great sonorous bells of the cathedral boomed over the city, the hours drifted on; still they waited.

So many hours had at last gone by that their patience, even the illimitable inextinguishable Italian patience, had begun to get ruffled. Pastorini had got up and gone so often to the gorgeous guardian of the doors to know if the Prefect had come home, that the functionary at last got angry and—*in irâ veritas.*

'His Excellency has never been out at all, simpleton,' said he. 'But you do not suppose he or the secretaries are here for the like of you? Mercy alive! if once they began to see the public, they would have the whole province here screaming. He has never been out, I tell you. He has got guests with him. He will now be coming out soon, because it is the time to drive in the park.'

Pastorini went back to Viola.

'He is coming out soon,' he said: 'they told us a falsehood; we will wait and watch the staircase. We cannot miss him.'

By this time all the long golden drowsy day was drawing near its close. Viola felt feverish and stupid; her head spun with the coming and going of the crowds, the noise of the carriages and carts, and the unwonted closeness of the city air. Her peachlike complexion grew yellow with the heat and fatigue, and her great eyes had a strained reddened look.

Presently there came into the courtyard a handsome equipage, with liveried servants and fine horses; it waited at the foot of the stairs. 'Now is our time,' said the miller; and he and his daughter-in-law stood up by the entrance.

In a little while there came down a lady very superbly dressed in surah of old gold colour and laces of price, and behind her a good-looking, smiling man, with long moustaches and a glimpse of ribbon at his buttonhole.

Breaking past the janitor of the gates the girl rushed to the foot of the stairs; her father-in-law behind her.

'Oh, let me beseech of his Excellency to hear me,' cried Viola, stretching out her arms with a piteous gesture; and his Excellency paused a moment on the lowest step.

'What is it, Cuccioli?' he said, glancing interrogatively over his shoulder to a slim young gentleman behind him, who was indeed his private secretary.

Cuccioli murmured that he did not know; he would inquire; and he looked unutterable furies at the porter.

Meanwhile Viola was sobbing so that she could not speak; and Pastorini, with his head uncovered, said beseechingly:

'Your Excellency, my brother died at San Martino! We are come——'

'Oh, a pension, a claim?' said the Prefect, lighting a long cigar. 'Based on military service? My good friends, you must apply to the Minister of War. We have nothing to do with such things——'

'But I thought,' stammered the miller, 'I thought that as his Excellency fought himself——'

Now, unhappily, there were few periods of which it pleased the Prefect to be reminded so little as this period, far behind him, when he had been a soldier of fortune. He frowned a little impatiently, and moved to get into his carriage; but Viola stood in his way.

'Oh dear, my lord,' she pleaded; 'if you would but hear me: my grandfather is such a good honest soul, and all he has is sold up, and he never owed any one a penny, and he is going mad; and if the money could be got back——'

'Cara mia!' said his Excellency caressingly, because she was a woman, and handsome. 'Believe me, these matters are not in my department. If I listened to petitioners I should be deluged with them. What is it you want? If it be a pension——'

'It is not a pension,' said Pastorini. 'It is the cruelty of the municipality, your Excellency. They have ruined me; taken my ground; never paid me; and this poor old soul of whom the girl rightly speaks has been treated——'

'Oh, I cannot hear anything of that sort,' said the Prefect very decidedly. 'The communes are autonomous. Whilst they are within the law no Prefect has any right to interfere in any way. Your commune, wherever it is, is self-governed: if you do not think it ruled well, change your Giunta; change your Syndic.'

Which was as though he had said to one who complained of bad weather: 'Change the sun; move about the moon.'

'But your Excellency——' began Viola and the miller in one breath.

'Make them understand this, my dear Cuccioli,'

said the Prefect with a wave of his hand towards the slim youth: then he smiled affably on the upraised face of Viola, and hurried to rejoin his wife in her carriage: the tall high-stepping horses pranced rapidly from the court to the street, and he was gone.

His Excellency had had a rough time of it in those early wars, and he wanted to enjoy himself now. Why else were rewards given to men for public service?

The slim youth turned to Pastorini with the true official expression.

'It is quite beyond our department. No one can interfere with municipal administration. It is quite impossible. You have your Syndic. You must rely on him. Pray be so good as to remember in future that the Prefect never can have anything to do with any personal grievance.'

'Who has then?' said the miller desperately.

'Well, no one exactly: you see the government of every commune depends on itself. Nothing can be more satisfactory. Each commune has the rule it desires. Good day,' said the youngster; and he too slipt down the steps, and went his way to saunter in the park, and turn his eyeglass on the ladies.

'We must go home, Viola,' said the miller with a groan: he would not reproach her; but in himself he thought if the Virgin could not help them better than this she might as well reveal nothing. The cost of the horse's stabling and of their own noonday meal was all that this pilgrimage in search of justice had brought to them.

Carmelo said nothing when he heard. He had guessed very well how it would be.

Viola stole down to her grandfather's in the

moonlight, weary and worn out though she was, and made a little supper in a little earthen pot; her tears falling all the while.

'It is a hundred scudi they have taken from me in all,' said Pippo to her for the five hundredth time, following the old mode of coinage that he had been used to as a lad, and which indeed country people most naturally use still.

'I know—I know!' sobbed Viola.

'A hundred scudi; it would buy a cow,' muttered the old man, with his hands set on his knees, and his eyes fixed on the boiling pot. 'I am sorry to hear you are with child, my dear; there'll be no bit nor sup for it when it grows up; and it will have to sweat, and toil, and hunger, and then at the end they'll sell the bed from under it. That is what they'll do.'

Viola could not see the burning charcoal nor the little brown pot, for the thick mist of her tears.

It was true: what use or joy was there in the children coming to the birth to know only pain, and privation, and hard injustice of God and man?

In this lovely land that brims over with flowers like a cup over-filled, where the sun is as a magician for ever changing with a wand of gold all common things to paradise; where every wind shakes out the fragrance of a world of fruit and flower commingled; where, for so little, the lute sounds and the song arises; here, misery looks more sad than it does in sadder climes, where it is like a home-born thing, and not an alien tyrant as it seems here.

Then, whilst so lovely is the land, most unlovely does this tyrant make the homes of the poor; the alternate dust and mud of the roads, the greed-clipped trees, the human filth strewn over the fields as compost and putrefying in the sun, the dark, grimy, foul-smelling houses, the starved and beaten animals panting in the heat, or shivering in the cold; these all come in the train of this alien misery, and are more horrible and comfortless here than anywhere else on all the earth. More so because, as you look on it all, you know that it is the greed of the State, and the greed of the landlord and his steward, which, working side by side, and striving to outwit each other, do it all. Get away from the grasp of these, and it is the Italy of our Raffaelle still, and smiles as his child-Christs smile, with a light on its face that is of heaven.

## CHAPTER XXXII.

The months went on and brought the winter round and the spring. Things went ill at Santa Rosalia. The place was littered with dirt and lumber from the public works so nobly begun in it; the people did not dare say their souls were their own, with the guards striding up and down the roads and lanes, or watching from the winehouse windows; the tramway company had made up its quarrels with the Municipalities; moneys had passed quietly from hand to hand; a few schemers had got the richer, and the rails had finally been laid two-thirds of the way, and soon would be completed; the diligence man said he would cut his throat come Pasqua, and no one was content except Messer Gaspardo Nellemane who found all the new laws and new inventions working well, from the steam-mill that poured its black vapours down the once bright Rosa water, to the mendicancy clauses which had cleared the land of some scores of useless old people.

Messer Nellemane, sitting behind his desk, felt that he had in him the soul of a statesman. In his mind's eye as in a magic mirror, he beheld himself already at Montecitorio, already with his portfolio, demanding a hundred millions for military manœuvres, and increasing the grist tax by an added third.

He was only a clerk, it is true; but what of that? He had studied to perfection the modern science of success, and he knew that he had in himself all the modern requirements for eminence. Already the prefect and the sub-prefect had murmured to him, 'You are wasted here, you shall not be forgotten;' and already Luca Finti had promised him, 'When we are in office you will be remembered.'

Here in the little room of the communal palace, with his maps around him and his piles of papers before him, Messer Nellemane, though his imagination was slow, was almost deluded into imagining himself a minister already; and his fancy leapt at a bound the stairs he had still to climb.

Besides, Messer Luca Finti, with his father-in-law, were bringing into notice a scheme for turning the catacombs of Rome into an underground railway; he had got a syndicate of Jew, American, and Scotch bankers to consider the matter, and he could trust to his own party's power of worrying the Government into a concession. The sale of concessions is as flourishing nowadays in Italy as ever was of yore the sale of indulgences, and Messer Nellemane, in a strictly private manner, had been associated in this great project which promised well, as it was thoroughly adapted to the temper of the hour.

There was a fine flavour of desecration and utilitarianism about it which would be quite certain to take with the Press and the Bourse. All the Liberi Pensieri would be delighted at the use made of the early Christians. To an age which has decided that martyrdom was a kind of hysteria, and faith a sort of meningitis, there would be something peculiarly fascinating in making of SS. Gianetta and Basilla a booking-office, and of St. Hippolytus a junction. To drive an air shaft and a corkscrew stair straight through the soil that Scipio and Gracchus trod, down into the twilight, where the ashes of S. Agnes and S. Felicita rest, would be an enterprise full of peculiar sweetness and suitability to a generation that submits to the March Decrees, Irish murders, Cook's parties, the pickel-haube, wooden nutmegs, and Paul Bert.

Europe, as it is at present constituted, would be seduced in a second at a prospect that would turn the Quattro Santi into a chief station, and make of the Callimachus—last resting place of so many martyrs and early popes—a depôt for the goods-trains.

Messer Luca Finti knew the motto of his generation was a paraphrase of Voltaire: 'Souillez, souillez, souillez! Toujours quelqu'un gagnera!'

And when M. Jules Ferry is a Minister, and M. Herold lives in the Louvre, why should not Messer Nellemane be a statesman and Messer Luca Finti date his letters from the Consulta or the Palazzo Braschi?

The deputy had that first and most useful of all talents: he knew how to hit the tastes of his own times, and he foresaw that the Catacomb Metropolitan would be a name to seduce the world and sell a million *actions*. He had paid Messer Nellemane the great compliment of divulging this grand scheme to him, and even employing his command of florid language in the composition of a prospectus. Messer Nellemane had proved himself equal to the task, and was assured he should be entitled to preference shares. He felt that he was already passed many milestones on the high road to public greatness, and when he slept at night dreamed of portfolios and grand cordons.

As for his passion, he had conquered it with that strength of will which was his characteristic. Messer Nellemane was nothing if not moral; when Viola Mazzetti had wedded another, he had said to himself virtuously that it would never do to compromise his career; besides, after all, she was very thin, and her mouth was rather large, and she had been only a common, hard-working girl: so he dismissed her memory and saw her reality pass by him without emotion. But passion departing left hate behind it; the not uncommon ashes of unholy fires.

His love was a short-lived thing, but his hate smouldered on, unquenchable.

The little square house with the blue and white Madonna was a blot in the landscape to him. True, he had accomplished much against it; the mill smoke drowned it night and day in black vapours and foul smells; the tramway cars would plunge right across its very doorway, and to lay their rails down, the trees of the bank that had shaded it were felled; inside it all was bare and desolate.

Yet the sight of the little old man sitting on the threshold weaving his rush-work was to the eyes of Messer Nellemane as the vineyard of Naboth to the great king. Old Pippo was not crushed into the earth, his sturdy little spirit was not stamped into the dust; he was very miserable indeed, and his brain was dull and his hand infirm; but still he lived on, and seemed to the irritated pride of the ruler of Vezzaja and Ghiralda to have an insolent and jeering pertinacity of existence.

As Messer Nellemane sat this day before his desk, he perused some long law papers with satisfaction: 'a quarter of a year more,' he thought, 'and that stubborn old fool will know what mockery of the State costs people.'

For through all these months he had not been idle. He had been on the contrary constantly employed in the affairs of Pippo; constantly engaged in the courts of Pomodoro in the old rebel's affairs; the impudent brook still ran across the road, and the impudent old man still existed: but in three months Messer Nellemane promised himself that the law should be respected.

Law is a slow and complicated luxury to indulge in everywhere; in Italy it is especially so, but Messer Nellemane loved it, and in this great love knew how to caress it and cajole it, so that it became for him a pliant and almost quick-footed thing. He had not been clerk in a notary's office without learning how to get on the right side of the Law, and it was this knowledge especially which made him so efficient a public servant.

Now again and again had legal summons of all kinds been brought to Pippo, but he was all alone now; there was nobody to see what he did, and he lit a match and burned all these papers and chuckled as he did so. 'They can't get bark off of a peeled pine,' he said to himself. 'They may call, and call, and call; they won't get nought any more out of me.'

And the simple old soul thought that if he did not answer, they would get tired of calling, and he never knew the nature of these many documents.

'It is all along of the water,' he said to himself, and thought so; but what could he do to the water? 'And I would not do anything if I could,' he said obstinately, as he sat all alone.

One day Cecco the cooper said to him: 'You have never paid your interest on your mortgage, have you, Pippo?' and the old man answered him: 'Not I; he will have the house after me; where is the harm? I have not got any money to pay with, he knows that; if I get a bit and drop, and a snip of tobacco in my pipe, it is all as I ever can do: lawyer knows that.'

Cecco scratched his head thoughtfully; he was afraid. He did not understand these things, but he knew that Pippo's name was often spoken at Pomodoro, and he was afraid, Pippo gave him no heed; he understood even less than his friend, and it was of no use at his age to learn, he said angrily.

'My house is my house,' he said doggedly. 'They will get it when I am dead. They can't get it before.'

So he believed.

Hypothec was as Greek to him, and of all that these law-papers said which rained in on him, and which he burned, he had no idea. He could go about, and he could make his wickerwork, and he could do his little bit of cooking and mending, but he grew rather childish, and no one could make him understand things.

He had left off going to mass.

When the priest sadly reproved him, he said always : 'I don't see as any one of them cares about me.'

By them he meant the Trinity in which he had been taught to believe, and all their holy army of angels, of martyrs, and of saints.

'For sure nobody ever would disturb you, and you nigh seventy,' said Cecco the cooper a little uneasily, for he had heard rumours that had troubled him.

'Disturb me? what mean you, you ass?' said Pippo hotly. 'The house is mine, it is all mine. I pay no man rent. I thought it would go, when I die, to my girl, but I suppose now it will go to the lawyer. He will want something for his money.'

'But if they should take the house?' said the cooper, very timidly.

'Take it?' said Pippo fiercely. 'Take it? you long-shanked fool. How can they take it? It's mine, and I carry the key on me always when I go out. Take it! one would think 'twas a basket of eggs.'

The cooper said no more, being a shy soul, and not at best clear as to what he had heard, or what were the measures and powers of law. Pippo was huffed, and would not speak of the matter any more. He went and dug in his garden where the almonds were once more in bloom over Raggi's grave.

His head felt queer whenever he stooped, and his ears had always a sound in them like bees swarming, as he said himself; but he would never complain, and he managed to keep his bit of ground tilled, and in order. ''Tis mine till I die, anyhow,' he said fiercely, as he struck in his spade.

Meanwhile, at the house of Pastorini things were nearly as bad as with him. With the unequal rivalry of the steam mill no water-mill could compete, and all that the year had brought to Carmelo's people were debts, and the promise of a new inmate in the shape of a small swaddled child.

'Your children will come on sad times,' said Demetrio Pastorini to his son; 'God knows whether they will find a crust or a drop of goat's milk.'

A great despondency had fallen on the mild and mirthful man; he grew helpless and weary, only not apathetic, because of his strong affections for those about him. The accursed iron rails had been laid down on the ground where his trees had been, but no money had been paid to him.

They knew very well that he could not go to law to command it, and that if he did there would be long delays granted to them, for they called themselves 'public utility,' and so claimed public respect.

Like the Duca di Ripalda before him, he saw his trees carried away to fill the furnaces of factories or rot in ship-yards, and never received a penny for them from the law.

All destruction is condoned under the parrot phrase of 'public utility.'

To the municipal mind of Italy all that is new and artificial is good; all that is old or natural is worthless. They say of Rome like M. Cardinal: 'C'est une ville à faire disparaître de la surface du globe. Je n'ai jamais vu Chicago, mais je préfère Chicago.'

The great wheel of the Pastorini mill was motionless on nine days out of ten, for there was no work; novelty and expediency alike took the neighbours to the iron wonder of Remigio Rossi.

Cesarellino, the next son to Carmelo, came home from his conscript's service much the worse for it, as country lads usually are; they go away innocent, homely, laborious, dutiful youths, and they return from the camp and the barracks too often vicious, lazy, discontented, contaminated by vice, and utterly unwilling to work.

'As well send a lad to the galleys as to the army,' say the country people, and they are right.

You cannot take a man away from his duties for three of the most impressionable and important years of his life, or even for the lesser term of eighteen months, and expect him to return to those duties the same docile and industrious creature that he was. He will have brought with him many a low sin, many a foul oath, many a vile memory; he will be unhinged, moody, good for little; that conscription does not make a blackguard of every lad that falls under its curse is due to the good and kindly temper of the nation, not to the system, which is a very factory of devils.

Cesarellino, coming home to the mill, with bad words in his mouth, coarse talk on his tongue, and a nature for ever stunted, soured, and vitiated, added to the gloom of the household; the youngster had seen Milan and Turin, and was disposed to be insolent and contemptuous of the stay-at-homes. Now that Cesarellino was home, the third son, Dante, had to go; he was a gentle, timid lad, and suffered greatly.

'What a pack of slaves we are!' said the father

bitterly. 'Has a man not a right to refuse the flesh and bone he begot to the makers of war?'

'There is no war going on, father,' said the returned conscript with scorn for his father's ignorance.

'Then where is the excuse to take our boy from us?' said the old man. 'Nay, nay, we are a pack of slaves! no better that I see for driving away the *stranieri*.'

But kicking against the pricks was of no avail. The drawing of the year had given Dante a bad number; there was no money to buy a substitute, if even they had dreamed of such a thing, and the poor little fellow went off weeping like a girl.

'If it were not for Viola,' said his eldest brother, 'if it were not for Viola, I would wish I were of the age to go in his place. I would do it.'

'But Viola you have, as you wished to have her,' said his father, 'and many children, I daresay, you soon will have too; you must do your duty at home, my son. Would to heaven it had not been made so bitter to you. You have to eat fennel with sour bread, but you must bring a man's courage to it.'

'I lack not courage, father,' said Carmelo simply. Then with an effort he added:

'What cuts me to the quick, is to see the old man so poor and ill dealt with; and you so tried, and the mill wheels motionless, and that rascal Bindo strutting to and fro as a cock on the green:— father, sometimes I fear me I shall never hold my hand off him.'

'Yes you will,' said his father tenderly; 'yes, you will for your wife's sake and mine. But you brood on these things too much, my lad. Thinking makes no bread.'

'Thinking may make free men,' muttered Carmelo; he dared not tell the miller all he dwelt on; all the schemes, and hopes, and views with which the German mechanic on his sickbed had filled his mind. Carmelo knew that down in the city there were many of the same way of thinking as himself, and not long before he had received a secret bidding to join an association there that was a branch of the Figli di Lavoro: that international league to which no one pays any heed because it has so harmless a title.

All the nature of Carmelo, all the temper he had been born with, bound him to his native soil; to a simple and pastoral life, to innocent affections and pastimes, to the old roof-tree, and to the familiar ways and habits that had been his forefathers as well as his.

The Italian is homely and strongly conservative, as I have said often before, and Carmelo, let alone, would have asked nothing better than to live and die as his grandfather had done before him, by the Rosa water. But it is the policy of Messer Nellemane to let no one alone anywhere; and the result is that the peaceful become restless, and the patient become restive, and in the stead of content there is rebellion, or at the best a profound if impotent disaffection.

What would Mazzini say if he were living?

I believe he would curse the *oppressor rusticorum* as he never cursed the Austrian or the Frenchman, the soldier or the priest.

We put up statues to him, but we forget this.

## CHAPTER XXXIII.

ALL those papers that Pippo thought he abolished by burning them as he lit his pipes, were rising in a heap over him, in truth, at Pomodoro, till they grew into a mighty mound of contumacy, and under this pile justice required that the contumacious one should be buried alive.

In a word, as he did not appear and did not reply, and no one appeared or replied for him, the lawyer who had his mortgage, and the lawyer who acted on behalf of the municipality, had it all their way, as no doubt they would have managed equally to have if he had appeared and had replied; and after the many ceremonies and formalities of the law had all been observed, he knowing nothing of it all the while, due notice was sent him that his property would be sold to satisfy the just demands of the mortgagee, and of the debts due by him to the commune for works not done by him, and repeated contraventions and fines for the same, all unpaid for a term of eighteen months.

But as this notice also took the form of a paper half printed and half written, and was delivered by the Usciere, Pippo twisted it up, set light to it, and pushed it blazing and smouldering under the little earthern pipkin containing his dinner, then boiling on the fire.

He was no wiser than before.

The lawyers and Messer Nellemane had had a great deal to do at Pomodoro in this matter, and all the engines and battering-rams of the law had been set in motion against the poor little house by the river, but Pippo knew nought of it.

'They can't get bark out of a peeled pine,' was all he said; and when the man of law left these long papers upon him, with all their formidable array of writing and printing that he could not read, he set light to them and thought that was an end.

'They will tire before long,' he thought. 'They can't get anything more out of me, and they'll give over.'

Pippo often went days on only a bit of bread, and once passed twenty-four hours without eating at all; but he shut up his pains in his own breast and would not take them to worry the girl: she was always the girl to him.

To Carmelo he did speak a little, for he and the young man were victims of the same torturer.

'Lord's sake, lad,' he said one day, 'when I was a middle-aged man, even so near as that, the land was all at peace and fed us all. Wine—why you could get it for the asking, or buy it for a soldo a flask. Bread—ay, there was bread for the dogs and the pigs then; loaves were as thick as stones in Rosa's bed. We were all quiet and happy. The gentlefolks didn't go roaming away to foreign parts, and didn't dine nigh midnight as they do now. They all got their dinners at three, and there was plenty for a hundred, if a hundred came by and wanted sup and bite. They bided in villa all summer, and they went down to their own city, whichever it was, for winter. Oh, lad! Then the cities were alive and pretty, with all the money spent honestly in them, not taken out to this, that, and the other foreign place as it is now. All the old feasts and fairs were kept, and the laughing and dancing all winter, and the pranks and bravery of Carnival kept the cold out, and, Lord! on a holy day, what poor soul denied himself a chicken in his pot. It cost but two soldi. Now a chicken—why you might almost as well talk of getting down the moon to eat. The fowls are packed off to foreign parts, and here we all are starving. Can you tell me the right of it?'

'I can tell you the wrong of it,' said Carmelo, his mind reverting to all the German communist had told him. 'The pot has boiled till all the scum is up; the knaves are saddled on us because they bellow "Liberty!" while they cudgel our bare bones. As our gentlefolks don't care how we starve so long as they go and cut a figure in Parigi, so the knaves don't care how we perish so long as they get soldiers and ships, and put money in their purses.'

'I suppose that's it,' said the old man, not much the wiser.

'I know twenty years ago there was a rare screaming about "Italy for the Italians;" and who's got Italy now?—the Jews,' said the elder Pastorini. 'Jew here, Jew there, Jew everywhere; and the poor sicken and die, and what d—d Jew dog of them cares? It is all the fault of the gentlefolks; they flare through their money to look fine, and then, when they're all burning up to waste, the Jews come in behind them. I never knew much, but that I do know. Look at what the old Marchese was, Palmarola, I mean; every soldo spent by him amongst his own people, and every hour spent by him here on his own soil. What's his son? A monkey-looking thing that scarce ever comes nigh his land, squanders all he gets out of it in Rome, or that place you call Parigi, and is whittling away every bit of the old property in gaming and harlotry, and trying to look like a foreigner. It's all the fault of the gentlefolks. Why didn't they send them adrift with the *stranieri*?'

'Ah,' said Pippo. 'Palmarola died in time; it would have broken his heart to see that youngster, always dwelling with foreign folks, and keeping bad women, as they say he does. And what a fine-looking man was the old Marchese, and what a shrivelled-up looking *monellino* is this youngster! It seems to me as if the men now were all so small——'

'Of course they are,' said the miller. 'They smoke at fourteen, and they keep bad women as you say, at sixteen, and they gamble all night long, and they drink strong spirits to get their courage up in the morning. Of course they are weaklings, that is all that the foreign craze has done for our nobles. And those who don't do that, are like Count Saverio there in the town; all they think of is buying scrips and stock, and they would sell the Madonna herself to get a share or two in a foreign railway, or be the first to suck the gilt off a bit of jobbery down in the city. But I don't know what we're to do; I have heard that the Inglese and the Americani have done it all, bringing in their mad ways and midnight dinners, and their craze for killing things: it may-be.'

'I've heard tell the Inglese worship foxes. They're heathens then,' said the cooper Cecco, timidly. 'I never knew much about them.'

'This I do know, for I have been told it,' said Carmelo, scornfully, 'that they're such poor shots that, if they want to hit a bird, it has to be shut up in a box, and let fly right in front of them! But, oh! father, not Inglese nor Francese nor anybody would be able to hurt our Signori if they bided at home as of old, and had human hearts in their breasts, and clean hands. But they have not, they have not! They will not trouble themselves about anything, unless it is to get money, and they give us over into the claws and teeth of the Impiegati as a shepherd gives over his lambs to the butcher's knife. They do not care whether we live or die. What they care for is their own ease, their foreign travel, the money in their bank——'

'I remember a chicken two soldi,' said Pippo, reverting to his original thoughts. 'Two soldi, and fine and fat; not a thing blown out just for market. And now they send all the poultry away by the rail.'

Then he fell to recalling in silence all the easy plenty and merry, simple festivities of his youth, when black Befana had knocked at all doors at Epiphany and when the Maggioli had brought in the spring to every village.

Carmelo with a sigh got up in his cart and went on his way; he had some sacks of 'torbo' (lignite), to leave at one of the very few farmers who still were bold enough to show friendship to the Rosa millhouse, and employed the young Pastorini in divers homely ways; the 'torbo' was wanted for the threshing-machine that would soon be in motion on the hills; one of the 'pillars of progress' that came to break up for ever the old gracious pastoral ways which were like pictures from the Bible, and, making labour less, make hunger more, and benefit the few to distress the many.

The farm was many miles off; on one of the green hillsides, clothed first with the olive, and higher with the umbrella-pine, that stretched along both sides of the plains through which the Rosa wound.

It could be seen from the valley, a long, low, white house with an old tower, and the pines standing all around and above it. The way to it was steep and long; a good, well-made Roman road of the ancient times when work was not 'scamped,' since engineers 'scamping' it, would have been beaten with rods or hung to a cross.

The mule was fatigued, for the lignite was very heavy, and it had been fetched from Pomodoro.

Midway on the hill road Carmelo, who was by nature merciful to beasts, checked the poor thing, lightened the cart of three sacks and set them down by the roadside, meaning when the mule had, thus relieved, climbed to the top of the steep slope facing it, to carry them up one by one on his own shoulders.

The road wound through wild scrub of myrtle, and cistus, and arbutus; young chestnut trees were growing in clumps; it was quite solitary; no one ever scarcely came there except a woodman, a sportsman, a hill hare, a fox, or a flock of goats.

Carmelo left the sacks by the wayside and began to walk up beside his mule, encouraging it in its toil with kind words and a bunch of sweet hill grass.

He was busy thinking: very simple, honest thoughts; of how best he could labour in the future for his own children, and his brothers and sisters, for Carmelo foresaw that, with six months more, the mill-house would most likely be no more over their heads, his father being no more able to pay his way. He had a stout heart and strong affections; he tried to think how best he could carry his father on his shoulders away from the peril; a humble Æneas bearing a homely Anchises.

He never saw coming through the myrtle and bay the figures of Bindo Terri and old Angelo; their pistols in their hands: when they had any leisure from tormenting the public, they took a turn at shooting thrushes and merles.

'Stop!' shouted the rural guards.

Carmelo glanced up, grew red, then white, and continued to pace beside the straining mule.

'Stop!' thundered the officers of the law.

Carmelo for all answer went behind the cart, and pushed it to aid the mule.

The men went in front of the beast and checked it with a jerk; the incline was great; the cart recoiled, the mule reared, the lignite rolled most of it on the ground; it was with a great effort that Carmelo saved the animal and the baroccino from destruction. He clenched his hands and ground his teeth in his struggle not to resent and avenge the offence done him.

Bindo Terri, keeping his pistol at full cock stood in the middle of the road.

'You are in contravention,' he said, with pert authority. 'Your sacks are lying on the public road. It is an offence against the municipal police. See Art. XV. of Rule 103. Angelo, inscribe the dereliction.'

Angelo opened his book and pretended to write. In real truth he wrote very ill.

Carmelo, whose heart was heaving and whose

whole body was shivering with rage, stooped over the fallen 'torbo' and employed himself in thrusting it back into the sacks.

He would have given twenty years of life to have been able to wrench the pistol out of the hands of the murderer of Toppa, and blow his brains out on to the turf. But he remembered Viola, he remembered his father, he controlled the justice of his bitter wrath, and bore in silence all the insults and gibes of his tormentors. Tired at last, as they could provoke him to no retaliation, they left him alone with his mule and his fallen lignite and went away across the chestnut woods: the land lay within their beat, being within the commune of Vezzaja and Ghiralda.

The next day the Usciere served a summons on Carmelo, citing him to appear for contravention of the law in having obstructed the public road.

## CHAPTER XXXIV.

Annunziata, since she had come out of prison, had never been quite the same. What she had thought the dire disgrace of it had gone deep into her honest old soul, and had ploughed it up as vitriol ploughs the flesh.

'If my poor dead man knew!' she would say, with a burst of sobbing. It seemed to her as if she were branded with an ineffaceable infamy. But never would she allow she had been a beggar.

'Not I,' she said: 'I only take what they give me. I never beg.'

All the winter she was very quiet; quiet perforce, because her old enemy of the 'rheumatics' seized her and pinned her down on her low pallet-bed. Carmelo and Viola and the Pastorini children did their best for her, and the old women in her room were always sisterly and kind, though racked themselves with nearly every ill that flesh is heir to; and in her exceeding joy at being at home in that cold tumbledown corner of a room again she was quite content, and bore her pain and nibbled her bit of bread cheerfully, Dom Lelio being as usual good to her, and going with a patched cassock and a rusty hat that he might spare from his meagre means for all those who had nothing.

No doubt it seems a very stupid and incredible thing, but old 'Nunziatina was happy so long as she could see those four walls and the square casement, that was filled with the poplar boughs, and hear the other old women chatter, and chatter too, and see the scrap of charcoal in the copper-pan warming the pipkin of bread-soup. Yet it is a fact, and it is a fact also that life, which goes out of youthful queens, and bright children, and cherished heirs, who have all done to save them that wealth and science and love can dream of, often keeps itself alight in these old, worn, and half-starved frames.

'You must never go about, dear, again to the villas and the farms,' said Viola, weeping, to her. 'They will be on you again if you do. You know they think it begging.'

'I never ask for aught,' said Annunziata sturdily; 'I take what they give me.'

And for her life she could not see that she did anything amiss.

All the winter she had kept perforce quiet from her rheumatism, and Viola begged and prayed her so that even when the tulips were all yellow in the fields and all the force of old instinct and old habit moving her, she still kept within doors, or only just went and sat under the deep shade of the old ilex that had the shrine set in its trunk.

She cared not at all for the municipal laws, this old rebel, but she cared to please the girl, as she still called her, 'who was getting so near her time that one can't cross her,' she said to her four old friends in the little room.

And indeed with the March tulips Viola's little son came into the light of the bright spring days, and promised to resemble his father in his big blue eyes and fair complexion, and was a happy little child that seldom cried.

This child was a source of great occupation and absorbing interest to its old great-grand-aunt, and 'Nunziatina spent most of her time at the mill-house with the little closely-swaddled bundle on her knees.

But also, indirectly, it was a reason for her to be more restless, and to wander a-field again; for she said to herself that now there was a baby, and no doubt dozens to follow, and so much trouble and straits at the mill-house on the Rosa, she could not and would not rob them of so much as a bit of bread, when all the people on the hillsides and down in the valley farms would be willing to give to her out of their plenty.

Carmelo and Viola endeavoured to make her understand that this taking of free gifts was her offence in the eyes of the law, but they could not succeed. She could not understand that she did anything wrong, and the habits of forty years could not easily be shaken off her daily life.

'I only take what they give me,' she said persistently.

By vigilance and persuasion they kept her in a few weeks, but their lives were too full of work for them to have leisure for perpetual watching. 'I never did do a bit of harm,' she said to herself, and she could not stay indoors this bright weather of the opening summer, and though she left her basket at home, as they told her to do, she began to wander about as of old. She was much weaker than of yore, and, like Pippo, her head buzzed.

'It's always like the bees in the acacia trees,' he and she agreed, sorrowfully. She did not readily comprehend what was said to her, and she confused names and dates. 'I want to be in the air,' she said to the old women, her companions in her little square room. 'I have always been in the air all my days.'

So she took her stick and trotted hither and thither, and naturally her feet, of their own accord, wandered into the old familiar paths, and up to the old houses. All her old friends at the farmhouses were delighted to see her, and gave her bit and drop as she wanted it. She would not take anything home.

'No, they tell me not; the dear lad who took me out tells me not,' she said always, and all she would do was to eat a plate of soup, and drink a little *mezzo-vino* when it was offered her. Her brown wrinkled face, all crinkled up like a walnut shell, had lost its mirth; her mouth often trembled, and she had grown very deaf; but she was as sensible as ever to kindness, and brightened up under it.

She was a picturesque little figure still in her round black hat, and her clothes that were made of all colours, and of odds and ends that had been given her.

One day, when Viola's boy was some three months old, and the weather was growing sultry, she had been up in the hills to a *massaja*,[1] who was very fond of her, and she had done some work up there with the poultry by way of payment for sitting and eating at the long table where all the contadini dined off maccaroni and salad and broth, and on her way home was so tired that she sat down to rest above the village, on a felled pine by the edge of the hill-road.

There was a pony carriage coming slowly up it, and in it, with a servant, was the pretty foreign child with the blue eyes, who lived at Varammista. When the English child saw her, out she sprang, and came lovingly up to the old woman, her golden hair hanging about her shoulders.

'Oh, 'Nunziatina!' she cried to her, 'We have been away all the year, and we are just come back, and we have heard you have been in prison. It is not true? It cannot be true?'

'Yes, carina; it is true,' said Annunziata. 'They took me the very day I was coming to bid you good-bye, and I had got a rose for you—such a beautiful rose. Yes, dear, I have been in prison, and perhaps your mamma would not wish you to speak with me.'

'Oh, mamma *would*!' said the English child,

---

[1] The *massaja* is the woman (usually the wife of the *fattore* or bailiff) who is set over all the womankind on an estate and directs their labours.

with a quick breath of indignation. 'You never did anything wrong? I am sure you never did.'

'No, carina, not I. I took what they gave me, and they said that is begging. I never have understood it.'

'Oh, what a wicked thing!' sighed the child, with her fair cheeks hot. 'I will tell mamma. Do you come up to Varammista and see her, and, dear 'Nunziatina, I must not stop, because it grows dark so soon, but take this and come up and see us.'

'Is it your own to give me, dear?' said Annunziata, holding the two-franc note with hesitation.

'Really my own,' said the child. 'You know I have so much money; and buy something nice with it, will you?'

'The saints bless you, carina,' said Annunziata, 'and I'll tell you what I will buy with it. I will buy a little shirt or two for Viola's child, that was given to her when the daffodils blew.'

'Oh, do!' said the child, 'and you will come and see us soon, Annunziata; to-morrow, won't you? I will tell mamma all about you, and she will be so sorry, so sorry.'

Then the glad little girl went away up over the hill, with her little rough pony, and the old woman went down it quite light of heart.

'I will buy something for Viola's child,' she thought, and slipped the money in her apron pocket.

That night, when Carmelo drove through the village with some flour, Gigi Canterelli ran out of his shop and stopped him.

'Do you know they have taken 'Nunziatina again?' he said to him. 'They say she was begging; they say they saw her take money on the hill yonder, just coming into the town; she is gone to Pomodoro.'

Carmelo turned crimson, then pale.

'But I paid forty francs for her!' he cried; 'I sold my watch.'

'What has that to do with it?' said the grocer. 'They have got her again. They will want eighty francs this time.'

'How shall I tell Viola?' said Carmelo, and he trembled like a girl. 'Oh, my God! Oh, my God, Gigi!—when shall we get justice or pity?'

'My lad, we have big ships, and sham battles, and a hundred men in every office-door to kick us out when we ask a civil question,' said Gigi Canterelli. 'That is as much as we shall get for twenty years to come, I am thinking. Your mule is tired; I will harness my own beast, and go over and see where 'Nunziatina is. Go you home, and tell your wife to keep up her heart.'

Carmelo thanked him, and drove to the mill-house with a bitter spirit, and a broken one; the old grocer did as he had promised, and went to Pomodoro.

There he found that the old woman had been taken by Bindo Terri, for the offence of begging for money on the road; she was in prison, and no one would tell him more, or let him see her. He returned to the mill-house and made the best of the sad facts that he could.

'To-morrow we will have her out,' he said cheerfully to Viola. 'Never you fear, my beauty. We will have her out. The foreign folk at Varammista will stand her friends, and we will all club together, somehow or other, if pay she must.'

Now as officials, all the land over, are convinced that the public never should be told the truth on any occasion—the public, in fact, having no business ever to inquire for it—they had not told the truth to Gigi Canterelli in the town.

Annunziata had been taken there by Bindo Terri, and told by him very sharply that nobody was ever let out after a second offence; she, for her part, was dumb with horror and amaze, and only found her voice when they took her two francs away from her as *pièce de conviction*, at which she screamed loudly.

'The little lady of Varammista gave it!' she shrieked, 'and I am going to save it for Viola's child!'

But no one attended to this; she was bundled away into the prison, and her case was to be heard in the morning. However, the Count Saverio chanced to see her, and took the matter into his own hands. He had always regretted that he had been cold to her; he was a man who set great store on his charitable reputation, and he knew very well that he had seemed very indifferent when they had worried him about her, just as he was in council with his stockbroker.

Now the Count Saverio was a man who was nothing if he were not charitable. He had made himself conspicuous solely by charity; it had been a career to him, and a successful one; these professors of that divine virtue which covers a multitude of sin are common to every country. They may be said to flourish especially here, because there are so many fraternities and endowments in which they can plant themselves as snugly as a scolytus in an elm tree. So he saw an admirable investment in this old woman whom he had refused to assist, and he exerted himself so greatly, to the admiration of everybody, that he obtained her removal from the prison of Pomodoro to the Montesacro of the city.

The Montesacro was also one of those institutions which had come down from obscure ages, and had been illumined by the light of modern common sense. It had originally been a purely charitable asylum for aged folk, with large funds bequeathed by a pious prince, who was also an abbot. But the State had taken a good slice out of it at that illustrious period of the Birth of Liberty, when Garibaldi and others were driving Scialoja to madness by drawing cheques on the public funds every day, and this modernised Montesacro nowadays made perpetual appeals for assistance, private and public.

Most people said it was managed magnificently.

Count Saverio said so, for his cousin was at the head of it: a few grumblers averred that the frescoes had been cut off the walls of the vestibule and corridors, the oak seats of its chapel gone, nobody knew where, and its altar-piece by Sodoma vanished from its place. A famous gold Reliquary, also, the work of Benvenuto Cellini, had disappeared: it was supposed to have been destroyed by rats.

But no one can help what rats may do, and these grumblers were not attended to, and Montesacro was always pointed out to strangers as one of the features and glories of the glorious and lovely city. It was divided into two parts; it had youth which did a great deal of work that was sold for their support, and the profit of its direction; and it had age which served as a reason for all kinds of donations, subscriptions, bazaars, lotteries, and theatricals on their behalf. Count Saverio, whose cousin was director-in chief of this beneficent asylum, had old 'Nunziatina carried there in the ambulance of his own fraternity, a coffin-like cart drawn by a weak old horse; and she was deposited on one of the narrow little beds of the dormitory, and expected to be grateful.

She was a stubborn old soul, and she was not so.

'What have I done, what have I done?' she screamed at every minute. 'Let me get back to my home. Let me get back to my home.'

For this silly old woman would persist in calling her corner in a room, with her bit of sacking for a bed, her home—*casa mia*.

She was in a long corridor, with those white-washed walls, off which the frescoes had been cut; there were some seventy iron beds all in a row; there were some lofty casements carefully blinded, with grey shutters, through which little chinks of light blinked, as a cat's eyes blink in the darkness; as long as she would live she would be set in one of these big rooms, have broth and bread found her, and be allowed to go outside once a fortnight for three hours.

Instead of being gratified and grateful, perverse old 'Nunziatina screamed till she was black in the face.

'*Casa mia! Casa mia!* Take me there. I am not a criminal. I won't be put in prison! I want the air, I want the sun. Take me to *casa mia*!'

If Messer Nellemane had been there, he would have had once more occasion to moralise upon the ingratitude of the poor.

A female likeness of him, who was there, gently gagged Annunziata without more ado, observing that discipline in an institute must be preserved at any sacrifice of the individual, and as the aged rebel tore at the gag with her hands, they tied those down to the bed rails.

Then the unwilling old woman was told that she ought to be piously thankful; tens of thousands of old women died, and there was no account made of them; she was exceptionally fortunate and blessed in having been selected to enjoy the refuge of Montesacro.

In the night she was delirious.

In the morning she was stupid.

But as no one thought her ill, and everybody knew she was stubborn, they paid her no attention, till an attendant shook her, made her get out of bed, and tumbled her into a bath. Annunziata, who had the common holy horror of her nation as to water, shivered, and was very sick, but as she had ceased to scream, they thought she was getting reconciled, and put her on the clothes of the institute, and placed her in the common room of the old women.

There she sat quite still, and dumb, shivering all over.

The old folks around her were busy working, some plaiting, some sewing, some knitting, some picking linen to make lint, some only staring vacantly and mumbling—who shall say what wishes, what regrets, what memories?

Annunziata stared with her eyes at the dull wall, the high barred windows, the great, unfamiliar, hateful chamber, but all she really saw was her own little den with the poplars waving green against the little window, the sunny roads where her feet had carried her so many years, the green hillside where she so long had wandered, the broad blue radiant light, the rose of daybreak on the plains.

You cannot cage a field-bird when it is old; it dies for want of flight, of air, of change, of freedom. No use will be the stored grain of your cage; better for the bird a berry here and there, and peace of gentle death at last amidst the golden gorse or blush of hawthorn buds.

When night came, and they made her go to her bed amidst all those other beds again, Annunziata was very cold; cold as marble. No one had been unkind, for she had been quite mute and passive all through this long dreary colourless summer day behind the grey blinds within the four walls.

'*Casa mia, casa mia*,' she murmured feebly, when they laid her down on the hard pallet: it was a stifling midsummer night, but she was still quite cold.

She was so cold that the woman in attendance called for help: there was no doctor near at hand, and the director was away at a dinner party of the Prefect.

They tried to put some warm drink down her throat, but she spat it out; her lips began to grow blue, and her eyes fixed.

'Let me get out, let me get home,' she muttered, with a tremulous voice. 'There is no air here; I can't breathe——'

The women were not frightened, for they were used to death-beds in Montesacro; yet, awed to some show of gentleness, they lifted her up and opened a casement to let in the coolness of the night.

But Annunziata knew nought of that. She gasped for breath still, and the little life there was in her was chilling into stone. All at once she opened her eyes wide and forced herself free of their hold:

'Lord! let me see the sun again; let me see the hills!' she cried aloud, stretching out her arms; and in that last prayer she died.

Will she see the sun again, free from all cloud, a sun that never sets? Will something greater than ourselves, and more pitiful than the State, let that poor, dumb, tired little soul of hers arise and rejoice in the green hills of an everlasting world?

If this be the last of her, this death on a strange bed, in a prison that hypocrisy calls a refuge, then let us weep for her indeed; ignorant, valiant, true, busy, and most harmless creature, almost as dumb as the dogs, quite as cheerful as the birds, having borne heat, and cold, and hunger, and pain without complaint so long as she was free.

'Be good to me, O God, for my boat is so small and the deep sea is so wide,' is the prayer of the Bréton fisher. Alas, how many boats go down, and where is the pity of God?

## CHAPTER XXXV.

The misery at this time grew yet greater at the mill-house; greater for this family, which had for so many centuries been the possessors of a homely abundance, than for those who by long usage were accustomed to hardship and penury. All Pastorini's savings had gone when Carmelo was in prison, and the mill brought in not a farthing. People who a few years before would have given him ten years' credit now did not like to trust him for a month. Popular favour is a fickle thing, and comes and goes alike without reason. He took the good grey horse to a distant market and sold it, being reluctant to keep it to want; the old mule he knew would soon have to follow; without grist to grind the mill only cost what it could not pay; the usciere began to call with summonses for trifling debts, for when one tradesman turns crusty, all turn so.

The little butcher Sandro had become bankrupt, and had disappeared from Santa Rosalia; the big one, he who was in good odour with the municipality, would give nothing without money down on the nail. The old man was shrunken out of all likeness to himself; the baby alone throve in the midst of the desolation, and there was likelihood of another coming; more hungry mouths and no food for any of them was the future that faced Carmelo and his father. The summons for having encumbered the road with the sacks of *torbo* had been served on Carmelo, and as he had not appeared to answer it, and could not employ any man of law to dispute it, it was passed as a matter of course on to Pomodoro, where the Pretore, merely seeing that Carmelo Pastorini was in question, decided without further examination that his late prisoner had been at fault, and so the matter with fines, penalties for contempt of court in not appearing, &c., ran up to a matter of thirty-eight francs. As for looking for thirty-eight francs in the mill-house till, you might as well have looked for emeralds and rubies. After due course a *gravamento* was instituted for the payment, as it had been done with poor old Pippo; and Carmelo, possessing nothing of his own in the world except a gun, his clothing, and the little coral earrings he had given his wife in the bridal week, these were seized and taken off by the usciere. Carmelo laughed aloud when he saw the distraint warrant.

'He set down three sacks on a hillside road to lighten the mule for a minute!' said his father piteously. But he himself said nothing. He only laughed till those were frightened who heard him. His father, without letting him know it, persuaded the usciere to take some of his own clothing instead of his son's. If he had still had the mule he would have sold that, but three months had gone by since the offence had been committed, and the mule had now gone to other masters, and the price of him and of the baroccino had bought food for the many mouths round the mill-house table.

Viola, who could do nothing, grew so wretched that she reproached herself bitterly for having married Carmelo; alone, she thought, he might have done better; he could have gone away, he would have had only himself to keep. It began to seem to her that she had done nothing but harm to all she loved.

When on this day of Annunziata's removal to Montesacro they heard only that she had been once more arrested, Viola felt her timid and patient soul grow desperate.

'Oh, Carmelo,' she sobbed, ' and it was they who killed Raggi, though I never told you!'

'Dear,' said the young man with a bitter smile, 'I guessed that long ago. These are the wretches that have our lives in their keeping; dog-butchers, thieves, extortioners! The people are like the steer who goes peaceably to be murdered when he could toss and gore.'

'But would it be any better if the people rose?'

'Who can tell?' said Carmelo gloomily. 'I have heard say that twenty years ago, when they first drove out the *stranieri*, it was our people, the soldiers of the people, the leaders of the people, born out of them, who were the first to plunder and pillage all the people's treasuries. And how can we do anything; we who have no union, no chief, who cannot read, who can only struggle blindly just as the birds do in the nets? That is the misery of it. Our people are timorous. They scurry like mice before a uniform; they crouch and crawl before a drawn sword. Yet anything were better than this. It would be an easier death to be shot down by artillery than to be bled to death slowly like this, a drop every day.'

'But what will be the end?'

'Who shall tell? This I do believe, that when they deal with us as with criminals for every little action of our days they will make us devils. If the army were with us, then, indeed—I have heard tell that the soldiers are muttering and growing restive; but alas! there will be always men found who will point the cannon on the poor.'

Viola listened, and understood enough to be alarmed and very disquieted for the safety of her beloved.

This day, made bold by the pains of what she loved, as does will be and mother-birds, she took heart of grace and resolved to essay a last chance for help and hope. It was a very faint one, and if she had not been a simple, ignorant, and most trustful creature, would never have dawned on to delude her for a moment.

As it was, she tied a handkerchief over her shapely head, took her little apple-blossom of a boy in her arms as a shield and prayer in one, and went straight, unknown to any of her family, towards the communal palace, and there asked with beating heart if she could see Messer Nellemane.

Now Messer Nellemane was growing very indifferent to Santa Rosalia; he knew very well that he would soon leave it for some higher official grindstone under which to squeeze the body-politic; and he was beginning almost to be high and mighty with his own master, the Most Worshipful the Cavaliere Durellazzo. Therefore he very seldom deigned to see any petitioner of the populace, and such were always dealt with now by the chancellor, the conciliator, or Bindo. Nevertheless, when he heard that the wife of Carmelo, the granddaughter of Pippo, wished to see him, he bade her be shown in to him; Messer Nellemane not being one of those who believed in the virtue of women, had a sudden evil notion come up in his mind of what her errand might be. But she would come in vain, he said to himself; such philandering was not to be indulged in; ambition was his sole Venus; he knew the mischief that one weakness may work in a public career; he meant to go through life with a blameless, a snow-white morality. There is nothing more useful.

Nevertheless, he let her enter.

When he saw the baby in her arms he frowned, and his face flushed angrily; when Helen comes to woo, she does not thus cumber herself.

'Signora mia!' he hastened to say, however,

with benevolent courtesy, 'it is long since we met. I have been so much occupied. *Un bel bimbo davvero!* What is his age?'

Viola, trembling very much, and with her great dark eyes wide open and strained, took no heed of his words.

'I am come to beg you to be merciful to us,' she said in a low gasping tone. 'Sir, dear sir, we are in great wretchedness. My father-in-law is ruined. My husband thinks of going to Maremma to work as a day-labourer. My poor old aunt is taken again, and my grandfather—oh, my grandfather——'

There her sobs choked her.

Messer Nellemane's black eyes shone with a pleasure he could not conceal, though all his features were composed into a regretful and sympathetic gravity.

'I am very pained at all this,' he said blandly. 'I had heard something of it——'

'Oh stop, stop it! you can!' murmured Viola, her whole form trembling, and clasping the baby to her convulsively.

'I!' cried Messer Nellemane in amazement. 'I! *cara mia signora!* What have I, what can I possibly have to do with the misfortunes of your relatives? Alas! would I could say they were altogether undeserved misfortunes, but when the law is obstinately set at defiance——'

'Oh, it is you!' cried Viola, forgetful of all wisdom, and borne away on the tide of her own strong feeling. 'You rule all; at a word from you all is done or undone. 'Nunziatina would be left in peace, and my husband could stay in his own place, if only you would cease to persecute us.'

Messer Nellemane drew himself up, the most rigid monument of offended dignity and unutterable surprise.

'Persecute?' he repeated; 'persecute? *I?* Signora mia! you cannot know what you are saying! What am I here? Nothing. The mere instrument of the will of the council and the syndic; the merest pen in the hand of an unblemished and most benevolent magistracy! You must see, if you reflect a moment, that the troubles of your relatives all arise from their own neglect of repeated warnings that, if they pursued certain modes of conduct, the law— the law which is absolutely impartial and impersonal —must take its course.'

'No!' said Viola, stung out of all prudence, and holding her little child close to her breast as she spoke. 'No, no! these are all words. When I was a maiden you had wicked and cruel thoughts of me, and you have revenged yourself on me and mine. If I had taken your gifts, and hearkened to your dishonest wooing, you would have spared my grandfather and the Pastorini and the old woman, who has no sin in all the world except to belong to me!'

Offended majesty and insulted virtue reigned together on every line of Messer Nellemane's countenance.

'You are mad, woman!' he said very sternly. 'How dare you use such indecorous language to me? I never saw you but twice, and then I regarded you as the betrothed of the youth Carmelo. Foolish fancies are not my foible. My time, like my heart, is in the service of the nation!'

Viola was vibrating and throbbing with passion. She scarcely heard him.

'It is because the dear old creature brought your presents back to you that you hate her, that you hate them all!' she cried with tremulous indignation and emotion. 'It is because I feel they suffer through me that I know not how to bear to see them suffer. Carmelo and I can do well enough; we are young and strong, and we have love and health to bear us up; but the old people—the old people— and it is all because you hate them. It is all through me!'

'This is insanity!' said Messer Nellemane, lifting his hands. 'It is worse: it is defamation! You are using the language of libel. All, I repeat, all, that has befallen your family is the simple and inevitable result of their inattention and disobedience to the laws of the land. Their contumacy has met with its natural, and I must say, however private compassion may plead for them, its just chastisement.'

'Oh, hypocrite!' cried Viola, with her pale cheeks flaming as the sun flames in the west on an autumn night. 'I did ill to come to you. You have a face of brass, a heart of stone!'

'You are excited,' said Messer Nellemane coldly. 'I am sorry that you ever misconstrued my charity to a poor man's granddaughter. I should have hoped that innocent country maidens had had purer thoughts. I fancied that it was only women of light life who put evil constructions on simple courtesies! Your child is crying. Will you excuse me if I request you to leave me now?'

The child had burst out sobbing loudly. Viola pressed it to her bosom, and turned and left the room.

Messer Nellemane had been to the last victorious; he had made her feel an unwomanly, unwise, ill-spoken creature, who had fancied an unholy passion as existing in a mere commonplace and benevolent compliment!

Her cheeks burned; her hot tears fell.

'O *bimbo mio!*' she wailed to the wailing child. 'Is it indeed only the law? Will the law follow us out into the sickly Maremma and seize our last crust there? O *bimbo mio!* if you were not so dear, so sweet, so fair, almost for your sake I could wish you had never been born!'

'What a fortunate thing I resisted my momentary infatuation for her,' thought Messer Nellemane, left alone with the prospectus and estimates of the Catacomb Metropolitan. 'Really she has grown quite plain, and how very painfully thin! If factories were established, there would not be this class of useless, hungry, most unhappy women.'

And he stretched out his hand and unearthed from the mass of the Catacomb circulars a plan for the Giunta to turn the old Convent of S. Francesca Romana into a manufactory: it would be hideous, it would pollute the river, and it would bring to the municipality a clear forty per cent. per annum. What could be more public-spirited?

## CHAPTER XXXVI.

THIS night that Annunziata died, Carmelo and his father were sitting up by the light of a three-branched lamp, and poring over their accounts. They kept these ill; they could make clear figures, but the miller wrote ill, and the young man, who had always been lazy in these matters, could not write at all.

Still, even their scanty education enabled them to perceive very clearly that the miller was deeply in debt, and that, unless things mended, they would share the fate of Pippo. And there was no chance that they would mend; the steam mill would every month take more and more. Santa Rosalia did as bigger societies have done a million times, and followed self-interest and the breeze of the hour.

The father and son felt this bitterly; both had fancied it would have been otherwise, for they were simple enough to expect that, as the whole village hated the *oppressor rusticorum*, the whole village would have courage to show their hatred; neither of them had great knowledge of human nature, and both had simple and trustful characters.

'Who could have thought all our folks would be so mean?' muttered Pastorini.

'They are taught to be mean,' said his son. 'They are ruled by a spy and a sergeant of police. What would you? All the fault is with the government.'

Pastorini sighed; he was thinking of all his dead brother had fought for; he did not understand politics, but it seemed hard.

Carmelo had his elbows on the table, and his face was resting on his hands. The yellow light of bad oil, the dregs of the oil-jar, flickered on his hair and on the papers before him. It was midnight; Viola was upstairs; the moon shone in through the kitchen lattice.

'Father,' he said abruptly, 'it is no use my staying here; I cannot help you; I only do you harm.

Alone, when Dina is married, there will be enough perhaps for you, and Cesarellino and the girls; and the others, when they are grown up, will do for themselves after they have gone through the hell which they call soldiering. Father—never did I think to do it, but I see now that I must. I will go away, and try and work elsewhere, and my girl will go with me, and perhaps the old man, for he will lose his mind where he is——'

'Go away? You? The eldest son?'

Demetrio Pastorini grew ashen white, and his breath came shortly; never in all the course of the centuries had the eldest son gone from the mill.

'It will be best so,' said Carmelo, sadly; 'there is not enough for us all. There is ruin here,' he added, striking his fist on the book. 'Unburdened, may be you may pull through it. As for me, I am strong, I can do anything in the way of work.'

'A *bracciante!*' groaned his father.

'A *bracciante*, if need be,' said Carmelo. 'I will go into the Maremma next month. There is plenty of work there, they say. I do not know rightly where it lies, but one can ask. I have no money to go over seas, or else I would. But anyhow, I have a strong arm. I will not let Viola starve, nor her children when they come, nor the old man if he will trust himself with us. You will let me go, father? You will not say nay?'

Carmelo, if his father had forbidden him, would never have stirred; he was as obedient as though he were still a child; in those old homely families, the old homely virtues linger.

Demetrio Pastorini was silent: his mouth was quivering with an emotion he repressed:

'Do what your conscience tells you,' he said huskily. 'I would not check you, not I; I have nought for you at home but bread, broken with bitterness. And yet—O Lord—the pity of it!'

Then the old man laid his grey head down on the table and wept.

He would not say that it would not be best for his son to breathe another air than Bindo Terri; but it cut him to the quick. For so many years he and his had dwelt here, father and son, one after another, the old broad house-roof sheltering all. That his eldest born should be driven out like an Ishmael, and be forced to wander and work on other land than the place that had given him birth, seemed so terrible to him that, for the moment, he thought that he would sooner see Carmelo dead upon his bed. Yet he would not say him nay.

'Go if you will,' he said to him. 'When the trees went, I knew the luck of the house went with them. As for me, I shall soon be no more.'

'Nay, nay,' said Carmelo gently. 'It is I who bring ill-luck to the house. Our honest hearth should not have a gaol bird by it. Cesarellino will be better master here after you than I, father. Though I lived for fifty years, they would never take the iron out of my heart, nor the blot from off my name.'

His hands clenched as he spoke; and in his soul he cursed those who had cursed him.

He panted to be gone: it wrung his very heart-strings to leave his own land, to think that he should live no more by the water that had sung to him since, in his babyhood, he had pattered in its shallows with rosy tripping feet; yet he thirsted to be gone.

He feared at every moment that rage would master him, and some utterance, or act, of it again fling him to his foes. The glance and the gibe of the guards, the estrangement of old comrades, the sight of the waste ground by his father's house, the shrug with which the youngsters went away and left him on the first Sunday afternoon when he had gone to take up his old place on the *pallone* ground, the sufferings of old Pippo and of 'Nunziatina; all these things were to him as is the fly in the galled side of the horse. He was afraid of what his pain and rage might make him do.

He was very young, and he panted for a fresh field, a free life, a place where he could work and play without a neighbour's pointed finger and an enemy's jeer.

He was very ignorant, and knew nothing even of other communes than his own; but he said to himself that anything was better than bringing ruin on his father; and he felt that he had strength in him to cut a new road out for himself, and get bread for his wife and the old man. He thought that somewhere there must always be bread enough for a willing labourer.

So little did he know, so little did even his own poverty make him realise, the poverty that gnaws tens of thousands of empty bodies in this land, eaten bare by the locusts of the State.

That night Carmelo sat up long by the little window that looked over the river, talking to his wife of this new hope of his. Viola had never heard of Ruth; but Ruth's heart throbs in every loving woman, and she said in her own way, 'Where thou goest I will go.'

'But grandfather?' she said, almost as soon as the idea of flight to other land had ceased to scare her, for another province to her was stranger than it would be to us to go to lands behind the sun, could we get there.

'We will take him with us,' said Carmelo stoutly. 'Nay, sweetheart, never would I ask of you to leave him. They are driving him mad here amongst them. We will persuade him to trust to us.'

'I think he never will come away,' said Viola with a sigh. 'His very life does seem as if it were wedded to those stones, as the roots of an aloe are fixed to the rock——'

'Dear love,' said Carmelo bitterly, yet tenderly, 'they will soon tear him off those stones, I fear. The beasts will never leave him in peace, and besides the house is mortgaged.'

'Then, perhaps, he would come,' said Viola, 'only he is old; you cannot get new ideas into him any more than you can get new resin into a dry pine. And there is 'Nunziatina too.'

'Father would let her live here,' answered Carmelo; 'I know he would; he is so good; and she would have our bed and our share at table.'

Viola kissed him with tender passion.

'As long as father lives he would always find a crust to keep an old woman out of prison,' said Carmelo. 'And to-morrow, Viola, I will go over and tell her so; and perhaps they will let her come out if I promise she shall never go again on the highway. I have no money.'

She kissed him again; and as they leaned there one against another, looking at the white moonlight on the Rosa water and the bats that were flying in and out of the ivy upon the wall, they were almost happy.

'If,' murmured the young man—'if we can only go where we can get bread enough to eat, Viola, and where your children will never hear that I was once in prison. Not but that I would do the same over again; just the same; yes. Poor Toppa!'

There is a great fair in August in Santa Rosalia; a cattle fair, a horse fair, and a merry-making all in one, that is always opened by a service and procession of the church.

It comes once in three years, and so does not lose its attraction from too constant repetition. It lasts two days, and all the country folk for twenty miles round come to see it.

There used to be at this gathering only good chaffing and good fellowship, followed by blameless mirth; now there is often a good deal of quarrelling, in which the knife is arbiter, and a good deal of drunkenness, for people's tempers are on edge in these days, and the wines and other drinks at the caffès are not wholesome and unadulterated, as they were before shopkeepers had to pay such taxes that they must recuperate themselves by cheating.

The preparations had been already made for this fair, and the booths and the flags enlivened the dusty piazza, and there were already groups of bullocks, white, dun, and grey, shaggy ponies and lean asses, bearded rough shepherds, and goats as bearded and rough, and lean sheep that fed on what they could crop by the road-sides; and little, indeed, is that, in these days, when the communal regulations forbid the poor creatures ever to pause in the highway

The place was full of movement, sound, and

laughter, and the noise was increased by the lowing of the cattle, and the braying of the asses, across which sounded now the chimes of San Giuseppe, and now the bells of San Romualdo.

In other years there had also pealed from across the river the beautiful, solemn, deep tones of the convent bells, but they were gone far away; they had been melted down into cannon which rusted on bastions that no one ever dreamed of attacking.

Carmelo, going towards the house of the Madonna to see how Pippo fared, had a heart less heavy than it had been since his return.

He had talked with the cattle drivers and the shepherds, and all had told him something of different places; he had also met with a horse dealer, bringing in a string of young horses from the Maremma, and he had asked the road from this man, and had been assured that a strong young fellow was always welcome in the woods there all winter. It was very far away, and very vague, but still it comforted him.

Here were men who came from the place he had thought of, and told him he might find bread there; what they related of the wide, marshy plains, of the great blue sea, of the dark forests of pine and chestnut, sounded to him wide, and fresh, and alluring. Surely, he thought, there would be no petty laws there to sting at you all day long, like a mosquito swarm in a swamp.

He was so young that any touch of hope was enough to lift him from earth like wings; he thought he would make haste to tell the old man; it would be hard, he knew, to get Pippo away from his little square house, but still he would try. He would urge it for Viola's sake. She never would bear the thought of leaving her grandfather to die alone.

He brushed his way through the crowd on the piazza, his thoughts intent on this, and not noticing that the people were all looking, not so much at the cattle or the booths, as at the iron rails that had recently been laid down along the river-side.

'Take care!' said some one roughly, and pushed him off the line just as a great, black, smoking traction engine roared along with some cars attached to it. It was the first journey of the tramway.

'The accursed thing!' cried Carmelo, while the people around him stood sullen and sorrowful, and a few partisans of the novelty tried in vain to shout and wave their hats, and excite enthusiasm.

In the cars were seated in triumph the Cavaliere Durellazzo, Signore Luca Finti, Signore Zauli, the Giunta, and others who had profited by this form of progress; Messer Nellemane sat in a corner of the first car, a smile upon his face, and a crimson rose in his buttonhole.

The ugly thing rolled out of sight amidst the dead silence of the people.

'I'm ruined,' said the diligence man, very quietly. 'I'll as well go and smoke myself out of the way as Nanni did. Nobody will miss me *now*.'

'Why do you let those things be settled and done behind your backs?' said Carmelo, with suppressed fury, as his eyes flashed. 'You are like the poor sheep yonder; you go to the slaughter-house as much as you go to your bed. Who rules here? A few knaves who have the wit to get on your backs, and ride you as we ride an ass.'

'And that is true,' said the people, ruefully;

'but what's to be done? They talk a deal down in the city——'

'Talk! Any fool can talk,' said Carmelo passionately. 'Talk is reeled out here by every rogue and every dunce, as thread reels off the women's wheel. It is action that we want. Every householder, every honest man, should dare to use his vote in matters of his *borgo*; things should not be done by a few picked knaves behind the backs of all the people. Can't you understand that much?'

'Yes, yes! Bravo! bravo!' the people nearest to him said, and the cattle drivers shouted to him to go on, and Carmelo, warmed and touched by the applause, and having all these months longed to pour out what he had heard in prison, threw his head and raised his voice.

'I have thought much about these things,' he said simply. 'Prison is a rude teacher, but one that tells no lies. There was a dying man there, who told me that we are all slaves. And what are we else? We sweat and labour from day-dawn to night, only that they may wring out of us the last penny that we have. Our mothers weep, and our fields lie half tilled, whilst our youngsters are borne off to swell the army and starve under their knapsacks. Our shipping lies idle in our ports, they tell me, weighted with taxes, till their owners dare not go afloat, and their timbers rot in the harbours. Inland, our little tradesmen are beggared like the merchantmen, and put their shutters up, and go and starve somewhere unseen. Here, in the country places, no man can say his soul is his own; if his dog stir a foot, or his child spin a top, the brutes are down on him; he must pay or be sold up. The

King, say you? Nay, he knows nought; he is set round with liars and deceivers like a hedge of aloes and cactus that lets nobody in; the Queen, in mercy, they say many a time pays the fines to redeem the workmen's tools, for these devils seize the spade, the pickaxe, the hammer that the man works with, if there be nothing better. If a man make ten centimes a day he pays the *tassa di famiglia!* you all know that. We are free, are we? And in the cities the barracks are full of bersagliere to shoot us down if we say a word, and in the country there are blackguards with little swords to spy on every act of our days! Our lives are no more our own. We must pay, pay, pay, till the sweat of our bodies is blood. They grind down our hearts and our lungs, and make them into money to squander. In the accursed factories they have built, the women work for forty centimes a day, and the children for half of that. They tell us we are prosperous and happy, and they tell the world so, at their banquets, and all over the land the people are sold up, and turned adrift and left on the highway, groaning and dying—dying in silence, because they are foolish as sheep, or holy as saints!'

The tears rolled down his face, the dew stood on his forehead; he was but echoing what he had heard in his sick bed in his prison, but he felt every word he uttered with all his heart, and with all his soul.

The people listened to him, entranced; the guard, Bindo Terri, on the outskirts of the crowd, heard too.

'They are true things that you say, lad,' muttered the diligence driver at last. 'But what can we do, my dear? If we say a word, if we fire a shot, there are the soldiers, as you say, and the prisons.'

'Then let us say we are slaves, and bow our heads,' said Carmelo, bitterly, as he pointed to the flag that floated from the caffè of Nuova Italia, 'and let us say that flag is the flag, not of freedom, but of famine, of oppression, and of fear. We starve, and a million leeches are sucking our mother Italy dry. We starve, and a million idlers sit in the public offices and fatten, and do nothing all their lives, and then are pensioned. We are cowards all.'

'Go away, my dear, they are looking at you,' said Gigi Canterelli in his ear. 'And if we all rose, what could we do, my dear? We have no weapons except a few old guns to shoot thrushes, and they would bring cannon against us like lightning.'

'What use would their cannon be if they could not get our conscripts?' said Carmelo; his breast was heaving, his eyes were shining

Bindo Terri advanced to him.

'Instead of talking sedition before witnesses,' he said, very sharply, 'you had better keep your wife's folk out of want. 'Nunziatina died the night before last in Montesacro.'

Then he slipped behind the shelter of a carabinier.

'What?' said Carmelo, with a scared glance on those around him. 'That brute is saying this only to hurt me. Tell me—tell me quick, some of you. She is not dead? She cannot be dead!'

Gigi Canterelli, who was nearest to him, put his hand soothingly on his shoulder.

'Dear lad,' he said, with hesitation, 'I did hear

something of it this morning from some one who came from the city, but surely they would have sent you word?'

'No, no,' said Carmelo, stupidly. 'No one has said anything to us. Who took her to the city? We knew nought of it. If she be dead—oh, if she be dead! What shall I say to Viola?'

Bindo Terri, safe behind the shelter of the armed carabinier, answered him.

'We had the official notice of it this morning from Montesacro. You will get it by post this afternoon. She is dead, that you may take my word for; and you had better have worked, and kept her in bread and soup, than come chattering republican balderdash that will clap you *in carcere* again.'

The young man sprang forward to seize the ribald throat that mocked him, but Gigi Canterelli and the others held him quiet.

'Dear lad,' cried Canterelli, 'remember your young wife. Get not into trouble again through this fellow. You will only rejoice his wicked soul if you do.'

'The old woman dead,' muttered Carmelo. 'Dead *so*, without one of us!'

His voice failed him; he drew his hat over his eyes and turned away.

'If you loved her so much, why did you not keep her off begging on the highway?' called Bindo Terri after him, but he did not hear.

'For shame, Bindo!' said Canterelli, sternly, and the crowd listening around echoed the reproofs.

The guard stuck his feathered hat on one side of his head, and thrust his short sword under one arm.

'If you jeer at me you are summoned,' he said,

with the pertness that he thought was dignity. 'I represent the Law.'

'Lord, Lord!' muttered Gigi Canterelli, 'and the times that I have spanked you for stealing my string and my sugar!'

Bindo, in his majesty, had his head too high to hear.

Meanwhile the tramway cars were rolling through the summer-scorched fields towards Pomodoro, and there were met by the Count Saverio, and the Syndic his brother, and the officials and gentry of that place; all, in fact, who had got a nice little pat of butter to sweeten their daily bread out of the concessions and the commissions of this iron apostle of progress.

Carmelo went across the piazza blindly; he was stunned and broken down by the tidings of the death at Montesacro.

She had been only a poor old woman, indeed, but Viola had loved her, and Carmelo himself had grown fond of the cheery, sturdy, little soul, blithe in privation as a robin in the snow.

The poor lad went on rather by instinct than by sight across the square to the house of Pippo.

'He will come with us now,' he thought; 'surely he will come with us, or he will die as she has done.'

When he reached the house his heart stopped with a spasm of fear; the door was shut: a thing never seen except at night, and the wooden outside shutters were closed and fastened too.

What could have happened to Pippo?

'He is ill!' thought Carmelo, but then he remembered that, were he ill within, he could not have fastened to those shutters, and never since he had been a child had he seen those windows thus closed.

He shook the door, and tried to force himself against it; failing in that, he looked round at a few loiterers who were near; the crowd was all on the other side of the piazza.

'What has happened to Pippo, do you know?' he asked of them.

'Not I,' said the man he spoke to, but he grinned as he answered.

Carmelo went round, vaulted over the wall enclosing the little back garden, and saw the house was shut in the same way.

'Good God, what can have happened?' said Carmelo in his bewilderment and terror. Had the old man been murdered? But who should murder one who had nothing?

Remigio Rossi from the mill-house across the river saw him thus standing, rigid and gasping, staring at the house. He shouted to the youth:

'The house has been seized for debt. They turned your grandfather out of it last night. He went away. I thought he went to you. Did nobody send you word? But, to be sure, it was nobody's business. Come in, my poor fellow, and take a drink of wine.'

Carmelo hurled a bitter curse at him.

'Where is he gone?' he shouted.

'Nay, that I know not,' said the owner of the steam-mill. 'We thought he came to you. Lord, boy, I mean none of you ill-will because I put up this black servant of mine and fill my pockets——'

But Carmelo had no ears for him. He had left the garden as he had entered it, and was gone across the fields. He had seen in the damp ground a print of a foot without shoes: he thought it was Pippo's.

'I never can meet my girl's eyes again if both are dead,' he thought. 'Surely he has killed himself like Nanni.'

He heard a step in pursuit of him, and the friendly hand of Gigi Canterelli touched him.

'Carmelo, Carmelo!' he cried to him, 'I have just this minute heard that your grandfather was turned out last night. They did it so quietly, none of us knew. It seems the lawyer in Pomodoro had a right to the place because the interest on the mortgage was not paid, and there were sums Pippo owed to the municipality, fines and what not, God knows, about the water, and so the *usciere* came and took the thing, and locked it up, all in the name of the law, and it has been sold at auction: so they say. That is what Angelo, the beast, has just told me. He saw you coming here. How it was we none of us saw or heard I cannot think, but the lawyers and the other folks kept still tongues in their heads, and the door of the house is turned to the river, and Pippo can never have made a sound——'

'He is gone away to kill himself,' said Carmelo under his breath.

He paid no heed to what was told him of the seizure of the house; all he thought of was that Pippo was lying dead in the Rosa water, or hanging dead from some bough in the fields.

'Nay,' said Gigi Canterelli in a hushed and solemn way, 'I think he will not take his life. He is a God-fearing man, is Pippo, and he thinks that in the matter of our living or dying it is the good God that fans our breath or stills it.'

Carmelo did not hear; he was looking to right and left of him wildly, as though he saw the corpse of the old man swinging in the air.

'If he be not dead,' he said, with a burst of weeping like a woman, 'he has gone to try and hide, so that we should not know. Look, here is a footmark; it goes along the fields; he would not stay by the river, I think, to see that iron beast roar along it; he would get away into the fields, away from the accursed smoke.'

He strode away as he spoke, and his old friend followed him.

'His brain was not right,' said Carmelo with a sob. 'It has never been right since he signed away his house to pay the thieves yonder. And I, who came to ask him to go with me to a new life——'

'O Lord, have mercy on us,' groaned the other. 'Nobody ever killed themselves when I was young; but nowadays the rivers are choked full, and the charcoal is used for naught but death.'

'Let us look,' said Carmelo in a low tone. He felt as if he were choking.

He broke off with a loud cry.

Under one of the maples of the vine fields that stretched all around he saw the old man sitting. The tree was heavy with green grapes, and the leaves were golden with sunbeams. Pippo was bare-headed, and his head was sunk on his breast.

Carmelo ran to him and threw himself beside him.

'Grandfather, don't you know me? Speak to me! look at me! Don't you see me, *me*, Carmelo? don't you hear?'

The old man's clothes and long white hair were

wet with dew; he had been out all night. He lifted his head, but his face was quite vacant. He chuckled a little; and he kept a great old rusty key in his hand. Carmelo saw it, and understood, and his heart stood still.

'They won't get in,' said Pippo in a whisper, clutching the key. 'They won't get in; I've got the key. It is my house, and I am master. There were many of them, so I took the key and hid. It is my house; it is my house.'

That was all he said; he hugged the key against his breast and chuckled.

'It is my house; they'll find I'm master. They've taken a hundred scudi from me, and all the things, and the bed that the girl was born on, and the bit of glass she saw her pretty face in; and the little dog is dead, and the reeds in the river are wanted for the king; but they won't get in the house; I've got the key.'

His hands clenched the thing closer and closer; he laughed a little feeble laugh of foolish triumph.

His mind was quite gone.

When the law had seized his house it had given the death-blow to his poor old brain, that for so long had been 'buzzing and muddling,' and seeing nothing anywhere in the air or in the water, in the sky or on the land, but those figures that had puzzled him so.

'I've got the key, they can't get in; it's my house, it's my house; and when I'm dead you'll bury me under the almond-trees where the little dog is, and you'll make the house into a chapel,' he muttered, clasping the key to his bosom, and looking with blank and foolish eyes into the sunshine that played with the vines.

At that moment, at the banquet in the Pretura of Pomodoro, the Cavaliere Durellazzo was reading out with much applause an oration compiled for him by Messer Gaspardo Nellemane.

In this eloquent speech he spoke of the prosperity of the country, of the excellence of the laws, of the admirable economy that was observed in every public department, of the necessity for Italia to be heard and respected in the councils of Europe, and of the large army that must be one of her chief glories as a great Power.

The discourse was received with great enthusiasm, and was duly reported in the local press, and praised in the organs alike of the Opposition, the Dissidenti, and the Ministry.

'I recognise your hand,' whispered Signor Luca Finti to Messer Nellemane. 'You must become a deputy at the next election; and I make no doubt that you and I some day shall sit as Ministers round the same council-table.'

Messer Nellemane smiled modestly as he slipped away to send a telegram in the name of the two Syndics to the King, announcing the completion of the great work opened that day.

He saw no reason why the prediction should not be fulfilled; nor, I confess, do I see any. He has every qualification for the honour.

## CHAPTER XXXVII.

At this moment Santa Rosalia pays two francs a day for Pippo, who has to be kept at the public cost at the asylum of St. Bonifaccio in the city. He is imbecile, and at times violent, but his old frame is tough; he does not die. At times he weeps for days together, and then they punish him. He is always searching for a lost key.

Viola was so unnerved and distracted at the calamity befallen her grandfather that she fell into a fever, which, coupled with her distress of mind, killed her as it killed young Mercédes of Spain: but Viola was not so soon forgotten and replaced. The little *bimbo*, bereft of his young mother, soon followed her to her grave. Carmelo, maddened with grief, joined himself to some few fiery and chafing spirits, nourished like himself on the bitterness of endless wrong; they tried to burn down the communal palace which held all those accursed documents against the poor, and, failing, were taken prisoners, and after a long trial sent to the galleys. The Italian and English press described them as a band of ignorant and brutal socialists; and then no one remembered them any more. They are in the mines of Sardinia.

Demetrio Pastorini died broken-hearted; his sons were unable to compete with the steam-mill, and sold the old place to the commune for a pittance; they are some of them day-labourers, and some are taken as conscripts.

Cecco is dead, and his sons are also conscripts. Gigi Canterelli, having the municipality against him, became bankrupt, and is now a beggar; the old convent on the hill is a factory where the women and children earn a few centimes a day with loss of all their health. The little house of the Madonna has been bought and enlarged by Bindo Terri, who has married well and entered into a wine business with the money he saved in his service of the State. His brother succeeded to his uniform and sword, and is as like him as one ferret is like another.

Messer Gaspardo Nellemane meanwhile flourishes like a green bay-tree in the service of the State: he is full of ambition, and in all probability will live to attain all his aims and die in all honour.

Santa Rosalia soon became too small to hold so great a man.

He has been translated to Rome.

When the Dissidenti become the Possidenti he will be with them in power. If, on the other hand, the Right return to office, Messer Nellemane will know how to take profit from the fact that he has always been moderate; he has been always on the side of order and the law.

Whatever party reign at Montecitorio it will be said of him, 'Verily he has his reward.'

# APPENDIX.

MARK TWAIN has said that an appendix gives a great dignity to a book. Despite this joke at it, it does not scare readers away, perhaps, as greatly as a preface does. At any rate, I will risk the addition, because I want to assure all who take up this story that there is no kind of exaggeration in it.

No doubt the public will be tempted to think that the municipal tyrannies, here depicted, are over-coloured, but I can assure them that I have in not the slightest degree overdrawn the power of those little communal councils, and the terrible suffering that they entail upon the poor people of this beloved country.

Travellers, and even foreign residents, do not, as a rule, know anything about this. You must know the language intimately, and you must have got the people's trust in you, before you can understand all that they endure. The system is, as I have said, professedly autonomous, but practically it works in the manner I have depicted. The frightful taxation of the noble and gentle is bad; the taxation of the commercial interest, of the shipping, and the trades is still worse; but more cruel by far than all is the municipal extortion by tax, by fine, and by penalty, that crushes out the very life-blood of the peasant part of the nation. There are, of course, communes where some good and wise man is chief proprietor, and then it is fairly well governed. There are others in which the blacksmith or the carpenter is at the head of affairs, and then, though things may go ill, the populace cannot complain. But these are few exceptions, and, in the main part, the twopenny Gessler that I have endeavoured to sketch disposes of its destinies at his will.

It is entirely useless to change the ministries of Italy so long as this municipal system remains what it is. It has ruined Venice, Florence, and Naples, and is ruining Rome; as it has done on a great scale in the cities, so it does on a little one in the small towns and villages. An enormous bureaucracy enriches itself at the public cost, and the people perish.

I believe that these municipal tyrannies might often legally be combated, but the populace cannot afford to do this. I won a cause lately against a municipality, and a shoemaker said to me, 'Oh, there is one law for you rich folks, and another law for us poor!'

And practically it is so; the poor man cannot afford to employ an advocate, and his pleading against false charges or extortion is never attended to; the tax-gatherers or the communal clerks are believed, and the poor man is beggared at a blow. Against the decisions of these small courts, also, there is no appeal.

It is no question here of the Right, or of the Left; it is a question of a method of so-called self-government, which goes on and impoverishes and distracts the country just the same, whether Cairoli or Sella, Minghetti or Nicotera, rule at Montecitorio.

It is this which the public of other countries never understand, and which the correspondents of the foreign Press never endeavour to point out. Here Garibaldi does in vain rail against it; nobody attends to him. In vain has he again and again declared the misery of Italy to arise from the locust-swarms of the *impiegati*, and the crowds of pensioners who live on and bleed the State to death. If I ruled Italy, I would ship nine-tenths of the *impiegati* and the pensioners to New Guinea: we might then get public business done, and the public coffers filled, without wrenching his last coin from the day-labourer. When the pensioner dies, his pension dies with him; but when the accursed *impiegato* leaves his stool of office, another of his breed is ready to spring on to it. He is an alligator that the hot sands of sinecure and corruption generate, and he multiplies without end. All political parties nourish him alike, as all alike continue to allow the local despotisms to cramp and starve the body politic.

One man arose and said this nobly in Montecitorio in the last session: no one listened to him; he was even shouted down; all they care to hear about there is Tunis or Albania, or a new loan.

It is a common remark that Italy wants a Bismarck: she wants nothing of the kind; she wants a minister, temperate, just, indifferent to bombast or display, resolute to destroy corruption, and convinced of the great truth that the first duty of a State is the prosperity of her children. But, alas! when a good man comes, he has no chance; his party split into schisms; the Dissidenti, disappointed of place, sting him like wasps; to be popular with Parliament and the Press, he must talk big of armies, of ships, and of the councils of Europe, and, even if he be premier, it is fifty to one that the great bulk of the populace never even know his name. Harassed, weary, and impotent, he will leave his good intentions to pave a lower deep than Dante ever visited, and, out of heart with all things, will let them drift on in their old fashion, knowing that you must be a demigod ere you can sweep clean this Augean stable.

I know the Italian people well; I mean the poor, the labouring people; I am attached to them for their loveableness, their infinite natural intelligence, their wondrous patience; they are a material of which much might be made.

They are but little understood by foreigners, even by foreign residents; they are subtle and yet simple; of an infinite good nature, and yet sadly selfish; they are very docile, yet they have great sensitiveness, and I see no more greed in them than in the poor of all countries; if we had not bread for our hungry children, I daresay we should be greedy too. There are sundry people, very, very poor, to each of whom I give a little sum weekly; *not one* of these people has ever asked for more than the allotted sum, not one has ever made it an excuse to plead for further gifts. Dear readers of mine, can you say as much of your countrymen?

They are ignorant, no doubt, and they are likely to remain so, for the public free education is a farce; the communal schools, when they have taught a boy his letters, set him to teach some smaller boy, and so on *ad infinitum*. They are ignorant, no doubt, and it is the interest of the municipalities, as much as ever it was that of the priesthood, to keep them so. As it is, they endure all these extortions and tyrannies that I have endeavoured in some measure to depict; endure them patiently, knowing no remedy, and incapable of the general action that can alone make a people's strength felt. Now and then there are clamourers for bread, but very few and gentle ones; there are troops and carabiniers everywhere ready to shoot them down, and if they murmur they are clapped in the Murate, where poor diet and low fever do the rest for most of them.

The nobility and gentry are supine, where they are not tyrannical.

Consequently, the municipalities conduct all affairs high over the heads of the persons concerned, and all sorts of important public works, sales, demolitions, or constructions are effected against the will of the people, who stand helpless.

The Left is inclined to make each commune still more self-governing and independent of the State: should this be done, the effects will be distressing on the populace; on the contrary, it would be far better to confine the syndics of all districts within the limits of imperial law. Their changes and caprices are a source of continual distraction to the country; for instance, at Genoa, a syndic (a well-known general) forbade dogs being given by the city to the vivisectors; a few weeks after came another syndic, who decreed that all dogs found loose should be seized and sent to the vivisectors' laboratories. This is only one instance out of many.

The illimitable and captious powers of these momentary

rulers are a source of worry, grief, and extortion to the people, greater than I can hope to make any one believe. The whole system is execrable, and leads to endless abuses.

The greater number of the nobles are so absorbed in their own grievance of paying 45 per cent. impost, that they have no ear and no inclination to pity any woes of the poor. The inexhaustible generosity of France has no counterpart in Italy. Even subscriptions for a charitable purpose are very niggardly given, and when given are usually filtered through so many hands in their passage to the poor that little reaches them. Save here and there an asylum, to which it takes strong interest and recommendation to get admitted, there is nothing for the poor; the man or woman who is starving has nothing to do except to die. The great difficulty in Italy is the apathy of the higher classes, and their absolute indifference to the state of the poor. When they do take interest in public affairs, it is too often only for the sake of the personal advantages, the nepotism, the contracts, or the *kudos* that may grow out of it. An Italian, in office of any kind, will always hear you amiably and courteously, but when you plead for the people he will only think you a fool, and say, 'Cara mia, why trouble yourself? They do very well, and they are all of them cheats.'

'How can you write books about these *birbonaccie*?' said an Italian nobleman to me, meaning about the contadini in *Signa*. 'They spend their whole lives in fleecing us. You should never believe a word that they say.'

Now, I would be far from declaring that this is the only view that the proprietor takes in Italy, but it is, alas! a very general one.

The number of vagrants and idlers is largely increased by the absurd law of the code which forces every parent to maintain a son, every brother a brother, every husband a wife, &c., however vicious, vile, or incurably lazy they may be; a law which indeed puts a premium on idleness, and attaches a penalty to industry; a law which, in its effects on the youth of the country, is beginning to be dangerous. On those who are industrious and saving, the insatiable taxes bring oftentimes wholesale ruin; every trade and every employment is taxed as if it were a crime; every labouring man must pay his quota, and if he do not pay, his tools and all that he has are forfeited.

A recent Italian writer on the terrible state of the Romagna and the Marches observes very rightly that the great bulk of the people derive no sort of benefit from all the mass of money thrown away in the alterations of the old streets, and introductions of new methods in the cities. He justly observes that where the pilgrimages, once so continual, took money into all the villages and small towns, the railways take it all away, and render nine-tenths of the provinces through which they pass poverty-stricken. The tunnels of the Alps have the effect of drawing away the food that the nation itself requires. A few contractors are enriched; but the markets of the populace are denuded, and only the worst of the products of the soil, and of meat and poultry, finds its way to the nation's mouth. Any night that you go down to any railway station when the goods-trains pass, you will see tons on tons of vegetables, fruits, and butchers' meat going to France or Germany. What can be more disastrous, also, for a country whose populace chiefly depend for all their bodily strength on wine, to sell their grapes to French and German merchants? Yet this is what the landowners have been doing this year right and left. Dazzle the eyes of an Italian with a little immediate profit, and alas! you may plunge him headlong into any folly, make him consent to any speculation.

It is irritating to see the foreign press, which knows nothing actually of the condition of things, laying down the law on Italian affairs. The English press attributes all the official evils of new Italy to the transmitted vices of the old *régimes*. Now I did not live during the old *régimes*, and cannot judge of them; but this I do know, that the bulk of people regret passionately the personal peace and simple plenty that were had under them. The vices of the present time are those of a grasping and swarming bureaucracy everywhere, and of the selfishness which is the worst note of the Italian character.

'Why do you care for that horse being hurt? It is not your horse,' every one will say to you; an impersonal interest is a thing they cannot conceive.

'*Una vanità enorme, un' aspro cinicismo ed i suoi interessi,*' says an Italian journalist of a living Italian minister, alone govern his conduct. Substitute for the bitter cynicism an indolent amiability that never exerts itself, and you have the characters of most Italian public men. The well-meaning have no power to cope with the vast inert mass of nepotism and corruption that block the way to all real economy, to all true justice. Whatever names and parties change in the government, these always remain the same. *Plus ça change plus c'est la même chose.*

As an ounce of example is said to be worth a pound of precept, I will cite the following cases which have come under my eyes in the last three months:

1. A man living in one commune, but on the borders of another, having paid his taxes in the first, naturally refused to pay them over again in the second. As he would not submit to be twice taxed, the commune got a summons out against him with its usual result of distraint. He had nothing of any value but a gun; they seized that. A gentleman took the case up, and obliged them to confess the man had been in the right; they promised to return the gun, but as yet they have 'not been able to find it.'

2. A contadino was going up a steep hill with some very heavy barrels of wine. Being a merciful man, to lighten his beast he placed two barrels by the roadside, meaning to fetch them later. He was seen by a rural guard, though it was in a wild and lonely part of the hills. He was subsequently summoned and fined ten francs! There is a rule in rural police laws that a man must never let his horse pause in the road to rest; *it would be an obstruction.*

3. The wife of a navvy who remains in a city of central

Italy while her husband is gone to work in Sardinia is in very great necessity and almost penniless; she has only a few sticks of furniture in a wretched room. One of her children fell ill with fever, and a gentleman sent her in a little bed for the sick child. The officers of the law saw the bed going in, and immediately assessed her for eight francs *tassa di famiglia*. She had not eight pence for the week's bread. They might as well have asked her for a million.

What can one say of a municipal government in which such a state of things is possible?

Meanwhile, in the public offices, tens of thousands of dawdling youngsters lounge in for a few hours, and are subsidised at from a thousand to two thousand francs a year, to be entirely useless and grossly impudent.

A respectable man went the other day to pay something at a public office. Three young men were gossiping on the ground floor. They said, ' it is not our business, go to the first floor;' the first floor sent him to the second, the second to the third; the third to the fourth; the fourth told him it was business for the ground floor. When he returned there they yawned and bade him ' come back to-morrow.'

At the customs-offices, again, no one can be seen till nine; at three a great bell rings, and away they all go and the place is shut; a gardener of mine went to get a little parcel weighing half a chilo, and prepaid from Germany. They kept him four hours, then sent him away without it because the bell rang. He was kept from eleven to two the next day, and finally, with a sheaf of signed papers long enough to sign away a kingdom, he got the little parcel, which was only a book. Garibaldi used to curse the 'black shoals' of the priesthood; the 'black shoals' of the *impiegati* are a more ravenous, more idle, and far more cruel class; they are an unredeemed curse to the country, and if I could I would send nine-tenths of them to hard labour to-morrow. When a poor man goes to pay a tax for a dog there are all sorts of excuses from the *impiegati*; it is not the time to pay it, the books are being revised, he may come in a month, the streets are being renumbered, he had better call again when they are finished; anyhow, he cannot get his receipt. A little later down comes the Esattore of the commune for arrears of the dog tax. In vain the poor man protests; no one believes him. When he has paid, the demand is made over and over again. They assessed a poor baker the other day for two years' dog tax with penalties; happily, I had paid the tax for him and so worsted them, as I produced the receipts. But if he had been alone, his receipts would have been insufficient to protect him.

This whole, enormous, and insatiable bureaucracy is like a sytaris; a sytaris, as you know, hides on a bee's back, gets taken into the hive, then slips into the cell where the bee larva lies steeped in honey, and tucking itself snugly up in the cell, kills the larva and sucks all the honey; one fine day, having grown fat and mature, it flies away.

To the bureaucracy the whole public is what the bee larva is to the sytaris grub; a means of growing plump and living in sweetness. This is no question of ministries; it is a much deeper question; that of a gangrene putrefying in the body politic of the nation.

There is a little Almanac sold for a soldo and bought by tens of thousands of the poor of Italy, which, in a very well-written little article addressed 'Ai Signori Ministri,' speaks of the unutterable misery brought on the industrious and honest classes by the frightful taxation which makes the peasant of Italy scarcely better off than the fellah of Egypt.

Referring to the projected law of Seismet Doda for relieving the poor of these burdens (a law which is for ever being 'considered' by the Chambers, but never passed), it proceeds to point out how all the small proprietors and the respectable poor are being utterly destroyed off the land. All the working people who are ordered to pay fines, six, seven, eight, or ten *lire* to the tax-gatherer, or the municipal police, are sold up if they cannot pay—sold up to the very tools of their trade.

The Esattore (examiner of taxes) published in one day

for the little *borghetto* of Rocca Magna no less than fourteen forced sales[1] of the houses or land of very poor men, which had been seized in the name of the State; little houses of three hundred or two hundred *lire* in worth, and in one instance the tax-gatherer seized and sold a piece of arable ground at the price of a hundred and ten francs. Everything is confiscated, because, to the simple tax due, there are added all the expenses of fine, of execution, of law-dues, and costs of auction!

Let no one think that my poor old Pippo is an exaggeration. Pippo has a thousand, and ten thousand suffering likenesses of himself all over the land.

The little Almanac adds, bitterly and justly:

'If all these working people, once content and laborious, thus dispossessed and driven out, cumber the prison, whose fault will it be? Who has caused them to change from peaceful, happy, country folks to despairing beggars? In the last few years, nearly *two million* small proprietors have been ruined and sent into beggary; at the same time all beggary is treated as a crime deserving imprisonment.'

It concludes with the threat, *Guai a voi, Deputati e Ministri se meriterete la maledizione dei poveri!*

This is no vice of an old *régime*. In the old *régime* there was scarcely any taxation; it is the vice of a hard, grasping, and greedy bureaucracy, and of the fatal appetite for devouring public money, and manner of regarding every public place as a mere opportunity and occasion for private enrichment, which are the characteristic of all the public and political life of the country.

In addition to this overwhelming taxation, there is the blackmail incessantly levied from the poor by the penalties that the municipalities assess at their pleasure and discretion. Half of these go to the municipal guard, and in the advertisements in newspapers inserted by communes who want a candidate for this noble office, this share of the fines is advertised as one of the attractions and perquisites of the post. It is easy to imagine what the

[1] Vendita all' asta, *or*, al incanto.

public suffer when three or four of these legalised and interested spies are allowed to stalk about every country lane, and peer into every hedge and spinney.

The timid purchase immunity from their torment at heavy cost of bribes; the courageous suffer incessantly from their espionage and hatred. By the police regulations of these gentlemen every harmless act in a day of country life may furnish food for fine and penalty. The testimony of the guard is taken as witness enough; and the poor man, harassed and fleeced by those set over him, and who should protect him, has no resource but to submit and pay. It is not too much to say that this daily and hourly tyranny and extortion of the myrmidons of the municipalities are, all over Italy, sowing the seeds of a bitter hatred of all Law.

The honest peasant sees himself ceaselessly spied on, worried, summoned, fined for all sorts of harmless little things; his dog barks on his wall, his child spins a top on the road, or bathes in a river, he lays an armful of brushwood on a lonely forest path, he rests his old horse a moment by the wayside; forthwith the spy is down on him, and he has to deliver over all his wages for the day, perhaps all his wages for the week, to the petty officers and judges who are banded together in a body to pillage him. If he will bribe, he will be let alone: if he will not, he will be persecuted for all time till they make him a beggar.

Until this system is entirely abolished and replaced by something of real freedom for all honest men, I see no peace possible for the people; and were their rulers not blind as moles they would hasten to pluck out this 'thorn from the foot' ere its canker spreads over the whole body.

But alas! no one in office cares about any of these things. A week ago a famous Italian doctor rose in the Chambers and drew attention to the destruction of the woods of Latium and the rural guards' connivance at these repeated infringements (for base reasons) of forest-law. He was listened to with apathy; and the minister concerned coldly said—he would inquire!

But all those present could see that this inquiry would be the last thing that he would deem it worth his while to make.

It is strange that with the present state of Ireland before their eyes the whole of the public men of Italy should be as indifferent as they are to the perpetual irritation of all the industrious classes at the hands of the municipalities and their organisation of spies and penalties. But indifferent they are: whether Bismarck approve of their Greek policy, or Gambetta do not oppose their doings at Tunis, is all they think about; the suffering of a few million of their own people is too small a thing to catch their attention; they think like Molière's doctor—' Un homme mort n'est qu'un homme mort, et ne fait point de conséquence, mais une formalité negligée porte un notable préjudice à tout le corps de médecins.'

No one can accuse me of any political prejudices. My writings have alternately been accused of a reactionary conservatism and a dangerous socialism, so that I may, without presumption, claim to be impartial; I love conservatism when it means the preservation of beautiful things; I love revolution when it means the destruction of vile ones.

What I despise in the pseudo liberalism of the age is that it has become only the tyranny of narrow minds vested under high-sounding phrases, and the deification of a policeman. I would give alike to a Capucin as to a Communist, to a Mormon as to a Monk, the free choice of his opinions and mode of life. But this true liberty is nowhere to be found in Europe, and still less to be found in America; and this pseudo liberty meddles with every phase of private life, and would dictate the rule of every simple act.

Every noble-hearted theorist of a future of freedom has died in heart-broken disillusion; from the Girondists of the past century to those who, with high hopes, shouted in chorus to Silvio Pellico the *Bianca croce di Savoia!* Thousands of gallant and goodly lives are thrown away like water in the effort to create a fair Utopia of free action and untroubled peace; and all that, in the end, is born of their sacrifice is a horde of weazels and of leeches, who suck the body of the nations dry; vermin who bear upon their backs a swarm of smaller parasites as pestilent as themselves.

Gianbattista Niccolini, walking with Centofanti one day in Florence, shouted to two monks:

'Go and get a spade and dig, you good-for-noughts!'

This is what, nowadays, the poor man—laborious and honest—seeing the idle eaters of the public funds swarming in and out of every public office, every municipality, every custom house, mutters in his soul against the accursed *impiegato*.

It is a change of masters, it is true, but it is no deliverance. It is the old tale of Jeannot's knife; blade and handle have both been changed, but it is the same knife still, and here it cuts the hand that forged it.

Yet again one of the deepest sins of the State against the public is the Government lottery.

It is difficult to imagine a more absurd anomaly, a more entirely indefensible contradiction, than the severity exercised by the State towards all private games and street games, and the selfishness with which it continues to be itself the centre of the most demoralising system of gaming that can be devised for the ruin of the people. The interference of the State with private gambling is carried to an inquisitive and impertinent excess; yet at the same time, for sake of profit, the Government carries on a gigantic machinery more fatal in its effects on the populace than any Casino like Monte Carlo. In the Casino it may be said that none are victims save those who voluntarily seek the pernicious attraction, and they are most of them people who, if they could not play there, would play at home. Paris baccarat is ten times worse than Monte Carlo's roulette; but the public lottery is ten times worse than Paris baccarat, because the State comes out and seeks the poor man as he takes his hard-earned wages, descends amidst the populace, wooes, entices, enervates, intoxicates, and beggars them.

'Ah! the State is a clever one,' said a working man to

me the other day. 'It sells everything else to the Hebrews, but it takes good care to keep the lottery itself.'

And this is true; everything else, down to the rights of Octroi at the gates of cities, are sold to the Jew syndicates, but the Government retains the lottery; and it may be safely affirmed that so long as it does retain this vile thing, so long will the sin and the sorrow of the multitudes lie at its doors. Not merely does it foster the fatal superstition which makes the study of 'lucky numbers' and 'dream omens' the sole thought of the people, but in the rare cases where the poor man wins, the sudden delirium of riches has an effect like poison on him, and he spends all in a brief summer frenzy to perish afterwards in beggary or a madhouse. The lottery takes all the earnings of the labouring classes in all the cities, usurps all their mind and hopes, keeps them for ever in that fever of longing which is in itself a moral disease, and encourages in them alike the lowest greed and the most enervating indolence.

No one seems to dare to lift up a voice against it; but until a minister shall arise who will destroy it, the nation will have no faithful public servant.

I would sooner see a Casino like Monte Carlo in every city of Italy, if thus the lottery could be abolished, than I would see as I do, daily and hourly, the legalised publicity of this accursed destroyer of the people allowed all over the land, whilst boys playing *morra* for coppers are seized by the police!

The system, too, to which I alluded above, of selling the Octroi and other public taxes to individuals or companies, is productive of evils which it would be impossible, without volumes of statistics, fully to describe. A grasping speculator, or group of spectators, buys up the rights of taxation over a city or a province, and makes the most out of the speculation that can be made. I ask the reader to think over for a moment all that this implies, all that this permits.

Yet who speaks of all these terrible and frightful evils —evils by which the country is impost-laden till it sinks like the over-weighted camel?

No one. The journals write beautiful threnodies over the grave of Ricasoli, and Rochefort shakes hands with Garibaldi, and who amidst the mouthing and the posturing of it all cares one straw for the nation, for the people?

The ranting demagogues of Milan care as little as the *amnistié* of the Cité Malesherbes or the satrap of the Palais Bourbon.

The one shriek for Universal Suffrage and the others shriek for the Commune or for the March Decrees and the Scrutin de Liste; but when does the one speak of abolishing the lottery or the other of abolishing the conscription?

When Madame Roland spoke her farewell words to liberty, she prophesied the whole hypocrisy of the century to come.

I want people to get these facts that I have narrated well into their minds; to turn their eyes a moment from the Italian men-of-war joining the Naval Demonstration of the Powers, and the Italian troops deploying in the Val d'Aosta and the Mugello,[1] and look into these million humble homes, darkened and naked, and see these children without food, these men without hope, who suffer that the pomp and parade of an empty boast may throw dust in the eyes of Europe.

I cannot think to make you care for these people as I care for them; I, who know that they see their radiant sun for ever through a mist of tears, who know that their hard-won bread is eaten with the gall of fear and of oppression tainting the sour crust, who know that their little children tremble in their town alleys and country lanes, and fly with their hunted dog from the armed myrmidon of a relentless and ignominious law; I cannot think to make you suffer for them as I do, but still I think you will not refuse to feel some pity for them and some pain.

[1] The manœuvres in the Mugello alone cost the country two millions of *lire*; yet the men had but one ration in twenty-four hours, and were on one occasion kept from one noon to the next fasting, and without even a drop of wine. These few days of sham battles cost precisely as many francs as there have been small proprietors ruined by the taxes!

## APPENDIX.

Italy is essentially a pastoral country. Those who would turn it into a manufacturing one would be as those who should turn a tabernacle of Giotto's into a breeding hutch of swine. The people thrive on their pure ambient air, they pass their lives under their unsullied skies, they love laughter, song, dance; and still—with the pipe of Corydon and the smile of Adonis—welcome the harvest night and the vintage morn. Up in the hills and in the green places remote from cities, the old, simple, contented, pastoral life still prevails, and there the husbandman follows Christ and recites Tasso; maybe he cannot read the words of either, what of that? Raoul Rigault and Passanante, the murderer Prevost, and the murderess Virginie Dumaine, could all of them read. Were they the better for it?

In its simplicity, in its freedom, in its purity of family affection, and in its Greek-like habits of husbandry, I believe the unspoiled country life of Italy to be the best that remains to humanity on the face of the earth. When the childish pettifoggers of the new school scream with puerile ecstasy at the sight of a tramway, of a steam thresher, they know not all the beauty, content, and pious peace that they destroy only to enrich some Scotch contractor or some Hebrew usurer. There are 40,000 Jews in Italy, and to them are going all the old estates, all the old palaces, and all the old heirlooms; the Italian noble, no more content to dwell as dwelt his forefathers, aspires to be beggared by the *belles petites* of Paris or the baccarat of some fashionable hell; the Italian people beholding all their old plenty and ancient rights slipping away from them, stand sullen and full of futile wrath to see all that for twice a thousand years has been their own passing into the coffer of the foreign speculator or money-lender. This ruin is called Progress—and the whole land groans, and the whole people curse.

Beyond all else, I repeat, is Italy a pastoral country All its peace and its joy lie amidst its smiling fields. The conscription that takes all its country lads from plough and spade, from vineyard and chestnut wood, because its leaders are bitten with the mania of meddling and marring in the councils of Europe, does the same evil to the land that do the foreign speculators who cover the country with unfinished rails and demolished buildings in that cruellest of all greeds, the greed of the hungry gambler of the stock-exchange. The temptations to the peasant to leave his hillside for the cities, which those gamblers for their own ends put before him as improvement, is as merciless and fatal as any tempting of Satan to innocent souls of old. Most unhappily the rural life all the world over is spoken of now with scorn; yet it is certain that the rural life is the safest, the healthiest, the sweetest, and above all it is so here where the climate makes the mere living out-of-doors a poem and a picture.

Compare the mechanic of Wakefield or Blackburn with the pall of black soot hung for ever between him and the sun, and his superficial repetitions of Darwin or Bradlaugh urged as evidence of an enlightened mind; compare his automatic hideous toil, his hard hatred of all classes save his own, his dwelling one amidst rows of a thousand similar, his wilderness of dark, foul-scented streets, his stench of smoke, his talk of agnosticism and equality narrow as the routine of his life, his shallow sophisms, his club, his strikes, his tommy-shop; compare him and these with the Italian labourer of the Luchese hills, or the Santa Fiora forests, or the Val d'Arno farms, rising to see the glorious sky glow like a summer rose, dwelling in his wide, stout, stone-built house old as the trees around him, following in their course as the seasons change his manly and healthful labours, reaping and binding, sowing and mowing, guiding his oxen through the vines, having for ever around him the gladdest and most gracious nature; at noontide sitting down as the patriarch sat amidst his family and labourers to a homely plenty; at eventide resting to see the youths and maidens dance, and listen to the old pastoral love songs sung to the thrum of the guitar or the story of the Gerusalemme Liberata passed down by word of mouth from sire to son. Compare these two lives; they are no fancy pictures. You may see either of them any day you will; and tell me whether I am wrong when I dread, as the plague was dreaded of old, the false teachers who, to fill their own purse, try to persuade the southern peasant to covet the northern workmen; who try to say gas is fairer than the sun, and the oiled piston sweeter than the honey breath of the cattle, and the anathema of Fourier and Bakounine lovelier and wiser than the strophe of Ariosto and of Dante.

Italy for the Italians! yes; with the municipal extortions made a thing of the past like the Inquisition, and the Jew usurer, and the English and American speculator, denied the soil they covet and pollute. This would well be the fitting war-cry of the Italy of to-day, who has darker foes made welcome in her midst than even the Austrian and the Bourbon that she banished.

Let me give but one example of the delightful natural intelligence which the new schools are striving to replace with the scientific smattering of the factory and foundry mechanic, and I will weary you no more.

In a letter published in 1859 to the celebrated Tommaseo, Professore Giulianni narrates the story of a woman called Beatrice in the Pistoiese Apennines—a woman he knew well—a poor, hard-working, country-bred creature, who knew not a single letter of the alphabet, but who improvised on the death of a beloved son, in a passion of grief and weeping, the most perfect poem in the always difficult *ottave*. This woman was but one amidst others, who all had, in a greater or a lesser degree, this grand poetical faculty, and harmony of ear, and who, when asked to teach their power to a stranger, would answer with a smile.

>Volete intender lo mio imparare?
>Andar per legna, or starmene a zappare.

What can the communal schools substitute for that one half so ennobling, so inspiring, so sublime, as those natural bursts of song amidst the solitudes of the everlasting hills?

'If you would learn to sing like me,' she says, 'come with me to gather the hillside wood, or stay beside me to hoe the earth; this rich and kindly earth which flowers for ever for you, making the almond bloom in the winter cold, and the cyclamen in the autumn mists, and all spring and summer shower on you blossoms with both hands.'

How right she is, this wise old woman eloquent!

What can the schools give us that will equal what Nature offers? Let us dwell, as she does, face to face with the blue sky, the mountain solitude, the forest freedom, and we shall see as she sees. This is what I would keep for this lovely land which has become mine, for these beloved people who are now my own, this fresh, natural intelligence, this healthful Greek-like life. And this is what day by day is perishing, crushed out under the weight of the impost of the municipalities and the engine-wheels of the greedy contractor. As an Italian writer[1] has said aright: 'As little by little our beautiful forests and green woodland growth fall before love of lucre and greedy desire, and give place to the smoke and the stench of the machine and the shaft, as our hillsides crumble and fall away, and our flowering meadows and our fair cultured fields vanish with them, so does equal craze for gain possess our people in the cities, and, bringing amidst them a strange and foreign element, corrupts our hearts as it corrupts our tongue.'

She, who on the mountain side mourned for her son as Tasso might have mourned, is ordered to give place to the parrot-phrase and automaton-learning of the school-crammed puppet; the old happy innocent nights in the valley and on the hills, when the youths came with violin and mandoline to bid the maidens dance *trescone* or *galletta* in the moonlight, or gathered about the wood fire in the winter time singing *romanzetti* and *strombetti*, and telling the old-world tales of the Queen of Cyprus, and Ginevra, and Piramo and Tisbe, are bidden to change and render up their place to wordy dispute of windy politics, and feverish suppers in crowded winehouses, where the pure juice of the grape is lost in alcohol and chemicals.

[1] Professore Tigri.

The peasant-improvisatrice is to become the hollow-cheeked toiler of mill or machine; the happy husbandman is to become the sullen and savage mechanic with rotten lungs and watery blood; the songs, sweet and strong as wild birds' notes, are to be drowned in the hoarse shouts of the proletariat; and the luxuriant, vigorous, natural intelligence is to be poisoned with the false logic of communism or stifled in the lifeless mechanical repetition of the schools.

Forbid it, O Apollo Cytheroedus! here, where the echo of thy divine lute still may be heard at evenfall, when the shepherd pipes, and the maiden sings, in the green myrtle hollows and on the pine-crowned heights! Arise and protect these thine offspring!

Let the false guides not take from thy children alike the bread that is life, and the pure air that is health, and the music that is laughter and is love!

THE END.

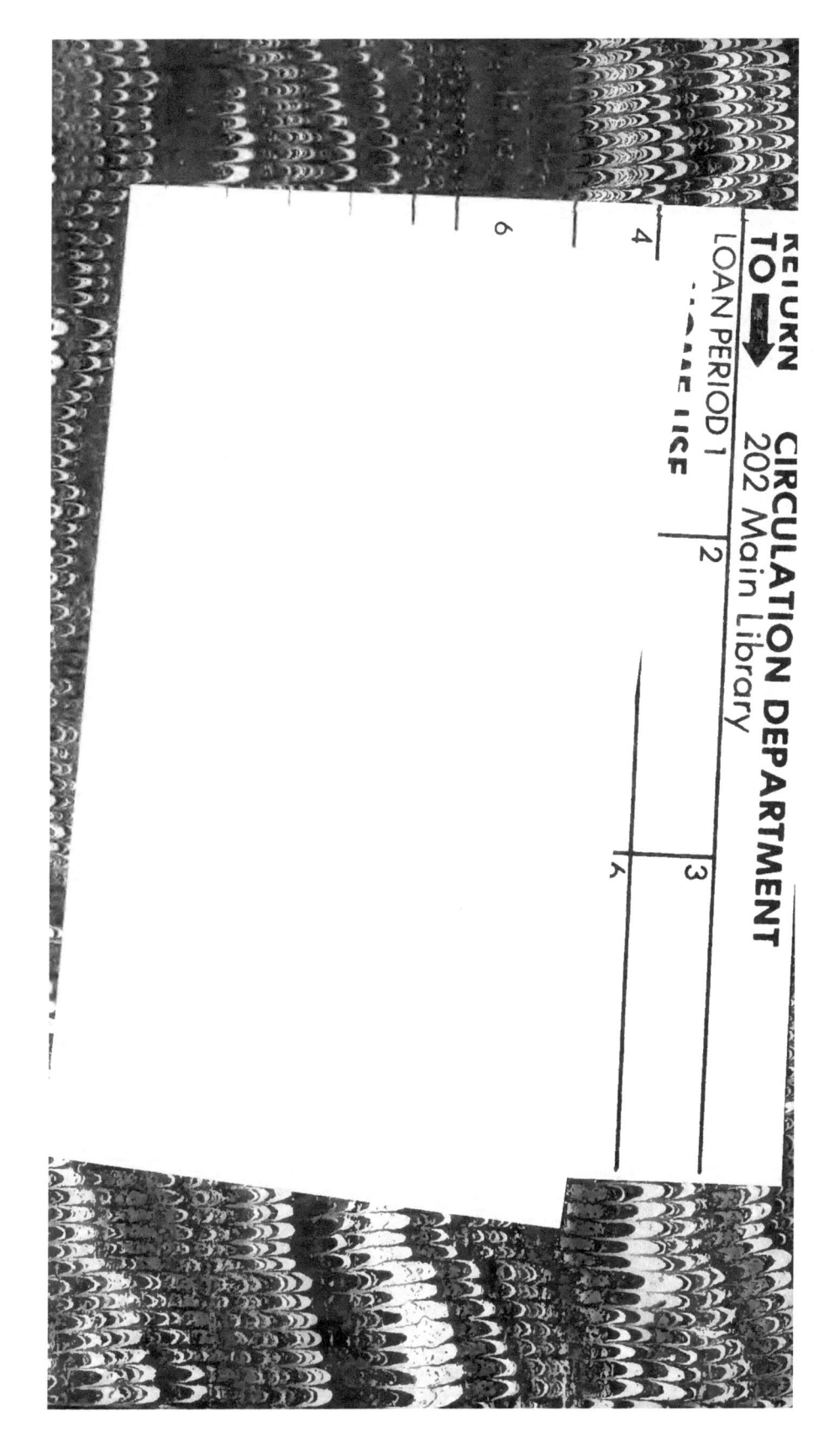

**RETURN TO** → **CIRCULATION DEPARTMENT**
202 Main Library

LOAN PERIOD 1
HOME USE

| 2 | 3 |